UNCANNY BODIES

Edited by
**Pippa Goldschmidt, Gill Haddow
and Fadhila Mazanderani**

Academia
Lunare
LUNA PRESS
PUBLISHING

First published by Luna Press Publishing, Edinburgh, 2020

www.lunapresspublishing.com

ISBN-13: 978-1-913387-22-8

Contents

Introduction
Pippa Goldschmidt, Gill Haddow and Fadhila Mazanderani

> What is the uncanny? Does it belong to philosophy or literature
> or psychoanalysis? *If* it belongs, it is no longer a question of the
> uncanny. Rather the uncanny calls for a different thinking of
> genre and text, and of the distinctions between the literary and
> the non-literary, academic and non-academic writing.
>
> (Royle, 2003, p.18)

This anthology started life as a series of discussions on, and a
shared interest in, the uncanny. We asked ourselves, what might an
exploration of the uncanny as a concept, a metaphor, an experience
and a literary product contribute to our own, very different, areas
of research and work? These early discussions culminated in the
organisation of the *Uncanny Bodies* workshop which took place
in Edinburgh in the summer of 2018. From its very inception the
workshop was an experiment in multidisciplinarity. We invited
social scientists, humanities scholars, poets and fiction writers to
collectively explore the uncanny in relation to their own work. Our
aim was two-fold; we wanted to update and extend the concept of
the uncanny in the light of scientific advances, looking specifically
at the intersection between the uncanny, human and animal
bodies, and biomedical science. We also wanted to encourage the
writers and academics to collaborate on creative outputs and in
doing so, to break down barriers that exist between disciplines.

A curious aspect of Freud's seminal essay *The Uncanny* (Freud
2003 [1919]) is its reliance on fiction to explore and explain the
uncanny; at the heart of the essay is an extended analysis of the

short story 'The Sandman' by E.T.A. Hoffmann (first published in 1816). Freud's discussion of fictional examples to illustrate his ideas makes clear the implicit fact that writers of literature have long explored the uncanny and made use of it in their narratives to achieve differing effects.

So, by inviting creative writers and academics, we wanted to encourage the latter to consider different modes of writing to explore their ideas. All modes of writing, including fiction (as evidenced by Freud's use of it), can be seen as producing knowledge about the 'real' world. Yet academics have few opportunities to reflect on, and experiment with, writing as a crucial mode of scholarly work, knowledge creation and research method. The need to do so is particularly heightened when dealing with topics that are hard to articulate, for example, emergent technologies that have yet to stabilise, concepts that challenge taken-for-granted ideas about the human body and mind, experiences that cannot be easily expressed in standard academic prose.

This is starting to be recognised in social sciences where researchers are becoming more open to exploring different writing devices such as autoethnographies (in which academics use their own experience as data, bringing the author's subjectivity to the forefront), dialogic formats (academic texts structured as dialogues), and text splitting (in which the text is broken up into physically distinct sections – a literary device appropriated by some social scientists). Innovative academic writing has appeared in journals in the fields of anthropology, the medical humanities, and science and technology studies.

After the workshop, each participant was asked to write a response to the uncanny, and was not given any direction about what form or shape that response might take. The creative writers generally wrote poems or stories, while Jules Horne's piece is a dramatic dialogue with commentary. The academics had the freedom to adopt a more conventional academic style or to be experimental. In some cases this resulted in standalone pieces of writing, whilst in others academic participants responded directly or indirectly to work produced by the creative writers.

Not all of the contributors to this anthology attended the workshop, afterwards we invited other academics and writers to participate in this project based on their research and creative interests.

Revisiting the uncanny, words and bodies

The uncanny evades any straightforward genealogy or definition. Its first articulation as a distinct phenomenon is usually traced to German psychiatrist Ernst Jentsch's 1906 essay 'On the Psychology of the Uncanny' (Jentsch 2008 [1906]), but is most commonly associated with Freud's essay *The Uncanny* (Freud 2003 [1919]). Freud, and indeed many who have followed him, is clear that the uncanny – or the 'unheimlich' in the original German – is not simply that which makes us afraid or uncomfortable, it's not the straightforwardly macabre or gruesome. Rather, the uncanny is the sense of discomfort or unease that emerges when something that appears familiar turns strange or hostile. It is (in Freud's words) 'the familiar turned strange'.

In his essay Freud discusses at some length the etymology of the German 'unheimlich' and its closest equivalents in various other languages. Unheimlich is usually translated into the English word 'uncanny', although this is inevitably not a precise translation. Actually, Freud's own suggested English equivalents were (in the following order) 'uncomfortable, uneasy, gloomy, dismal, uncanny, ghastly'. It is the first English translation of Freud's essay by James and Alix Strachey in 1925 that uses 'uncanny', and (to date) all subsequent essays in English have followed their lead.

The Stracheys' choice is an interesting one. The English word 'uncanny' is derived from the Scots 'canny', c.f. the Scots phrase 'ca canny', meaning 'proceed cautiously'. But 'canny' is a slippery term that can variously mean 'shrewd', 'safe', 'prudent' and even 'having supernatural knowledge', which is also a meaning of 'uncanny'. Similarly, in German 'heimlich' can mean 'secret', 'stealthily' and 'furtive', and as Freud commented, 'heimlich' and 'unheimlich' are not always antonyms but sometimes operate as synonyms.

The linguistic representations of the uncanny, like the concept, therefore defy categorisation and boundaries.

Given our research interests and the prominence of the body, or more accurately different bodies, we were particularly keen, both in the workshop and this anthology, to consider the uncanny in the light of medicine and illness. Many of the examples Freud draws on in attempting to describe and define the uncanny are related to human and non-human bodies: a dead, inanimate or mechanical object behaving as if alive; conversely, a live being behaving as if dead, inanimate or mechanical; encountering one's double or doppelgänger; dismembered limbs and body parts continuing to move; the sensation of a foreign body within one's own, or an estrangement from one's body.

Today, over a hundred years after the original publication of *The Uncanny*, our understanding of the body and its relationship to its environment is undergoing a radical transformation in the light of biomedical advances and new technologies. Implantable devices, such as mechanical heart valves, maintain life in their recipient organisms. Older technologies, such as prostheses, replace limbs but in doing so serve to remind us of what the body has lost. New technologies allow us to see beneath the skin, to follow blood flowing around the brain. They illuminate what has, until now, remained hidden. Technologies such as these can muddle our sense of what life is, and remind us that by looking beneath the skin perhaps we look into the future. When the German physicist Roentgen discovered x-rays at the end of the nineteenth century, the first image he made with them was of his wife's hand. In this image, the skin is invisible, the muscles and flesh appear ghostly, the bones are the most immediately apparent aspect of the hand. When Roentgen showed the image of her skeletal hand to his wife, she is reputed to have said 'I have seen my own death'. So, technology used to aid the prolonging of life, can also have the opposite effect in allowing us to visualise what will become of us after life.

It is not just medicine that renders us uncanny, illness can do so too. The self is not a compact and autonomous entity; we are more porous than we would like to believe, susceptible to invasive disease that may alter our behaviour and perhaps our very sense of who we are. The experience of illness can turn our own bodies, once perceived as stable and reliable, the physical 'home' of the self, into something threatening. Even without the presence of disease, 'we' are constituted by other species (such as bacteria) to function healthily. What does it mean to blur the boundaries between species? How does it feel to have a pig valve inserted into your heart? Does it challenge our sense of being a unique species to learn that we share most of our DNA with monkeys, and a fair amount with fruitflies?

These new (and old) uncanny experiences challenge traditional notions of humanity, and create new possibilities for thinking about the human and non-human body. The uncanny can tell us about 'ourselves' and how what we assume to be fixed and coherent is in fact more mutable, subject to influence and ingress both internally and externally than we have previously assumed.

By asking contributors to respond to the uncanny through writing, we were also thinking of how the body is represented and symbolised in words. When we use language to describe the human body we transform this matter into something less substantial and more ethereal. Language itself simultaneously creates both a bridge to, and a divide between, us and the material world.

Written language is 'embodied' in text, rendering it physical. Poetry recognises this embodiment more consciously than prose – the physical shape of the poem on the page is an essential aspect of the work, the poem marries form and substance. Indeed, part of the workshop was spent on a creative exercise using, and transforming, pages from Freud's essay. Led by the poet nicky melville, the workshop participants each took a page and, with the aid of coloured pencils, pens, Tipp-Ex, etc. converted it into another text with an altered meaning and purpose. (This process is perhaps similar to that used by the artist Tom Phillips to create his palimpsestic masterpiece *A Humument.*) In some cases the result can be read as a commentary on the original essay, or as a consideration of the underlying themes. We published the resulting pages as a limited edition pamphlet (Goldschmidt, P., Haddow, G. and Mazanderani, F., 2019).

Building on and moving forward from the workshop, this anthology explores different aspects of the uncanny, transgressing disciplinary and stylistic boundaries, staying with, while at the same time reconsidering, its parameters. As such it contributes to a wider body of work that has taken up, appropriated and reconfigured the concept of the uncanny in multiple ways and contexts (Eyre and Page, 2008; Masschelein, 2012; Royle, 2003; Sandor, 2015).

The anthology

We have broken the anthology up into three sections or themes, although we should point out that the work itself sometimes resisted being categorised in this way. The reader may be able to see other themes, or other ways of grouping the work within these themes. We leave it to you as an uncanny exercise. Rather than providing an exhaustive list of the contributions, we highlight a few examples below.

Pain, illness and healing

Perhaps the largest of the three themes is that of illness. The 'self' is housed in the body and when everything functions normally, the boundary between the two feels seamless, invisible. But when the body is affected by pain and disease its relationship to this 'self' becomes ambiguous, making the body no longer absent but a presence in which the boundaries between inside and out are permeable (Leder, 1990).

Ordinarily, the body appears obedient to the self's wishes and desires. But in the presence of disease, and related physiological effects such as pain or numbness, this seamlessness is revealed to be an illusion. In experiencing illness we become more conscious of our bodies as both separate to, and yet connected to, our innate selves. We realise that any control we have over our bodies is imagined, false.

Treatment for disease breaks down the apparently solid

boundaries between 'self' and other. Treatments often require ingestion of foreign bodies, and produce side-effects. They may even require additions, such as prosthetics, to our bodies, which makes us interact with our surroundings in new and unforeseen ways.

Dilys Rose's flash fiction 'Half Here, Half Where' humorously evokes the estrangement from one's own body caused by the experience of a stroke. The body's innate sense of itself, that extra sense known as proprioception, goes awry. The illness divides the body cleanly in two, half of which obeys the brain, and the half which seems to have its own 'mind'.

Pregnancy is not a disease, of course, however it is an uncertain and complex state in which the woman's body must shelter and support a growing fetus which, by definition, is both connected to it and reliant on it, and yet a separate entity. Jules Horne's dramatic dialogue 'The Stane Bairn' renders the unborn uncanny and the woman talking to her fibroid tumour (in an echo of the baby bonding process) evokes an uneasy feeling in the reader. Just who is she speaking to? Is this stane bairn alive? Furthermore, the dialogue is in Border Scots, a language not often represented on the page. Reading it here almost requires the reader's mouth to shape the words, to give them a ghostly presence.

Sarah Stewart's poem 'What I Haven't Told You' and the accompanying essay 'Unbecoming Animal' by Ritti Soncco explore processes of transformation, blurring the boundaries between humans and non-humans. Many of these works – including the ones written by the academics – follow the principle 'show, don't tell' that fiction writers are taught to obey in Creative Writing 101. Work that is produced with 'show don't tell' in mind allows the reader to experience vicariously the emotions of the characters on the page, thus the story gradually unfurls in the reader's mind without being explicitly spelled out. It is supposed to produce work with a greater immediacy than that 'told', which can distance the reader from the page. 'Show, don't tell' feels a little bit uncanny, when we read Ritti's essay initially we're not sure what is going on or who – or even what – is talking to us. But we see the world through their eyes and, in doing so, we 'become' them, we slip into their skin.

Situating bodies: the uncanny in the city and the forest
The workshop was held near our University department of STIS (the Science, Technology and Innovation Studies unit) in Edinburgh's Old Town. Edinburgh has a venerable reputation for medicine and science. It's famous for its contributions to the development of surgery (such as anaesthetics) and related advances in the understanding of anatomy, as embodied in the Surgeons Museum and the University's Medical School. The physical and human geographies of Edinburgh serve to illustrate its 'double' nature. It is a city of two halves, the Old Town and New Town face each other across the gap of Princes Street Gardens and the railway lines. The lower levels in the Old Town (such as St Mary's Close) are now not always inhabited and can be thought of as architectural analogies of the hidden subconscious. The resulting deep city canyons, such as Cowgate and Grassmarket, becoming physical renderings of 'uncanny valleys'.

Following on from the workshop being situated in the heart of Edinburgh's Old Town, some of these works are likewise based here. 'A bed of my own' by Christine De Luca is an, at first, apparently straightforward tale of a woman reminiscing about her student days in Edinburgh and the financially straitened circumstances requiring her to share, not just a room but a double bed, with a medical student. But other voices intervene, and we realise this city is crowded with ghosts who cannot go away and leave the living in peace. The living and the dead interact intimately in this story.

Writers considered the transgression of the boundaries and the corresponding disturbance to the self. Some of them examined how Edinburgh shapes us. Jane McKie's poem 'Where the Edinburgh All-night Bakery Used to Be' illustrates how ever-changing cities create their own ghosts, and through our memories, ghosts of our former selves too. In 'Ma' by Pippa Goldschmidt, Edinburgh is a mysterious place, easier to navigate in virtual reality than in real life. Or perhaps its complexities – a city of unmapped alleys, streets with identical names, and buildings with more exits than entrances – exist only in the protagonist's mind.

In contrast, 'Little Cat in the Bronx' by Eris Young takes the reader to 1950s America and a situation in which the narrator, expecting to be in control of his domestic life (as promised him when he came home from the war), gradually realises that he knows nothing about the most immediate aspects of his home. The writing in this story shows how even the most mundane and domestic devices can turn truly uncanny. Nothing is as strange as your own home.

Donna McCormack's essay 'Haunted House' investigates the paradoxical situation of a human body with a transplant. A body has become a haunted house because something 'dead' has taken up residence in it, and yet this organ is now responsible for keeping its host alive, which would not be so if it weren't for the presence of the dead.

One of the uncanny examples from his own life that Freud discusses is a walk through a 'provincial town in Italy' in which he repeatedly gets lost (in the red light district, although curiously he doesn't discuss this aspect of the experience in any detail). His feeling of uncanny is engendered (according to him) by the repeated act of getting lost, of being out of control. But if he is not in control, then who – or what – is?

All the pieces in this section situate bodies within a particular environment, be this urban or rural. Each of them in different ways explore the uncanny within real and imagined landscapes.

Transforming bodies into Other

The third section considers how technologies (in particular information technologies) break down barriers between the human and not-human. This is both new and not-new, Freud's discussion of 'The Sandman' is itself rather unsettling because it ignores one of the most uncanny tropes of that story, namely the fact that Hoffmann's narrator falls in love with a woman who is in fact an automaton. The reader figures this out for herself as it's never made explicit; another example of the use of 'show, don't tell' rendering something uncanny (it's also humorous).

Naomi Salman's 'sur la comète' introduces us to the world of everyday cyborgs, and the very different reasons that people have for augmenting their bodies – do they do so because they want to learn more about the physiological processes that ordinarily remain secret beneath the skin, or do they want to establish a connection with the rest of the Universe? In Jane Alexander's story 'The Lag' the interactions between the protagonist, her prosthetic limb and her wider environment is closely observed. The story makes a connection between the spatial complexities of the interaction between her 'natural' body and its 'artificial' limb and the time lost as a result of having to accommodate this limb.

Vassilis Galanos' essay takes us on a chronological tour from Freud to the 'uncanny valley', a concept which first emerged in Japanese robotics science in 1970 and which strives to explain why we can feel so disconcerted by inanimate objects (a doll, puppet or robot, or even a cartoon character) that try, and yet fail, to appear human. Galanos questions the apparently straightforward link between Freud and this concept, siting it instead in Japanese culture, and asks us to consider how this phenomenon may change and adapt in the future as we become more accustomed to robots. This essay also points out the possibility that it is not just robots that trigger the unease we feel in the 'uncanny valley' but also other humans.

Ruth Aylett's sequence of poems explores the anxiety we feel when faced with a robot who may be usurping us, not just in intellectual abilities, but also in the ill-defined role of being human. Can we ourselves pass the Turing Test?

And finally…

Nothing has managed to explain the uncanny, not Freud's (unsurprising) attempts to explicate it as a fear of castration, nor more recent attempts to map the brain using MRI. It is this insistent ability to evade explanation and exhaustive categorisation that renders the uncanny a continuously interesting proposition.

And in spite of what Freud says, we cannot help thinking that the uncanny is not necessarily a negative connotation. The negative response may be the initial one but after that has died away, perhaps we're left with something more abiding, an interest in what it is that has caused the feeling. The uncanny can act as a tracer of something which wishes to engage us, which we should consider in more depth.

Ultimately it is for you to decide if these pieces either evoke or investigate the uncanny. Have we spotted it? Where does it reside? We leave this to you.

References

Eyre, S. and Page, R., (2008), *The New Uncanny*, Manchester: Comma Press.

Freud, S., (2003 [1919]), *The Uncanny*, (translator David McClintock), London: Penguin.

Goldschmidt, P., Haddow, G. and Mazanderani, F., 2019, *Uncan*, Edinburgh: Uncanny Press.

Jentsch, E., (2008 [1906]), 'The Uncanny' (translator Roy Seller), *Uncanny Modernity*, (eds. Jo Collins and John Jervis), Palgrave.

Leder, D., 1990, *The Absent Body*, Chicago: Chicago University Press.

Masschelein, A., 2011, *The Unconcept: The Freudian Uncanny in Late-Twentieth-Century Theory*, Albany: State University of New York Publishing.

Phillips, T., 2016, *A Humument: A Treated Victorian Novel*, London: Thames and Hudson.

Royle, N., 2003, *The Uncanny*, Manchester: Manchester University Press.

Sandor, M., 2015, *The Uncanny Reader: Stories from the Shadows*, New York: St. Martin's Griffin.

familiars
nicky melville

something long
known to us   once
very familiar

                                             what was once well
                                    known and had long
                                          been familiar

the familiar can become
uncanny and
frightening

                                     the familiar can become
                                             uncanny and
                                               frightening
                                      how this can be

I shall show in
what follows

                                    shall emerge in what
                                            follows

meaning

                                             may
                                    provisionally be
         belonging
                                             glossed
to
                                           feeling
the home
                                         at home
is frightening
                                           what is
because it is *not*
                                    novel may well
known
                                  prove frightening
and familiar

Naturally   the converse is not true
not everything which is new   not everything new
and ~~un~~familiar is   un~~familiar~~
                                                        frightening
frightening   Something   something
has to be   must be
added to   added to
what is novel and ~~un~~familiar   the novel
to make it   and the unfamiliar
beyond   if it is to be
this relation   come uncanny
to the novel and un~~familiar~~   to go beyond
with ~~un~~familiar   a mere equation
to other   with the unfamiliar
languages   and turn first to other
because we speak   languages
a different language   because we ourselves speak
                                                    a foreign language

belonging to   belonging to
the house   the house
not strange   familiar   tame   not strange   familiar   tame
on the one hand   one relating to what
it means that   all the more   is familiar
which is familiar   familiar   and comfortable
and on the other that   the other
which is concealed   did the man   to what is concealed
and kept out of sight   and kept hidden
                           now appear

a place free   a place that is free
from ghostly influences   of ghostly influences
familiar   familiar
friendly   friendly
intimate   confiding

the marked   a marked
or familiar path   or unfamiliar path
ends again and again   one comes back a
in a return to   gain to the same
one and the same spot

                                                                    spot
something familiar and old   long familiar to the psyche
                                                                familiar
established in the mind   to its opposite
still   in the dream   dream-states
place   through the empty
is familiar to me   and to me
I have been there before   unfamiliar streets

what was once   is what was once
            familiar
un   something familiar
                                                            that has been

is the token of repression   repressed
a hidden   and then reappears
familiar   traced back every
that has undergone
and then emerged

                                                                    time
the exact value
proceeds from   something that once
something familiar which has been repressed   was
to something familiar that has been repressed   familiar and then repressed

the realities we are familiar with   a world that conforms
                                                to the reader's familiar reality

This poem was made by extracting all phrases containing the word 'familiar' from two different translations of 'The Uncanny.' The one on the left is by Alix Strachey (1955) and that on the right is by David McLintock (2003).

Section One

Pain, Illness and Healing

Half Here, Half Where
Dilys Rose

When it happened, it was so unassuming. You were dizzy but in an airy, fit-of-the-vapours sort of way, your field of vision had a light dusting of snowy static but no hissing, then half of you evaporated—poof! And in its place, in half of *your* place, your *space*, was a simulacrum. You had become half girl (half *old girl*), half ghost.

The evanescing was painless. Disconcertingly so. No wrench of severance, no lightning-bolt schism or residual throb of loss. You didn't reach out to your flighty, fugitive side as if you hoped to corral the blown seeds of a dandelion clock or soap bubbles from a wand. Instead, you stood dead still, hoping that stillness might restore you—to wholeness, equilibrium, symmetry?

It was the day before midsummer. You were standing at a tall window in the cheerful living room of your friend's holiday home, gazing at sand yellow, sky blue and white-capped sea green. The coastline of France—oh, the romance!—was a faint smudge on the horizon. Around these parts, perhaps even just along the road, Turner had painted some of his wispy seascapes with, according to Constable, 'tinted steam'.

Your reflection in the window glass gave the impression that your right leg (which appeared as your left) was, in its share of floral-print trousers, every bit as solid and ordinary as its neighbour. Ditto your right arm, extending from the short, loose sleeve of a t-shirt. Your right side might have been able to fool a casual observer but it didn't fool you: it was as insubstantial as steam.

*

Later the same day. No longer a room with a view but a hot, crowded, A & E waiting room. There are no visible clues as to your altered state except that when you embark upon another trip to the loo, you peg and flop like a half-wooden, half-rag doll. For nearly five hours you wait, sitting, or propping yourself against a wedge of wall. There are fewer seats than patients, a logjam of wheelchairs and no clear path to the medical bays. You try not to dwell on the sorry state of the NHS. The reason you are here is that your blood pressure, to quote the triage nurse, is through the roof.

Head, shoulders, knees and toes. Eyes and ears and mouth and nose. In the continuing absence of a doctor you tap repeatedly at various parts of your body. Your weaker left side remains pretty much as before. The stronger, abler, go-to right side, with the larger, veinier and nimbler-fingered hand—you can't begin to compute all the fine motor skills you will need that hand for—is numb, weightless, absent. It might as well be a hologram. Any contact you make with it has to be seen to be believed. If you raise your right foot from the scuffed linoleum, it continues to drift upwards of its own accord. This is seductive rather than alarming, but something tells you this is the wrong response.

Your brain is not relaying the correct messages but you really don't want to think about what your brain is or is not doing; it is hard enough getting to grips with your wayward body. But what should the messages be and *where are they*—sequestered in a locked ward of the brain, until you locate, identify or recognise the key? Perhaps the correct messages are shambling around some cerebral waiting room, whining for attention, jostling for elbow room, fretting for their names to be called so they can sprauchle towards a fully functioning nurse holding a clipboard who will, if all goes to plan, direct them to a door at the end of a hitherto unseen corridor.

Forgetting
Alice Tarbuck

I do not presume to know how objects seem,
and I have probably looked at many things for the last time
without noticing. Several collected works,
cherry red gloves, a certain stone on the way to a holy well.

all[the[ache[is[a[sharp[pin[is[a[same[point[please[is[hysteria[is
[nownownownowhere

The chlorine smell
fades out of towels and back into dryness, the sticky gum
unsticks from the pavement in hard frost. Open the gate
to look at the path, open the path to see the bones,
open the bones and the miniscule holes whisper
incantations that dissolve like sugar.

unplace[pain[unplace[allplace[allsuch[allsudden[all[eyes[all
[mouth[all[nerves[all[undo

These daily leavings tax, our shoulders
braced, and all you can be is steady, still, animal,
while the person you love needs you. All you can do is point
at something in the rear view mirror and say huh,
a diner the shape of a peach, a cliff the shape of an open mouth,
a traffic light bent at an angle, like a hat cocked in farewell.

[against][against the blank white][of no goodbye[only delay][only return][
the shriek of the now
the shriek of the unmap
the shriek of the undone undo unmake body tunnel pain

Pain's Uncanny
Sara Wasson

… open the path to see the bones,
open the bones and the miniscule holes whisper
incantations that dissolve like sugar.
Alice Tarbuck

You're stuck in a secret story – and it's not on your side.

The uncanny involves a crisis of narrative. When Sigmund Freud tried to describe the feeling of the uncanny in his 1919 essay, he asks us to imagine that we are in the grip of a story that isn't under our control. For example, he recalls finding himself in a part of the city he doesn't mean to visit, yet to which he continually finds himself returning. 'After the third time, a feeling overcame me which I can only describe as uncanny… helplessness and …. Uncanniness' (Freud, 1919, p. 359).

In Freud's telling, in the grip of the uncanny we feel that something other than ourselves is controlling the meaning of our spaces, shaping our trajectories. There is an excess or mystery to the things we assumed were familiar. Freud argued that unconscious, repressed material is the most common cause of this disorientation, but even that does not domesticate the radical strangeness of the cryptic story. We don't know how it emerges, or how it ends. Something else is shaping the scene, and although we aren't sure who or what, we intuit that it's not in our favour. In the uncanny, the familiar becomes strange, and along with that strangeness comes a dim intuition of a secret script, one we cannot know, and shaped by an agency alien to us … something that we sense does not love us.

The experience of chronic pain may abound in such cryptic scripts and strangeness. Your body may become unfamiliar, aching and twinging, speaking of something amiss. Scans and tests may show your body's interior, but even if a cause is found the sense of the body's change can be disorienting. The cause can also remain elusive, even while the pain, shorn of any origin story, continues to live a vivid life within your body. Pain's paradoxical: it can provoke speech or can silence, sometimes defeating the ability to represent at all – 'unplace[pain[unplace[allplace[allsuch[allsudden[all[eyes[all [mouth[all[nerves[all[undo', in Tarbuck's haunting words.

Familiar/unfamiliar, and a secret script. Even time can run strangely under pain's narrative regimes. Cause and cure may remain elusive – why did it start? Can it end? – triumphalist story may not apply, but instead a different script, one we may not have chosen.

> '…All you can do is point
> at something in the rear view mirror and say huh,
> a diner the shape of a peach, a cliff the shape of an open mouth,
> a traffic light bent at an angle, like a hat cocked in farewell.
> [against][against the blank white][of no goodbye[only delay]
> [only return]…'
> (Tarbuck)

The strange, recursive temporality of pain experience can be uncanny, a return to a familiar state, experienced before, yet subtly different and strange even in the fact it is repeated, returned to, over and over – a repetition, a haunting, a curse. In pain, time may become circular, or static. It can be a thing of repetitions, of reversals, of returns. It can be a recalcitrant story.

Estrangement may also affect encounters with others—medical practitioners, family, loved ones, who may not know the pain and may not understand it, or even, sometimes, quite believe it:

'I try to speak to doctors about the severity of my pain. My words float strangely in the air. As I pronounce them, I myself become a spectator. As soon as I begin to speak, I am no longer there. Someone else is speaking these words. Someone who has not suffered the pain, for it is much worse than she says. [...] How can she, how can I, explain this prelanguage torment?'

Here, in her book *Inside Chronic Pain*, pain sufferer Lous Heshusius describes a medical encounter as so profoundly alienating and disorienting that she feels depersonalised. A sense of her own body and her own words as radically other emerges from the choreography of care.

Pain's uncanny.

A similar statement emerges in many of the entries in the *Translating Pain* online anthology which I run at Lancaster University. This anthology showcases short 'flash' writing about chronic pain experience. In my 'Creative Manifesto' inviting submissions of work, I invite flash writing up to 150 words which 'communicates in any emotional register, positive or negative', to 'communicate the vivid, contradictory, and diverse realities of living with chronic pain'. To date the 80+ entries from 8 countries have been passionate and varied, and the cumulative tag cloud gives a sense of the emotional trends and topics:

adaptation·alteration·body·cancer·cancer pain·class·
connection°credibility dark·disconnection·disregarded·economic·
erosion of spirit·escapism·family·fear/distress/grief·
fibromyalgia·frustration·gender·gratefulness·gratitude·grieving·hardship·
helplessness·hope·hopelessness·identity·insurance·
invisibility·isolation·language·living·in·pain·loss·
medical·observation·pain·sexuality·social·strangeness·
surprise·time·torment·trans·author·waiting·witness

Fear, distress, isolation, waiting, time and *strangeness*. All these words can potentially invite uncanny representation, a sense of dread and suspense and an intuition of non-benevolent change.

Roseanne Watt's haunting poem 'The Diagnosis' describes the experience of pain and the sense of changed time. The first person speaker describes her body as previously occupied by birds who suddenly left her when ill health struck:

'…they uninhabited,

leaving only their barbed-wire
residues, strung across the boughs

of my hips; all sticks and spit,
all hollows meant for holding

something small, still desperately
alive. I'm sorry – I'm afraid

I know only my own dark canopy,
its filtering bones of light.'

This poignant verse captures the estrangement, loss and dread that may afflict a pain-wracked body—the familiar made disturbingly strange, and apprehension of a cryptic future.

Why might anyone wish to represent chronic pain as uncanny? Why admit such unpalatable truths? In the Creative Manifesto that emerges from the *Translating Chronic Pain* project, I list many reasons why it is valuable to represent the full gamut of pain experiences. People living with chronic pain may endure profound challenges, personal, social and economic. A positive outlook can be deeply beneficial, but when positivity becomes an *imperative*, it can mean that some people may feel profoundly delegitimated. Unseen. Unheard.

As such, it can be a huge relief to have the difficult aspects of pain experience validated and recognised. Heshusius, for example, speaks of her tearful relief at reading Melanie Thernstrom's writing on pain: 'Every paragraph had me in tears. Finally, words that spoke to what I was going through. This was me. I was not crazy. I was not exaggerating. Thernstrom described ... the despair, the fear, the isolation, the terror' (Thernstrom, 2010, p. 24). There is emotional succor in recognising, witnessing suffering, respecting another person's story even if it does not fit the triumphant trajectory we all prefer to see. Such acknowledgement is all the more precious since many people living with pain may have had the experience of being disbelieved or doubted, or even seen by medical professionals as unreliable witnesses of their own experience. This attitude can become a form of 'epistemic injustice' (Fricker, 2007), for such people are not seen as able to know their own experience.

There is value, then, in finding ways to represent variously such trouble, disorientation, the familiar become strange, the future become mysterious and a thing of unease. In this spirit, elsewhere I call for 'a writing craft that deliberately draws close to the textures of pain, shame, and wounds. [...] Valuable work may be done by representations of time frozen and interrupted, images of impasse, stasis and repetition ... for some of us are indeed rendered spectral, strange and sad' (Wasson, 2020). Take the uncanny, its unease and dread, its creeping trouble. Let that strangeness validate experience that can be hard to accept, to acknowledge. Let some kinds of suffering be seen.

Show the shadows.

References

Freud, S. ([1919] 1985), *The Uncanny*, Penguin Freud Library, vol. 14, trans. J. Strachey, ed. by A. Richards, London: Penguin, pp. 336-376

Fricker, M. (2007), *Epistemic Injustice: Power and the Ethics of Knowing*, Oxford: Oxford University Press

Heshusius, L. (2009), *Inside Chronic Pain*, Ithaca: Cornell University Press

Tarbuck, A., 'Forgetting', this volume.

Thernstrom, M. (2010) *The Pain Chronicles, Healing, and the Science of Suffering*, New York: Farrar, Strauss, Giroux

Wasson, S. (2018) 'Before Narrative: Episodic Reading and Representations of Chronic Pain', *Medical Humanities*, 44.2, 106-112. DOI: 10,1136/medhum-2017-011223. Available at: https://mh.bmj.com/content/44/2/106, accessed 3 December 2019

Wasson, S. (2018), 'Creative Manifesto' and Online Anthology of Flash Writing, *Translating Pain*, Available at: http://wp.lancs.ac.uk/translatingpain /, accessed 1 April 2019

Wasson, S. (2020, forthcoming), Spectrality, Strangeness and Stigmaphilia: Gothic and Disability Studies, *Routledge Companion to Literature and Disability*, ed. by Alice Hall, London: Routledge

Watt, R., (2018), 'The Diagnosis', *Translating Pain*. Available at http://wp.lancs.ac.uk/translatingpain/2018/03/29/the-diagnosis-by-roseanne-watt/, accessed 1 April 2019

The Stane Bairn
An Uncanny Play
Jules Horne

Characters: **Mother**
                   Stane Bairn

Mother: You're growing, bairn. You're growing fast. I've loosened my belt another two notches this past week. (beat) Speak to me, bairn. Tell me how you're doing in my wame. Is it warm enough? Have you plenty room? Speak up, my darling.

Stane Bairn: A deh speak, mither. Am the Stane Bairn.

Mother: Away with you. Everybody learns to speak. Maybe not now. Maybe not stuck in my wame with your mouth full of wet and veins. But soon.

Stane Bairn: All never speak, mither. Am the Stane Bairn.

Mother: Away. You'll learn to speak fine when you're out of here, sprung into the world with breath in your lungs.

Stane Bairn: Braith, mither? Am the Stane Bairn. All never breathe nor spring.

Mother: You'll sing, though? You'll surely sing, bonnie bairn?

Stane Bairn: If a could sing, ad be the gravelliest voice on the hale land mass. But a cannae sing. Am stane.

Mother: It's a sair fecht, bonnie bairn. And here's me shopping for bonnie clothes for you. Soft wee stretchy clothes in pink and blue and yellow.

Stane Bairn: What makes ee hink am bonnie? Am the Stane Bairn.

Mother: All bairns are bonnie to their mothers. Even the pugliest bairns like hers up the close.

Stane Bairn: No mei. Am heavy and hard wi a stiff grey face. Am stane.

Mother: What kind o stane, bairn?

Stane Bairn: Whinstane. The heaviest kind. The quarry stane. The road stane.

Mother: The kind I skipped on to school. Danced on to dances.

Stane Bairn: The kind that weighs doon the hale o Scotland. Which wioot whin wad be a light, airy country wi a 6/8 jigging step in her. But insteed is a ponderous trudge across the drookit cobble-banes.

Mother: You're a cheery sowel. Are you ready for your scan?

Stane Bairn: A ca sei, mither. Am blind.

Mother: Look! There's you. Aw. Sitting all snug. No wonder I can hardly move! You're a muckle bouncer, all right.

Stane Bairn: A ca bounce.

Mother: That'll do! I can't wait for the day you're out of here. Take the weight off, straighten my back, ease my legs, walk free.

Stane Bairn: Ee dinna love iz.

Mother: I do.

Stane Bairn: Cos am no bonnie.

Mother: You are!

Stane Bairn: Cos ee ca tak iz oot in the buggy in soft blue claes and show iz tae the neebors.

Mother: Blue claes?

Stane Bairn: Aye. For preference. Forget-me-not.

Mother: I will take you out.

Stane Bairn: Ee wull?

Mother: Aye – in this! I knitted it. It's stretchy. It'll fit. And I'll put you in the buggy and we'll up and down the street and they'll all stare-

Stane Bairn: - an swallae -

Mother: And say 'bonnie'. 'What strong features.' 'Sturdy.'

'Strapping'. 'What a rare bairn.'

Stane Bairn: 'What a grey face.' 'What a gliff a got.' (beat) Am a bonnie?

Mother: To me you are. Look! A glint! There and there! In the scan light. Glitter. Sparkling. You'll look bonnie in the sun up on Wellogate Hill.

Stane Bairn: Where's that?

Mother: Your home.

Stane Bairn: Am biding wi you.

Mother: No.

Stane Bairn: Eer ma mither.

Mother: I can't. (beat) You'll be with all the other stone bairns, sitting in the grass, toppling and wearing moss. Whins and marbles, granites of every colour, with all their names.

Stane Bairn: Cun they speak?

Mother: To each other. And their mothers.

Stane Bairn: A want ti meet them. A want oot. Av grown enough.

Mother: Soon.

Stane Bairn: Now.

Mother: Soon.

Stane Bairn: Eer seek o iz. Am seek o yow.

Mother: Let me hold you a wee while longer. It'll be funny to have a flat wame. Wearing my old clothes. Light. (beat) Aye, it's soon be time.

Stane Bairn: Mither.

Mother: What?

Stane Bairn: How?

[ENDS]

The Stane Bairn

Talking to yourself – a sign of madness? Or sanity?

I'm interested in how dialogue might be used as a way to help manage a foreign body, physical condition or illness, or at least the thoughts around it. Something unwanted and distressing. Something you can't run away from, but carry around as part of you.

For around a year, I carried a heavy fibroid (uterine tumour) that made me look 7 months pregnant. I was on the NHS waiting list but not a priority for surgery, because it wasn't life-threatening. It became very heavy, and I was often mistaken for pregnant. Then I got pregnant with twins. I didn't think this was possible. The three grew rapidly alongside each other. A successful outcome was never likely.

As a fiction writer turned theatre maker, I've learned to externalise, physicalise and use objects to bring inner life out onto the stage – a basic technique of dramatization. This strategy gives abstractions such as love or status a form or totem. The totem can then be literally and cognitively grasped and engaged with – far more easily and robustly than an inchoate thought, memory, wish or concept. As an example, the throne in Rona Munro's *The James Plays: The Key Will Keep the Lock* (2014) is a dramatic device which externalises the concept of kingship and can be acted upon, undergoing transformations of meaning in the process.

Taking this further by adding the dimension of movement, such totems can also be animated or puppeted, to create the illusion of life and character. This creates the potential for monologue to become dialogue, even if the interlocuter is silent. A good example of this in action is Wilson the volleyball in the Tom Hanks film, *Cast Away* (2000). Hanks' introspection is directed outward and solitude made more bearable through the existence of the Other. What's more, Wilson is fun. The illusion (character) and the reality (prop) can enjoyably be held in the audience's heads at the same time.

At a further stage of dramatization, these mean-imbued things can themselves be allowed to speak. Given agency, even if of a thudding and passive aggressive kind.

The Stane Bairn is my experiment in turning a solid lump of muscle into a character, to see what it has to say. During the experience, I was confused by a yearning to will the fibroid into a baby, to play the role of being pregnant, to go shopping *as if*. At some level, I *was* pregnant – to others, to myself in the mirror, looking down at and holding the lovely round shape.

This was over twelve years ago. Last year I was diagnosed with trauma and given NHS mindfulness training, which is a detachment and refocusing strategy. The dramatic technique of externalization onto objects is also a strategy of detachment and refocusing.

I'm convinced dramatic techniques can help to process trauma much quicker. I recently found out about 'psychodrama' and the work of Jacob Moreno. It's interesting to see that his techniques use uncanny tropes of doubling and mirroring.

Why does *The Stane Bairn* speak in Border Scots? Maybe because it's the voice that lives deepest in my body. It seems to be channelling the part of the Depressed Egg played by Gavin Mitchell in *Pass the Spoon* (David Shrigley/Magnetic North, 2012). A character like this can be dramatically inert and hard to sustain for a long time. As I wrote, I felt a change when the Stane

Bairn became its own gravestone, two states coexisting. Then the ending opens up a horror image. Although drama is written for speaking, it's possible to write unspoken images which are all the more powerful for being created by the audience themselves. I've found myself wondering how far uncanny techniques are the very stuff of drama.

Glossary

wame: *womb, belly*
deh, dinna: *don't*
mither: *mother*
Am: *I'm*
braith: *breath*
hale: *whole*
sair fecht: *painful fight (life's a struggle, usually mocking)*
bonnie: *pretty*
ee: *you*
hink: *think*
bairn: *child*
mei: *me (emphatic)*
stane: *stone*
pugliest: *from 'pug-ugly'*
wioot: *without*
drookit: *drenched*
banes: *bones*
ca sei: *can't see*
sowel: *soul*
muckle: *big*
iz: *me (unemphatic)*
claes: *clothes*
neebors: *neighbours*
wull: *will*
swallae: *swallow*
rare: *fine, exceptional*
gliff: *fright*
biding: *staying*
eer: *you're*
Av: *I've*

Response to 'The Stane Bairn: An Uncanny Play' by Jules Horne

Aoife S. McKenna

Reproductive Loss and the Uncanny Margins of Life/Death

The Stane Bairn play raises an uncanny confluence of topics around mal/functioning bodies, reproduction, personhood and death. Freud's seminal essay on the uncanny outlines how the concept has peculiar qualities that make it distinctive within the broader category of the 'fearful' (Freud 1955 [1919]). Exploring births and deaths, or "the margins of life," allows scholars to examine "the making and unmaking of persons and relationships, social and corporeal bodies, and life itself" (Kaufman & Morgan, 2005: 318). When reproduction itself goes awry, multiple physical and social boundaries can be crossed. This may lead to experiences of grief and loss, however at times it can also produce particularly horrifying or uncanny effects. 'Reproductive loss' refers to experiences including miscarriage, stillbirth, and perinatal, infant and maternal death. The term also denotes, more broadly "the loss of 'normal' reproductive experience" (Earle, Foley, Komaromy, & Lloyd, 2008: 259); a situation that is clearly conveyed by Horne in 'The Stane Bairn'.[1] In this response, I will draw upon social science and phenomenological approaches to pregnancy and reproductive

---

1. Miscarriage is defined as the cessation of pregnancy before 20 weeks gestation (cannot survive outside of the womb). Stillbirth is defined as the cessation of pregnancy after 20 weeks ('viable' outside of the womb). Perinatal is the period immediately before and after birth and is defined in diverse ways (nhs.co.uk). As I am interested in the experience of pregnancy and pregnancy loss rather than the status of the fetus, I will use the term pregnancy loss in its broader sense, which is more relevant for 'The Stane Bairn'.

loss in relation to Freud's concept of the uncanny as evident in 'The Stane Bairn'. Poems from two other authors are also included, and my own erasure poem response to Horne's play concludes the essay.

Although there has been relatively more focus on reproductive 'success' and technological innovations, reproductive loss has also been examined in the social sciences (Bledsoe, Banja, & Hill, 1998; Scheper-Hughes, 1993; Simonds, 1992; van der Sijpt, 2010). Studies have explored, for example, differential rates of infant mortality by race, gender and nationality (Greenhalgh 2003), as well as social responses to pregnancy loss (Cecil 1996; Layne 2003a). Anthropologists have illustrated varying cultural practices and understandings of infant death, infanticide and abortion (Bastian, 2001; Hardacre, 1997; Scheper-Hughes, 1984). It is clear, however, that infant death in general is threatening to the Euro-American social order. Research demonstrates that dead fetuses and embryos[2] emerge into public consciousness under certain conditions (Kaufman & Morgan, 2005). For instance, Layne's (2003a) ethnography of pregnancy loss support groups in the U.S. shows how miscarriage is silenced and miscarried embryos rendered socially invisible. Morgan's (2002) work details how dead fetuses are brought into social existence and assigned significance at particular times and places. Events that disrupt socio-cultural conventions around conceptualising or dealing with dead fetuses and infants can provoke reactions of horror. This is evident in the societal response to the discovery of a mass grave of 796 babies in a sewage tank in Tuam, Ireland (Finn, 2019). The Taoiseach (prime minister) at the time described the Mother and Baby institution in Tuam, where unwed pregnant women were sent between 1925 and 1961, as a "Chamber of Horrors" (Phelan, 2018). The extract from O'Brien's poem 'Child' provides an example of the horror evoked by disrupted social conventions around dead infants and babies. Instead of a warm, protective home or a caring family funeral, the children here are dumped into cold darkness and

---

2. 'Embryo' is the term used for the early stage of development of a multicellular organism. A newly developing human is usually described as an embryo until the ninth week after conception; it is thereafter typically called a 'fetus.'

stripped to the bone. O'Brien's use of 'poppets or shadow dolls' is particularly uncanny, as it blurs the line between the living and inanimate. Here, children's familiar play-time objects evoke a sense of the unfamiliar: the inhuman treatment of babies who were discarded like unwanted toys. The works on social conceptualisations of pregnancy loss will be discussed in further detail in relation to the Stane Bairn below.

Reproduction Awry and the Uncanny

A miscarriage at any stage can be extremely distressing, as varying socio-cultural and individual interpretations lead to differing emotional reaction (Sijpt 2010: 1778). Reproductive mishaps, however, can cross over into the realm of horror when the boundaries between bodies, and what is human/non-human or alive/dead become ambiguous. This is clear in "gruesome" examples from Layne's research within toxically assaulted communities in the U.S., where extremely malformed fetuses were described by participants in 'inhuman' ways, such as "alien"

Child

*They went, those children
into dark places, not of the soul
but into the cold earth and all
the while
the lean wind stripped their
bones...*

*Down, down they went
in tens, in dozens, like poppets
or shadow dolls.*

Jean O'Brien (2018).

(Layne, 2003b: 1884). For instance, Christine was admitted to hospital after a ten month pregnancy. Medical staff realised that her son had severe hydrocephalus and spina bifida[3] and was missing limbs and organs including fingers, toes and eyes. In the written testimony in the court case against Hooker Chemical Corporation she describes how:

> *"The doctor braced himself with his knee against the table and repeatedly tried to forcibly rip something from my body. I felt as though I was being eviscerated. I was sure I was going to die". The doctor asked the nurse to call in the anesthesiologist who exclaimed when he entered the room, "My God! Is it alive?" Apparently, despite the severe birth defects, "the baby had been alive until the doctor crushed his skull".* (ibid: 1884)

Christine's account can be seen to evoke Freud's notion of the uncanny in several ways. Firstly, the apparently healthy baby was revealed to have severe, fatal malformations (missing eyes was a particular focus in Freud's original essay [1955:226]). Secondly, the boundary between her body and the fetus is unclear, as it seems as though her own body is being violently 'eviscerated.' Thirdly, the fetus was expected to be already dead due to its 'inhuman/unlivable' state, but was instead revealed to be alive. Finally, the violent and accidental actual death of the fetus as a result of that confusion, at a time when newborns are usually handled with care.

The Stane Bairn

The ambiguity around whether the Stane Bairn is living, or not, is clearly evoked throughout Horne's play. The opening line sets out an "ordinary pregnancy practice," that of a mother talking to her baby in the womb (Han, 2013). According to Han's research in the U.S., talking, reading aloud and singing to the belly were frequently

---

3. Hydrocephalus is defined as excess fluid on the brain, often leading to severe brain damage or death; spina bifida is when the spine and spinal cord do not develop, leading to a gap in the spine and damage of the nervous system (NHS, 2017).

practiced by her participants, family members and others during pregnancy. These 'belly talk' activities were prescribed widely by experts as prenatal stimulation, and in popular culture as leading to the ideal pregnancy (ibid: 60, 61). The women described them as meaningful experiences; they did it, not because it was already a person, but because it was part of how the "little thing inside" becomes a baby, and how they, in relation, became parents (Han, 2009). Belly talk is an ordinary social practice through which babies and parents become imagined and embodied (ibid: 61).

In Horne's play, the mither speaks in a loving and affectionate way to her (yearned-for) child throughout: "*Is it warm enough?* […] *Speak up, my darling.*" She reassures her bairn in a caring way that it will speak and that it is bonnie. In reply, however, the Stane Bairn slowly strips away the features of a living child. In doing so, it is steadily rejecting or denying each hope of the mither's imagined future bairn, as well as her relationship with it, and identity as a mother. The Stane Bairn cannot speak, it cannot see, it cannot sing or dance. It is the opposite of a soft, delicate and warm living baby; it is "*heavy and hard wi a stiff grey face.*"

The physicality of the mither's experience is emphasised, "*take the weight off, straighten my back, ease my legs, walk free,*" as the heavy weight of the large "*bouncer*" is underlined throughout the play. The vitality and energy of a skipping child or energetic jig is contrasted with the Stane Bairn as heavy, dark whinstone and the weight of an entire, drenched country. Phenomenological studies of the body, that centre lived experience and break down distinctions between the mind and body, are useful here. (Merleu-Ponty, 1962; Beauvoir, 1949; Csordas, 1990). From this perspective, pregnancy is understood as "the embodied response to an Other whom I may or may not have 'conceived and given birth to,'" including an Other not born at all (Guenther, 2006: 139). Relational accounts of personhood thus acknowledge the profoundly physical dimensions of pregnancy (loss). For example, in her account of her own miscarriage, Marshall (1999) mentions that "the shift between being largely pregnant, a little bit pregnant, or not pregnant is a corporeal one with implications for how I stood and moved and was in the world; not merely a shift in some free-floating 'body image'" (1999:70). Narrative research with descriptions of bodies experiencing various changes (e.g. illness) highlight how bodily experiences can come to the fore or shift in and out of alignment with the psychosocial sense of self (Svenaeus, 2000; Warsop, 2011).

The image of a *"hard, stiff"* uterine tumour can be particularly painful because it disrupts the socially symbolic indicator of the beginning of a life/person, as opposed to the end, in Euro-American societies (as outlined above, see Kaufman and Morgan, 2005). Yet in 'The Stane Bairn' the mither and bairn continue their conversation as though it is alive. This uncanny incongruity is similar to the creeping dread associated with the confusion between the animate and inanimate, or the living and the dead in Freud's essay (1919: 249). At this level, the conversation also reflects the relational aspect of personhood, particularly during pregnancy. It illustrates the individuality and variablity in women's emotional and intellectual connections to

The Last Letter

And I wrote you every year
On the expected date of your birth.
Alas! I didn't have an address...
Yet I wrote!
Although I could not see you grow,
But I buy a dress each year
Just for you – that to see,
How you might be budding somewhere.
Although I could not see you toddle,
But I had bought anklets for you
Just to see how those jingle,
When you would have danced.

Varsha Bhardwaj Gaur

their fetuses (Parsons 2010: 12). It also highlights the fact that women assign meaning and value to their own pregnancies, despite the biomedically defined status of the fetus (Stoyles 2015: 93).

Other ordinary social practices and events documented in research on meaning-making in pregnancy are present in Horne's play. These practices also contribute to "calling a fetus into personhood" and "calling a person into a parent" (Han, 2013; Stoyles, 2015). Lindemann describes these as a series of interpersonal, communal activities that create a place in the social world for the forthcoming child to occupy after birth (2009). Aside from 'belly talk,' this could include calling a fetus by name or nickname, preparing a space for it to sleep or eat or buying clothes (Han, 2013). It can also include the engagement of a mother's social circle and wider society in these activities, such as gifting toys, or even public transport conventions that prioritise seats for pregnant women.

The extract from the poem 'The Last Letter', by Varsha Bhardwaj Gaur, illustrates how these ordinary social practices of 'calling a fetus into personhood' take on a different meaning in the context of pregnancy loss. Writing to, or buying gifts for, a dead loved one are practices that can help to process grief. In this poem they both bring the imagined child into being as well as highlighting her absence. This double action conveys a sense of tragic loss, but also evokes a feeling of the uncanny, as it creates uncertainty about whether the child exists or doesn't exist/is alive or dead.

Horne evokes these social practices of pregnancy and (creation of) motherhood identity in several ways. It is clear when the mither refers to shopping for and knitting "*soft wee stretchy clothes*" .The prenatal scan is additionally now an important milestone in the pregnancy process, often assisting in solidfying the bonds between the (becoming) child and parent/s (Ross, 2015). It is also evident in the mither's and Stane Bairn's discussion of the imagined interaction of the neighbours exclaiming over a newborn in a buggy. Stoyles explains that these practices involve "the physical expression of human beings' intentions, emotions, beliefs, attitudes, and other manifestations of personality, as recognized by other persons, who then respond by taking up an attitude toward the fetus of the kind that's reserved for persons" (2015: 94). However, the Stane Bairn again disrupts these images and hopeful futures, pointing out that "*am no bonnie*." It flips the script by shifting the neighbours' reactions to 'stare and swallow,' and contrasting the mither's positive descriptions of ("*sturdy*") with "*fright/gliff*."

Toward the end of the play, the ambiguity around death gradually comes to the fore with the introduction of Wellogate Hill. The mither reassures the Stane Bairn through describing a graveyard as its "*home*," with similar gravestones and/as (stane) bairns. The Stane Bairn thus is both itself and also becomes its own gravestone; it is a bairn belonging in the warm "*wame*," but it also belongs in a graveyard. This is suggestive of Freud's original discussion of the uncanny in German "*unheimlich*," which literally means "unhomely" and is the opposite of "*heimlich*" – "familiar" and "belonging to the home" (1919: 219) Freud, however, shows how the two terms can merge and overlap, where the uncanny is both familiar and unfamiliar at the same time: "*heimlich* is a word the meaning of which develops towards an ambivalence, until it finally conincides with its opposite, *unheimlich*" (ibid: 224). This dual status of the Stane Bairn similarly echoes the creepiness of the 'double'; another example of the uncanny discussed by Freud (ibid: 234). He describes how the double can become the psychological "ghastly harbinger of death" (ibid: 234), or also incorporate or reflect manifestations of "unfulfilled but possible futures" etc. (ibid: 235).

In addition, a feeling of ambivalence about the 'birth' is emphasised as the mither and Stane Bairn alternate positions on whether they want it to be "*oot*," or to stay in a "*while longer*." The pre- or non-pregnant body and "*old clothes*" have now become the unfamiliar. This finally leads to the focus on the actual 'birth', and the uncanniness of the ambiguous boundary between 'bodies' is highlighted. How can the Stane Bairn – as stone tumour/part of the mither's body, as the weight of Scotland and as gravestone – emerge from the mither? There is dread here at several levels:

in separating or cutting unclear bodies and body parts; in the opening up of a mither who is *"full of wet and veins"* and *"can hardly move"*; and in the moment of 'birth' as the moment of the Stane Bairn's death. These features are reminiscent of Layne's (2003) participant's birth experience (above), where instead of leading to life, a 'birth' can mean or be experienced as the violent ripping apart, evisceration and skull-crushing of vulnerable body-subjects. The play thus culminates in an uncanny, dread/ful end to a dream of a wanted future person, relationship and embodied identity.

Summary

In contrast to the earlier tendency to erase or dismiss women's (embodied) experiences, feminist writers have highlighted how important it is to give voice to the diverse experiences of women's embodiment in distinctive and expanding ways (Beauvoir, 1949; Wright, 2018: 138). However, experiences of reproductive loss are still frequently taboo in many Euro-American societies, and there is much work yet to do on the topic within phenomenological and social sciences approaches to the body (Layne, 2003; Wright, 2018). This response piece has drawn upon social studies of pregnancy and pregnancy loss, as well as feminist phenomenological approaches, to explore themes raised on the uncanny in the The Stane Bairn play. The Stane Bairn speaks to research that examines how boundaries around life and death are negotiated and affirmed, as well as the identity categories that these boundaries redefine and create. Freud's concept of the 'uncanny' can be used to trace out details of the effects of troubling these boundaries. This work highlights how ambiguous these life/death and body/subject boundaries are, and illustrates the ways that humans form and disassemble themselves and their embodied, social worlds.

Found Poem - Response to The Stane Bairn

A 'found text' is produced by using an existing text as a source to make a new one with a different meaning. I created the following 'erasure poem' using Part I of Freud's essay on 'The Uncanny.' I erased words, keeping those I had chosen in their original order, and added punctuation. The resulting poem, 'The Warm Room,' concludes my response piece to the uncanny themes raised in 'The Stane Bairn:'

The Warm Room

Not merely
feeling
kind,
sublime
and
fertile but,

foreign,
not
recognized,
terrifying.

Awaken
difficulties
attached to the
long known, familiar,
belonging to the home.

In the dismal night,
ghastly
intimate
family
secrets.
Wild

creatures.
Sense of peaceful pleasure,
it grows
still, quiet.
Flowing waves of the
cradle-song
at home. The warm room.
Buried.

Concealed,
Withheld.
Steal
away
sigh or weep.
Love
As secretive,
deceitful and cruel
magic.

Freedom is the whispered
roots
grown in the deep earth.
Eerie, bloodcur-
dling,
horror.
Motionless like stone.

Pale brewing heaven,
veil the divine shades.
Hidden,
withdrawn from the eyes.
Speech expressing
me
that died.

References

Bastian, M. L. (2001), ' "The Demon Superstition": Abominable Twins and Mission Culture in Onitsha History'. *Ethnology,* *40*(1), p.13. DOI:10.2307/3773886

Beauvoir, S. de (1949 [2009]), *The Second Sex*. Transl. C. Borde and S. Malovany-Chevallier, New York: Alfred A. Knopf.

Bledsoe, C., Banja, F., & Hill, A. G. (1998), 'Reproductive Mishaps and Western Contraception: An African Challenge to Fertility Theory'. *Population and Development Review,* *24*(1), p.15. DOI:10.2307/2808121

Cecil, R. (1996), 'The anthropology of pregnancy loss: comparative studies in miscarriage, stillbirth, and neonatal death'. Oxford, Washington: Berg Publishers.

Csordas, T. (1990), 'Embodiment as a Paradigm for Anthropology'. *Ethos,* *18*(1), p.5. DOI: 10.1525/eth.1990.18.1.02a00010.

Earle, S., Foley, P., Komaromy, C., & Lloyd, C. (2008), 'Conceptualizing reproductive loss: A social sciences perspective'. *Human Fertility,* *11*(4), p.259. DOI:10.1080/14647270802298272

Finn, C. (2019), 'Cabinet approves legislation to excavate site of Tuam mother and baby Home', *TheJournal.ie*: https://www.thejournal.ie/mother-and-baby-home-excavation-legislation-4925619-Dec2019/, accessed 12th December 2019.

Freud, S. (1955), 'The Uncanny', in Strachey, J., and Freud, A. (eds) *The Standard Edition of the Complete Psychological Works of Sigmund Freud, Volume XVII (1917-1919): An Infantile Neurosis and Other Works*. London: Hogarth Press and The Institute of Psychoanalysis.

Gaur, V. B., (N.D.) *The Last Letter…* <https://yourstoryclub.com/poetry-and-poem/poem-on-female-foeticide-last-letter/, accessed 16th January 2019.

Grennhalgh, S. (2003), 'Unplanned persons and gendered children – planned births, unplanned persons: "population" in the making of Chinese modernity'. *American Ethnologist*, 30, p.196.

Guenther, L. (2006), *The Gift of the Other: Levinas and the Politics of Reproduction*. Albany: State Univ. of New York Press.

Han, S. (2013), *Pregnancy in Practice Expectation and Experience in the Contemporary US*. New York: Berghahn Books.

Hardacre, H. (1997), *Marketing the Menacing Fetus in Japan*. Berkeley: Univ. of California Press.

Kaufman, S. R., & Morgan, L. M. (2005), 'The Anthropology of the Beginnings and Ends of Life'. *Annual Review of Anthropology*, 34, p.317.

Layne, L. (2003a), *Motherhood Lost: A Feminist Account of Pregnancy Loss in America*. New York: Routledge

Layne, L. (2003b), 'Unhappy endings: A feminist reappraisal of the women's health movement from the vantage of pregnancy loss'. *Social Science & Medicine*, 56, p.1881. DOI: 10.1016/s0277-9536(02)00211-3

Lindemann, H. (2009), '"… But I Could Never Have One": The Abortion Intuition and Moral Luck'. *Hypatia*, 24, p.41. DOI:10.1111/j.1527-2001.2009.00005.x

Marshall, H. (1999), 'Our bodies, ourselves: Why we should add old-fashioned empirical phenomenology to the new theories of the body'. In *Feminist Theory and the Body*, (eds) J. Price and M. Shildrick, p.64. New York: Routledge

Merleau-Ponty, M. (1962), *Phenomenology of Perception*. London: Routledge & Kegan Paul.

Morgan, L. M. (2002), '"Properly Disposed of": A history of embryo disposal and the changing claims on fetal remains'. *Medical Anthropology*, 21(3-4), p247. DOI:10.1080/01459740214079

NHS (2017), *Spina Bifida* <https://www.nhs.uk/conditions/spina-bifida/> Accessed December 2019.

O'Brien, J. (2018) 'The Child,' in Casey, E. (ed.) *The Lea-Green Down*. Dublin: Fiery Arrow Press.

Phelan, S. (2018), Tuam Babies: Remains of hundreds of children feared buried in mass grave to be exhumed, *Independent.ie*: https://www.independent.ie/irish-news/news/tuam-babies-remains-of-hundreds-of-children-feared-buried-in-mass-grave-to-be-exhumed-37450152.html, accessed 11th December 2019.

Ross, E. (2015), *Exploring tentativeness: risk, uncertainty and ambiguity in first time Pregnancy*. PhD Thesis, University of Edinburgh: Edinburgh.

Scheper-Hughes, N. (1984), 'Infant mortality and infant care: Cultural and economic constraints on nurturing in Northeast Brazil'. *Social Science & Medicine*, *19*(5), p.535. DOI:https://doi.org/10.1016/0277-9536(84)90049-2

Sijpt, E. van der (2010), 'Marginal matters: Pregnancy loss as a social event'. *Social Science & Medicine*, *71*(10), p.1773. DOI:https://doi.org/10.1016/j.socscimed.2010.03.055

Simonds, W. (1992), *Centuries of Solace: expressions of maternal grief in popular literature*. Philadelphia: Temple University Press.

Stoyles, B. (2015), 'The Value of Pregnancy and the Meaning of Pregnancy Loss'. *Journal of Social Philosophy* 46(1), p.91. DOI: https://doi.org/10.1111/josp.12088.

Svenaeus, F. (2000), 'The body uncanny – Further steps towards a phenomenology of illness'. *Medicine, Health Care and Philosophy*, 3, p.125.

Warsop, A. (2011), 'The ill body and *das unheimliche* (the uncanny)'. *Journal of Medicine and Philosophy*, 36, p.484.

Wright, J. (2018), 'Relationality and Life: Phenomenological Reflections on Miscarriage'. IJFAB: *International Journal of Feminist Approaches to Bioethics*, 11(2), p.135. ISSN: 1937-4577.

Bunting
Neil Williamson

'You'll be needing a spade.' Uncle Don indicates the blackiron pot by the door. It bristles with gardening tools the way other people have umbrella stands. Around it is a tumble of men's shoes in a litter of crumbled-off mud. A far cry from the kitchen at home, white-tiled like a science lab, or a hospital.

While Struan hovers, his thumbnail worrying the scab on the inside of his wrist, the dogs *tick-tack* out of the cave mouth of the darkened front room. The big one and the small one, rangy and unkempt. He thinks they might be mother and son. They slink past his legs to wait by the door. Two pairs of ghost-white eyes, eager to be loosed.

He's only been in Garsdale since lunchtime. A bus, a hitched car ride and then his own two feet getting him from Leeds to this dim cottage that stinks of soil and moulder, but he's not ungrateful for the suggestion of a walk around the neighbourhood. To show him the land, Don said, though Struan hadn't realised he'd be expected to work it too.

He withdraws a narrow-bladed spade from the thicket. The flat is rusted, the edge pitted. It doesn't look like it will stand up to breaking ground. He makes to put it back but Don says, 'It'll do the job fine.' Then his uncle chooses a spade of his own and opens the door and the dogs dart out, and the two men follow.

*

'How's your mam?' The question swoops out of nowhere, like the cars that tear around these Dales roads, forcing the walkers onto the verge. They are climbing a bend now and there's another one coming. Struan recognises the quickening vibration through his soles this time and steps off pre-emptively, taking another step almost into the ditch when he realises that this one is a van. It's going too fast for the corner, scything an arc through the tree branches right where he'd been standing. A decal of cartoon chickens obscured by a rain of twigs.

Walking on, Struan lets out his held breath, draws in another. The smell of the autumn air is clean, though lacking the antisepsis he's used to. Instead, something vegetable: leaf drop and conker shells; something animal: wool tufts in the hedge; something else, musky, perhaps the little brown mushrooms that proliferate here. The afternoon sun doesn't quite overpower the chill but he doesn't mind. It's a relief from the stifle of home.

Don's question is a complicated one. On the phone the other night—his first alone since his folks installed him in his new university accommodation—Mum had said she was feeling tired. Probably just fatigue from the long drive, not a genuine dip in the erratic skimming stone trajectory of her illness. Maybe fatigue, yeah. Or perhaps a stoke of his guilt for choosing a university so far from home.

'She's just the same,' Struan says, rubbing his wrist inside his sleeve, then snatching his hand away to stop himself from picking.

Uncle Don merely nods in response. And then they're in the verge again as three cyclists rattle-swoosh past, helmets and suits the colours of Struan's new floor-mates' vibrant Pride flags.

'Worse than the motors, them,' Don says.

Struan's turn to nod, although he suspects his uncle means something other than their flagrant confidence and assured trajectories.

*

It's another quarter mile before they come across the rabbit. The dogs scamper ahead and are circling, sniffing the carcass when the humans catch up. Don tongue-clicks them away.

It's a sad sight, Struan supposes, though sadness isn't exactly what he feels. He's never seen roadkill up close before. It's interesting. The animal is stretched, arcing like one of the ghosts in *Watership Down*. Otherwise, it looks unharmed. Its eyes are closed as if in sleep and the fur still has that tawny-grey-gold brindle. It looks so soft. Struan can imagine how it would feel under his fingers.

Don rummages for a bin bag. 'Hold it open.'

Struan looks away as he stretches the plastic. He hears the scrape of the blade, feels the jolt of the corpse. Then Don takes the bag back, swings it over his shoulder.

They walk on, the dogs trotting with happy tongues at Don's heels.

*

'It's for your Aunt May's memory.' Don shakes the frying pan and turns off the gas. 'Great big heart, that woman. Too much love in her to bear to see an animal left out there, reduced to dirty scraps. Always wanted them properly taken care of. You don't remember your Aunt May.'

Struan's sat at the table. The dogs are pacing and whimpering. Finding their restlessness contagious, he worries at the scab, feeling the tight skin give. Don's right. All he has of Aunt May are hazy recollections: a bosomy woman with a drowsy odour that wasn't astringent and false like the perfumes Mum wears, gentle hands setting a paper crown on his head at Christmas, cupping his scalp for a warm second after. Those few flitting impressions. He's not even sure if they're real memories. They're more like the daydreams he comforted himself with when he was small. The ones about changing his skin, about being different.

Mum never talks about her sister. The photographs he found with *Arbour Cottage, Garsdale*, pencilled on the back were from when the two of them were younger than he is now. He thinks they looked quite alike, but he suspects they really weren't. He clearly remembers May's death, though. Struan was old enough by then to sense that when Mum had cried in the kitchen, her tears were of anger more than grief. And he remembers Mum and Dad, sharp dressed and sombre for the funeral, pacing in and out of the living room where he was playing Mousetrap with the babysitter. Mum smoking. Mum snapping and sniping while Dad tried to calm her. Mum saying, *No, no, no, I won't, I won't go,* for the longest time before the car arrived eventually, and they did.

There was nothing between his earlier recollections and that day. No visits, no calls, no birthday cards or Christmas presents. Not a word from his mother's lips since then either, but he'd remembered all the same.

'Sorry,' he tells Don. 'I'm sure she was a good person though.'

Shaking the cooling meat into the dogs' bowls, Don says: 'Your mam'd disagree, as like.'

Struan wonders if that's meant to be an invitation for him to ask, but it's too soon. None of this is what he'd expected. He turns his gaze to the window where, in the deepening bleed of the September sky, he can see the rabbit skin pegged out. The soft brindle ruffles in the breeze. Next to it, the two stoats it had been his turn to scrape up.

'There you go, you two.' The second Don places the bowls on the floor, the dogs dive for the meat. As Struan watches them eat, he feels his phone buzz in his pocket. If Don can hear the insistent vibration, he doesn't say. Struan doesn't want to answer it. Doesn't even want to look and see if it's the University calling to find out why he didn't turn up at induction. Or if it's Mum, always Mum. The phone stops ringing, eventually.

'You'll be hungry too,' Don says. 'I'll go up the village for chips.'

*

In his absence, Struan gets the fire going in the living room. He used to do this for his grandfather when Mum, who considered it a *filthy business,* was absent. The scrunched newspaper, firelighters and matches are all there beside the coal scuttle. Soon there's a proper blaze and the cave-room comes alive with flicker and shadow. He perches on the edge of a corduroy couch, sagging under a heap of books, magazines and other stuff. Though there is an empty armchair, from the spectacle case and tube of haemorrhoid cream resting on the arm, that is Don's place. The comfortable niche he has made for himself in the world in the years after his wife went.

Her presence has even faded from the house she lived in.

In the fireglow, Struan's hands are black with coal dust but, when he moves his fingers, something sparkles. He turns his hands this way, that way, fascinated by his new alien skin. Imagines himself like that all over. A creature of void and starlight.

No, that doesn't feel right. Too cold.

He blasts hot water into the kitchen sink, scrubs the black away with soap and stiff bristles. Scrubs until his hands are new-born pink, scrubs until they're roadkill raw. Scrubs at his fat fingers. Scrubs at his palms. Scrubs at his wrists, finally knocking off the scab and revealing the potential of newness beneath.

Struan tugs the fringe of old skin with this thumbnail, working the delicate rag as slowly as the boiling anxiety inside him will allow. There is pain—there should be pain. He teases, pulling and lifting. The more he can shed, snakelike, in one piece, the closer he feels he will be to discovering who—*what*—he is.

In his early teens they'd tried to cure him of the dermatillomania: the urge to pick and peel. *I can't just be me*, he'd told Dr Manning, *if I don't know what that is.* Dr Manning had many theories; about gender, sexuality, body image, but they were all wrong. All those visits had left him with was a better idea of the question of himself: what he was *not*, if not what he was.

One time, Struan peeled off a strip four centimetres long but today it's barely one. The frustration floods through him, a tide of needles. He pops the skin scrap onto his tongue and, with a wordless prayer, swallows it. He licks the salty blood from his throbbing arm and pulls his jumper sleeve down.

He hears the door. Don's back.

*

They don't talk while they eat. The chips are too hot, too salty. Don moves some of the crap off the sofa for him to sit properly, turns on the ceiling light and the BBC News, banishing the magic from the cave, making it part of the world Struan already knows he has no place in.

The black dogs slink in to beg for food, jumping up one either side of him. He burrows his fingers into their coats, feels their hot flanks, the real, skinny-long shape of them hidden beneath the fur.

His phone goes in his pocket again. Must be Mum this time. The dog on that side of him grumps and shifts away. Struan can imagine the conversation playing out.

We got a call from the university, she'd say. *What's going on? Where are you?*

Nothing's wrong, he'd say, searching for a plausible lie. He's getting better at those. *I went out with some friends from the halls and we had a few drinks too many and we slept in.*

Friends? That would stump her, simultaneously feeding her conflicting fears that he was finally growing beyond her and that he wouldn't cope on his own. *You've only been there a couple of days. What friends?*

Just the guys on my floor. It's fine. We're going to register tomorrow.

That was how it would go. Unless, of course, he actually answered, and stammered apologies and lapsed into a paralysed silence that ended with the inevitable: *We're coming down tomorrow.*

Don is staring at the TV but Struan watches the fire instead, his fingers up his jumper sleeve, picking and peeling. It distracts him from the huffy buzz as his phone tells him the caller left a message. He watches the coals settle, basks like a lizard in the heat, couries into the dogs again and, inch by inch, relaxes.

'There's a bed,' Don says. 'If you're staying.'

Struan blinks. Realises that he has been drowsing.

'I don't want to impose,' he mumbles, but where else is he going to go?

As he stumbles out, Don scritches the older dog and murmurs something Struan barely hears. It sounds like: 'All the strays come here eventually, don't they?'

*

If there was no sign of his Aunt May elsewhere in the house, the bedroom is full of her. The dressing table holds a satin-backed hairbrush and mirror set, a box of kirbies in a crocheted cover, an atomiser of perfume. The tasselled bedside lamp illuminates a stack of romance novels and a pair of reading glasses. The pillowcases and sheets welcome him with a trace of drowsy scent.

Struan kicks off his shoes and collapses onto the custard-coloured candlewick.

He dreams of a rumble and occasional jolt in a darkness interspersed by flashes of sodium orange. In the dream, he is enveloped in Aunt May's scent, cradled gently and swaddled head to toe in soft warmth. In something that feels natural. His real skin.

Dawn wakes him. A soft, silver purity, a light of revelation. The bedroom, Struan understands now, is one person's remembrance of another. But it's just the veneer. No deeper. All the same, he suspects Don has slept in his chair for twelve years rather than desecrate this place.

The light, though...

Getting up, Struan approaches the window. He feels flushed. His skin itches. He's ready. He steps forward.

And waits...

But there is no transformation. His skin does not split and slough and birth the real him anew.

His skin is wronger than ever.

He needs a knife, scissors... Searches the dressing table, the dresser, and then the wardrobe. And finds this flat box.

And in the box is tissue paper. And, within that...

A tiny all-in-one garment. Exquisitely tailored from a patchwork of hides. It is cosy rabbit and bold badger. Dappled fawn overlaid with a collar of striped pheasant feathers. A magpie hood. Four little paws to keep a toddler's hands warm. Round the back is a fox cub's brush.

So beautiful. So perfect. Its rightness calls to him but he doesn't dare touch it.

Instead he picks and peels at his own traitorous flesh, because all he can think is that it's too *small*.

And it is far too late.

Skin Sisters
Bridget Bradley

This extract is based on ethnographic and auto-ethnographic research with people living with body-focused repetitive behaviours in the United Kingdom and United States between 2016 and 2018.

*

She draws with charcoal. She calls it compulsive because it comes from within, without reason.
She controls it well, keeping it safe, mostly, in the spaces where it can't bring her harm.
On the train. On the bus. Her head is down… immersed… drawn in deep… pushing it
out of her hands and on to the paper.
One
by
one
by
one
by
one
she draws.
Fast – and – focused – and – frantic – and – fearless – and – filthy.

*

It might seem unusual to the outside eye, but perhaps that's because you can't fully understand it or
appreciate its value without   looking in.
Really looking in.
Observing. Participating. Asking. Empathising.
I asked her, 'What does it feel like?'
She said, 'It feels like the disorder.'
The truth is, in some ways, I know what it feels like.
It's a deep-seeded urgency, under your skin, scratching your bones.
It makes you sit up.
Stand up.
It takes you away from the world, and lets you escape into one of your own – for a moment.
It's never just a moment.
Minutes
and
minutes
and
minutes
and
minutes.
Time moves.
Fast – and – focused – and – frantic – and – fearless – and – filthy.

*

Until
something snaps you back into your skin
where you can feel and see and know what *you have done.*
Is it pain? Pleasure?
Perhaps somewhere in between.
It's an aching < holdyourbreathuntilyoucan'tbreathe > kind of tension
and when your shoulders unravel and
you feel the muscles unwind and all the goodness that was there is gone.

Turned to guilt, disappointment, regret.
But for her, instead, it becomes something beautiful
something positive
something shared
with a multiplicity of values and meanings.
Fast – and – focused – and – frantic – and – fearless – and – filthy.

*

She is an artist.
She works with her body, and her body moves with her work –
through spaces
and places, with people, and things.
You may have seen her. In the city.
Perhaps she shared it with you?
Maybe you share it with her?
It's not so strange you know…
Scratch-scratching, start-stopping, scrib-scrabbling
up
and
down
and
in
and
out.
Fast – and – focused – and – frantic – and – fearless – and – filthy.

*

Liz has compulsive skin picking.

It is a condition that dominated her life for over twenty years before she knew it had a name. Dermatillomania. Excoriation Disorder. Derma. CSP.

It goes by many names despite having only been recognised as a psychiatric label in 2013 (American Psychiatric Association, 2013).

Skin picking is the sister condition to compulsive hair pulling. Trichotillomania.

They are part of a family of disorders known as body-focused repetitive behaviours or BFRBs.

Arguably, skin picking, hair pulling and related behaviours are common in all humans and animals. But it's estimated that 1 in 20 people worldwide experience BFRBs to the extent that they become compulsive, obsessive, and almost impossible to stop (according to The TLC Foundation for Body-Focused Repetitive Behaviors). With a complex blend of mental emotional distress and physical bodily damage, BFRBs interfere with everyday life causing shame and embarrassment. The limited understanding of these conditions and their lack of treatment options makes dealing with their effects a struggle for people and their supporters.

Liz started picking her skin when she was six years old. She has vivid memories of how it quickly became a daily activity that occupied her hands and her thoughts. Her first memory of trying to keep it secret was telling her schoolteacher that she had chicken pox. It would be the first of many lies. Skin picking covered her entire body. She would pick her face. Her chest. Her back. Her arms. The soles of her feet. She would pick in her sleep, and wake up with her bedsheets dotted in blood. She didn't own a t-shirt for ten years. Liz didn't tell anyone.

When I first met Liz, we were both far from home. Brought together by the world's only international conference for BFRBs, taking place in Dallas, Texas in the spring of 2016. These conferences happen each year, and connect hundreds of people with BFRBs and their families with clinicians and researchers. For many people, it is the first time they have ever met others who share their problem, and it can be emotional and overwhelming. I was sitting in the morning sun writing in my fieldwork notebook, taking a moment away from the busy intensity of the conference. Suddenly I heard a very English 'helllooooooo' from across the pool garden. I recognised Liz immediately from her social media profiles. Although we had never met in person, I had heard about her work (artist, advocate) and she knew of mine (anthropologist, advocate). I was excited to meet her, and jumped up from the poolside chair to introduce myself. Grinning widely, Liz opened her arms and gave me a huge warm hug. We chatted excitedly for a few minutes, and once again I had that feeling of familiarity, relatedness.

*

My hair pulling began around the age of eight or nine. For a while it seemed to go unnoticed by other people, but for me the sudden and uncontrollable urge to pull out individual hairs from my eyebrows quickly got out of control. Soon it was impossible to conceal, glaringly obvious, staring everyone in the face when I lifted my head. For ten years I genuinely thought I was alone. The only one in the world who did this thing to my body. But then I found the name, trich-o-till-o-mania. More years passed before I connected the dots with skin picking, nail biting – behaviours that most of my immediate family members shared. More time would pass before I could open up to them about how my hair pulling had affected us all. The silence was long and painful.

Now I dedicate my life to talking about it.

Recognising these shared attributes in my family was intriguing, reassuring. But meeting a complete stranger whose experience mirrored my own so closely, was powerful beyond words. A deep intimacy, a bond, an embodied understanding. So many of the people I have met over the years said the same thing, 'I feel like we've known each other our whole lives'. We can talk as if no one is staring. We can laugh about all of the absurd and time-consuming tactics we have used to hide. We can cry over the ridicule, the blame, the shame. We can forgive ourselves, and we can go on living our lives.

*

Liz Atkin is a London-based artist who combines her creativity with efforts to share her skin picking story with people all over the world. In the spaces where Liz is usually affected by skin picking temptations (on the London underground to work, for example), she uses charcoal to scribble attractive and unique drawings on free newspapers, which she hands to strangers along with an explanation of why she is doing it. She calls this her one-minute 'Compulsive Charcoal' series, and it is a beautifully simple and powerful metaphor for compulsive skin picking: fast, all-consuming, messy, visible. She uses her art to divert her skin picking away from her body and onto the paper, raising the profile of the condition and changing the way it is viewed by the public. Every day Liz gives away about 60 drawings, and very often she meets someone else who struggles with skin picking, or hair pulling, many of whom have never met another person just like them, some not even knowing the behaviour has a medical name. In my conversations with Liz, she told me, 'drawing saved my life', and she talked openly about her history with anxiety and depression which make her skin picking worse.

In October 2016, Liz had invited me to an event where she was asked to do a live drawing. It was early October 2016. I waited for her at Dalston Junction station in north-west London, which was busy on a Friday night at nine o'clock. I watched as the crowds of people ascended the escalator, emerging suddenly from underground, eventually seeing Liz among them. She was smiling and colourful, with bright red lipstick, multi-coloured rainbow high heels and a roll of paper on her back the size of a small tree trunk. She rushed towards me excitedly and we hugged. On our way to the venue, we popped in to a convenience store to buy baby wipes, an essential handbag item for her when she draws with charcoal almost constantly. She told me that because she had forgotten her baby wipes she was unable to draw on the train, as she wouldn't have been able to clean her filthy hands afterwards. She held up her little finger to show me the damage she had done to the skin all around the nail which had been peeled away, demonstrating how easily she slips back into her picking routine without the tools she needs to keep it maintained.

At the event that evening, Liz had been asked to do a large-scale charcoal drawing at the launch of a fashion magazine that features some of her artwork. We arrived at the venue ahead of the launch to get set up. Heading down the dark staircase into a basement, I felt as if we were on the set of *Doctor Who*, a long white corridor which looked like a tunnel made of cubes, decorated with twigs and sticks. In the rooms leading off the corridor were photographs from the magazine hanging from gold wire, bizarre props, and music playing in the background that sounded like noises from the seventies kids show *The Clangers*. Liz and I were shown where to get ready, and I helped her to tape the huge sheet of paper to the wall. Adding to the obscurity, the editor of the magazine approached Liz and requested that she wear a full-length white doctor's coat while she drew. Liz accepted politely, asking no questions, but quickly turned to me, and raised her eyebrows with a smirk. As the guests started to arrive, Liz began to draw, working surprisingly quickly as rough sketches of mountains suddenly appeared on the wall. I watched her as she travelled up and down the paper, her whole body moving and taking over the drawing. Her hands were instantly filthy, covered in black charcoal dust, and so was the white coat. I started to ask her questions while she drew, how does it feel? For Liz, the movement of her body, and the sensations associated with drawing replicate that of skin picking, and so she is able to replace her BFRB with her art. She described the similarities between the two: the energy and speed with which she moves; the itchy feeling of the charcoal on her skin; the pincer-like positioning of her fingers as she holds the charcoal which is the same position of her fingers for picking; the trance-like zone she enters that makes her feel calm; and the production of something satisfying at the end.

After completing the wall drawing, Liz decided to do some compulsive charcoal drawings for the guests who were milling around the room, enjoying the complimentary gin cocktails. I watched as she approached them, asking if she could draw them a picture. Her advocacy was in full swing as she told people why she draws and more about the disorder that she keeps at bay. When she was finished each one, she gave them to people as small gifts.

They were beautiful drawings, simultaneously messy and intricate sketches of hills surrounded by dark clouds. I asked her, is it ever hard to part with these drawings? She said 'I learn not to be precious with them because I see the value in *this*' - she held up her charcoal covered hands, showing me that keeping her hands busy and away from her skin is more valuable to her than the art she produces. The value in Liz's work goes beyond the personal self-care of drawing that she relies on, and also beyond the cherished artwork that she gives to grateful strangers for free. Through this embodied self-care, she maintains control of her disorder while she draws, but at the same time she is making skin picking visible in new ways to the public, reducing the stigma one sketch at a time.

References

American Psychiatric Association (2013) *The Diagnostic and Statistical Manual of Mental Disorders* (*DSM* 5). Fifth Edition. Washington D.C.: American Psychiatric Association

The TLC Foundation for Body-Focused Repetitive Behaviors: https://www.bfrb.org/, Accessed 10th January 2020

The Treatment
Helen Sedgwick

Say hello. Come on, little one. Say hello.

I wait patiently but you give me nothing.

Say hi. That's an easy one, isn't it? Say hi. Please?

There is no clock in this room, no sound other than my own voice. I smooth the edge of your sheet down over the side of the cot bed – you crinkled it when you pushed your hands out this morning, as you do every morning, as you have done since the staff took away the bars to celebrate your second birthday. Remember that?

Say hiya.

At last your eyes move from the window to my face and you give that deliberate blink of yours. Eyes closed. Eyes open. Your cheeks have perfect colour. Your elbows bend and you place your hands neatly over your tummy. The pinpricks left in your skin from when they took the drips out yesterday have vanished already – your body is doing what it was designed to do now, I've no doubt about that.

Through the window, where your eyes have returned, there's a shrub covered in red berries so bright and shiny they look plastic. They're not though; they are entirely real. I squashed one between my thumb and forefinger last time I was outside, while you were sleeping, and when the berry burst some red juice came out, more watery than I expected from the deep crimson of the surface. Before all this happened, I would have licked the juice from my thumb.

I remember when you were new. The snowfall was the heaviest there'd been in thirty-five years, the outside world buried under white and there you were; flawless with transparent skin and Cupid's bow lips. I let you lie belly down on my chest in the warm water of the bath – we neither of us wanted to move – and you kept smooshing your nose against me, like you were trying to burrow your way face-first into my heart. When I touched your head, my palm neatly cupped your scalp. Hello, I whispered. Hello, little one. Hello? I wanted you to make a noise. Perhaps I needed proof that you were okay. Your lips opened and closed against my bare skin, leaving cool patches where the moisture evaporated. You latched on easily; you fed for a while and then you dozed. The water around us was misted and thick so eventually we moved to bed and crib where you took in rapid, shallow breaths and I lay awake all night trying to do the same, watching the determined rise and fall of you.

Hello, I whispered to you every morning. Say hi. Say hiya. I had to give it time. We were acclimatizing to one another, while the snow fell silently outside, but then the snow stopped and I saw your fingers curl around the top of your crib. Carrying you gently in my arms, I wiped a hole in the window's condensation with my sleeve; it was warm in our room but standing there by the glass I could taste the frost, feel the slip of ice against my skin. A bird had been on the ground, a robin perhaps, or a chaffinch – something small – and her prints made a path of tiny arrows through the snow beneath our window. You reached out, your palm pressing flat against the glass and you made the purest sound I'd ever heard: a perfect, single note.

When the rains came we watched the snow turning to slush, and then to streams that flowed to the woodlands where pine trees were losing their caps. We spent more time downstairs, sitting on the rug by the fire, as I showed you how to reach, how to grasp, how to push. Gathering my courage, I wrapped you snug against my body in your sling, eased a hat over your head and the hood from your tiny raincoat over that, and then I opened the door. Big puddles, look! Your arms waved and your single note got higher.

Splash! Jumping into water with my boots. Splosh! You giggled and squealed and blew me a raspberry, little bubbles of saliva forming between your lips. You're doing so well, I told you as I laid you down inside again, checking your neck and face and hands were dry and warm and clean.

Then one day I took you deeper into the garden to see the crocus stems pushing their way out from the damp soil. One of the buds was about to open, its deep purple petals wide enough to reveal a pattern of delicate white veins. You were wriggling and excited, getting heavier too. Suddenly you lunged forwards. My grip tightened. Do you want to look closer, is that it? Say yes, muma. Say please. I sat down on the grass, forced my hands to loosen their hold and laid you on my legs, facing the fresh stems in the flowerbed. Your hand reached out, slowly at first, gently, then you pitched sideways, clasped mud and gleefully squelched it between your fingers. I grabbed you fast – no, sweetheart – turned you round as you kicked and squirmed, hands everywhere, mud everywhere. No. Your vocal cords creaked like an old gate. *Gaaaa*. Your legs pushed against my thighs, my stomach – you had some strength. *Gaaaaaaa*. That's enough. I held you firmly. Stood up. Time to go in. When I brushed my hair that night something snagged, pulling the tender skin where the back of my head met my neck. A clump of mud, caked dry. I looked at you: you'd kicked all your blankets off and were lying face down in your cot, knees bent and toes curled. From that day on, you refused to lie on your back like you were supposed to, no matter how many times I turned you over.

We stayed inside to play. When I left the room to make tea, I came back to find you lying under the window, head on one side, transfixed by the sound of rain pelting glass. We couldn't afford many toys, but there was a giraffe that you liked to chew on. You loved your soft felt cubes and yellow-cow blanket. I moved my face away from your line of sight, then back again, over and over, sometimes all day long, to see that look of recognition spark across your face. Say hiya. Say muma. Say hi? *Gaaaaaaaa*. You'd sit, then wobble, then fall, and I'd pick you up to soothe you, tell you how clever you were getting, that you were learning things so well. Then one day the air was warm and dry and we felt strong enough to venture out of the house, beyond the garden, all the way to the stream. That was what you wanted, wasn't it.

Say yes.

Say sorry.

The stream running along the dip in the hill behind our house, between the pines and blueberry bushes, over stones and twigs and the toppled branch that lies half out and half in, rotting, glittering in the sun. We followed the path through flowering gorse, you strapped to me in your carrier, until we reached the pond where the stream opens up like a mirror and dragonflies dart. You wanted out. Legs thrashing and arms grabbing, your head desperately arching over your shoulder so you could see the water. Okay, I said. Okay, little one. Here we go. I found us a safe spot on the grass by the edge where you could sit between my legs and look at the water and there: the little tadpoles! I pointed them out. Do you see them? Say hello. Wave at the tadpoles. We dipped our hands in and for a moment we both felt them, wriggling between our fingers. The next thing I knew, you had scooped up a handful of pond water and were slurping it into your mouth. I didn't mean to shout but it was the shock. You grinned at me and fast as a blink you were gulping more pond water and I grabbed you and ran through the gorse and pines until we got home, my panic hissing all the while that it was dirty and stagnant and filled with larvae and I needed to get it out of you.

Milk. Was that the answer?

I held you on tight to feed as you squirmed. You pushed me away to cry. I held you on tighter. You kicked and screamed. What can I do? What do you need? It took all my strength to keep you pressed against me until eventually I stopped and laid you down and you fell asleep on the floor at my feet and I began to search online. Pond water. Parasites. Bacteria.

Oh God. The noise you made when you woke up.

I tried to hold you, to calm you down. I kissed your head. Wrapped you tight in fleecy blankets in case you were too cold then cooled you down with a wet flannel in case you were too hot, and still you cried. Your face was red with the effort of it, your eyes wet and sore and angry. I thought that if I could make you sick then whatever it was you'd ingested would come out, so I dripped sugar water into your open mouth. You screamed and thrashed, you threw up, your nappies filled with brown liquid. The crying got worse. My head throbbed with the constant noise. Days passed, the air got hotter. On the rare occasions when you slept I lay awake, my skin clammy with sweat, listening to the sound of honeybees bashing repeatedly against the window.

I took you, screaming, to the doctor. The waiting room had pale green walls and posters about how to eat less and exercise more and stop smoking, and it was filled with people who stared at us as you cried. Shhh, please, I whispered, cuddling you close, but you were oblivious. If anything, the volume of your wails increased. Down the corridor, the GP placed you on the examination table, bent your knees and ankles, listened to your chest, felt for a pulse. Then she asked me:

What do you think it is?

If I knew that I wouldn't need to be here, I thought, but didn't say out loud. She had a window in her room that looked over the car park. My eyes were drawn out there; I had to force them back to her face.

There's been constant crying for nearly a week.

You could try paracetamol, or a little ibuprofen.

But there's something very wrong.

It's a normal thing, sometimes, to cry. It's a very human thing, don't you think?

I picked you up again, squeezed you to my chest.

Back at home, I squirted Calpol into your mouth with a syringe and you spat it all out, pink oozing from your lips in sticky trails down your chin. The next day I ran through gorse, collected a sample of pond water, returned to find you'd pushed your head through the bars of your playpen. The water was teeming with microscopic life: wispy particles, green tendrils, froth that had a yellowish tint when I held it to the light.

Another doctor claimed everything was normal. A third refused to examine the pond water. There were no GPs left for me to try in the surgery. Summer baked the ground and dried the burn, its heat stuck to my skin like melted liquorice and you screamed with desperate gasps that filled your body then left it hollow in my arms. I let you cry on the floor as I read about chlamydomonas and spongomonas, cyanobacteria and spirochaete, curling the names of bacteria and viruses and algae on my tongue. There were pictures of them online, bulbous pellets, hairy and fibrous. I imagined them in your mouth, latching on to your stomach's lining. The doctors wouldn't listen so I had to save you myself. Day and night I read online health forums and chat rooms and threads started by mothers with nowhere else to turn. There were suggestions of herbal remedies – we were beyond that, you and I – and the recommendation of a private clinic that we would never be able to afford. Then the advert appeared on the right hand side of my screen, beside a thread I'd been reading about klebsiella and gut inflammation.

It was called The Microbial Research Institute. Their procedure was experimental, still in the developmental stages. We would be part of a clinical trial – they would even pay us – but it wouldn't involve doing anything to you, not the true you; the treatment they offered only targeted microbes.

Are you in constant pain?

Do you suffer from stress or anxiety?

The answer could lie in your gastrointestinal microbiota.

Microbiota.

Microorganisms inside the digestive tract, crawling through your body. Living, inside you. And this company, this institute, was offering a way to clean them out. Start over. We both needed it.

I strapped you, wailing and struggling against me, into the baby car seat. The snow hadn't arrived yet, but I could taste it. I started the engine. We left our garden, the woodlands behind our home, and emerged onto the main road; low sun sparking off the still water of the firth, the grumble of tyres over uneven tarmac.

The mountains to the west were white-capped and soon they were in my rear-view mirror, and all the while your cries came in waves, a high pitched moan followed by the whimper of your inhale. Two hours to the city. Tall buildings on the skyline, blocky concrete, a winding river, an empty car park and we had arrived.

The institute doors opened smoothly on our approach: a wide reception hall of glass and light and polished metal handrails. They had come to meet us. They were waiting. We were led down a corridor where your screams echoed off the pristine white walls; guided through another large, empty space gleaming with internal windows. It was too hard to talk with you crying beside me, so they took you into another room while I was interviewed about your pain. I described it all – the milky water at your birth, the way you sucked on my skin, the mud, the tadpoles, the thrashing and wailing.

They listened, and they made notes by hand on yellow lined notepads. There might have been something in the pond water at the time, they said, pouring away my precious sample; but that'll be useless now. It might have been in a tadpole. It might have been in the soil. Or it might just be something in you. Imagine E. coli, they said. Some strains are harmless. They looked at me intensely then. While some strains act like poison to the host. My head was pounding from the drive and the worry and the crying and the dry heat of the air, but they kept talking:

The microbial ecosystem contains 1012 non-human cells per gram of intestinal content. Bacteria, fungi, protists, archaea, viruses – and in the human gut, most of these are beneficial.

I asked for a glass of water.

In fact, they make us what we are. More than fifty percent of all the cells inside the healthy human body are microbial. Firmicutes and Proteobacteria; Candida, Rhodotorula, Bullera—

Their words moved in and out of me, heard and not heard; my headache intensified, my eyelids tender and throbbing.

But if something goes wrong, it needs to be treated, wouldn't you say?

I nodded my consent.

Breastfed babies should be dominated by bifidobacteria—

Yes! I exclaimed, the relief as cool as ice water. I breastfed, I exclusively breastfed.

Not if your child swallowed a tadpole.

I didn't like to speak after that. But as I listened I began to see them, the bacteria, the viruses; I could see them crawling inside you, like slugs and leeches, feeding off you while you cried. They told me that your microbiome could be affecting your emotional state, your cognitive function, your entire personality. I couldn't help it. I ran from the room to where they were keeping you and I scooped you up in my arms and as you thrashed and kicked and screamed I could believe it: something was animating you.

I fell to my knees. They had a padded mat on the floor, so you wouldn't hurt yourself if you toppled. They had followed me into your room and I felt a comforting pressure on my shoulder, saw two hands reaching out for you, lifting you into the air and out of my sight.

You said you wanted water.

Please, yes.

My voice was croaked and dry; the glass they passed me was clear and slippery with condensation.

We don't know what's causing the problem, but we can start removing a species at a time.

What does that mean?

One type of microbe at a time. Sometimes we'll be able to administer the treatment via a drink. Sometimes it will be a pill. We might need to go intravenously. We'll keep going until the pain is gone. That is what you want, isn't it?

Down the hall a door closed. I could hear the silence. I sat back on my heels and at last I took a sip of water.

Your treatment began when you were eleven months old. The crying was relentless at first, accompanied by hysterical shaking. You wouldn't take the drinks so they put you on a drip and when you kept pulling it out I had to strap you down, just for a little while. The snow was lighter that year, a dusting, though I remember the sharpness of icicles hanging down from the gutters.

The temperature inside, of course, never changed. I slept in the institute with you – or rather, I lay awake there, listening to your sobs, sometimes sitting beside you. I tried to stroke your hair but you pulled away. From across your room the blank walls stared back at me. There were days when it felt like no time was passing at all, but spring melted into summer and they moved on to another colony and your crying became sporadic, less insistent. Are you feeling better? I whispered to you, one morning. Say yes? Please, say yes. Just try. You rolled away, replied with formless cries, but I noticed that your face didn't get as red as it used to; your eyes stayed clear and alert.

By the time autumn arrived you were much calmer. We still had to get through the wailing despair when you woke, but during the day you were able to toddle around the room – once I found you standing below the window, trying to lift yourself up. It's working! I told you. You're feeling better! Do you want to go home soon? Say yes. Say yes, muma. Your eyes turned to mine and your lips pouted and I picked you up and put you back in bed, quickly kissing your soft hair where it swirled around your crown before you could push me away. But you didn't push me away. Weeks passed and you didn't cry, not once. Months went by without a sound. You sat up in bed and offered your arms for the drips. At night you slept peacefully and I stayed up, breathing in time to your breaths like on our first night together. I whispered how much I loved you, how big and clever you'd grown, how well you had learned. Sometimes we listened to the chirp of the birds that feed on the berries. And look! They're here again, just outside your window. You sit up at that, shuffle around so that you can see; your eyes swivel this way and that, just like a little person. Your legs dangle off the bed and you swing them back and forth, making an insistent rhythmical beat with your feet against the bed frame, and your lips – your lips are working around an invisible shape in your mouth. Every contaminant has been removed; you are complete and perfect and you are preparing your first word. What are you going to say, now that you're finally about to speak? Now that I've got all the pain out and you sleep calmly on your back like you're supposed to and your eyes are dry as polished pebbles. You're not going to say hi, or hiya, or hello. You wouldn't say anything so mundane, not after everything we've been through. You're not going to say muma either – you'll probably have a different name for me, something special and unique. But you are about to speak. I can see it in the curve of your cheeks and the intensity of your gaze. And when you do, you are going to say thank you.

What I Haven't Told You
Sarah Stewart

I haven't told you   but you are beginning

to suspect   (the blue smudges   under my eyes

my drowsiness   the curtains awry)

that when you sleeping   I slip out I howl

at the blueblack sky   that globule of pearly moon

I tear my clothes   my teeth double in size

I crawl sometimes   sometimes I crawl

I like to roll in the dirt   you find me

mornings   sullen in sleep   sickles

of earth   under every fingernail

the start   of a smile   on my mouth

Unbecoming Animal
Ritti Soncco

The autumn fields stretch out before us as hardened moors, stripped trees, icy burns. The hard frost crunches beneath our feet as we trudge slowly along the mountainside. My group shuffles and lingers; leaning down to rummage at the plants on the earth, looking up to watch the Munros shift as we rise to meet them. Standing on the mountainside with a rare blue autumn sky we have a clear view of the mountain chain around us, mesmerising and humbling with its unapologetic silence, its unwavering magnitude and its glittering snowpeaks. The breath escaping my nostrils forms the only cloud in this world. I watch it hang like smoke before it fades. It makes me wonder about the fire that must be inside me. *There is something inside me.*

A ripple goes through my group. One of us has stopped the slow climb to stare towards the bealach. We pause, turning carefully to follow her gaze. There they are again, appearing as little dots chattering enthusiastically in their group. They haven't seen us yet, but they will. They came for us.

I don't know how the others feel but I don't mind their attentions. If anything, they make me curious. They've woken up before dawn, jiggled excitedly in their vans as they drove through the glens, walked up and along the mountains for hours, all of that to see us. Then they just stand around staring, their movements slow but their machines whizzing at high speed. If we linger, let them get closer, they shout to one another delightedly. They're a strange part of the seasons – they've always come, always been part of the landscape as far as I can remember – but recently the way

I think about them has changed. *I've changed.* Rather than look back at them with the rest of my group, I imagine myself crossing that line to stand beside them, to join them in looking *at me.* Can they see something I can't? Can they see how *I'm changing?* Is it visible from over there?

Until recently I never considered crossing that line between myself and the others, but now I wonder if the only way to really see myself is to cross over. Because from inside me, nothing makes sense any more. I can't tell you when the changes began, when I first felt something moving inside me that isn't me. Perhaps I lost my eyesight. I can feel this thing sink deeper and deeper into my folds, into places I haven't been to myself; making strangers out of my organs; dislocating me from my inner worlds. Of course I knew I wasn't completely alone before she came along; I always knew I was a superorganism of sorts, but those were microbes I had always been with. Old friends, so to speak. They lived with one another as buddies in my gut, law-abiding citizens of my colon, tax-paying neighbours on my skin. My health was never my own; it was always a multi-species collaborative dance project housed in the halls of my body. But she is new to this neighbourhood, and I am baffled at how easy it was for her to find space to move in. Did she nudge the others away from the table or am I riddled with more holes than I knew, more full of emptiness?

I feel her roam in me as she explores, deciding where to settle, how to inhabit me, and as she moves in, this new citizen is not the only one evolving, becoming new. Her very condition of citizenship reshapes *me.* I, who always thought of myself as an autobiography, a first-person narrator, am becoming an environment for someone else's story. I am no longer a citizen. I am an environment for something else to thrive in.

I know she won't hurt me. She hurts as little as I hurt the earth when I walk over it. She will unfold her wings and lay them out inside me, but nothing dramatic will change for me. As she takes a gentle asymptomatic stroll from my nose to my genitals; as she quietly shapeshifts when she ambles from my knees into the world of my gut, my new citizen will not unmake my health. The world around me hasn't changed nor has who I am in it changed. But in the secret places of my bloodstream, my organs, my brain, I am no longer alone with my old friends. A new being has moved in, become entangled with me. I am now infected but not sick. So if she won't hurt me, how can I complain?

This isn't a complaint. This is out beyond the ideas of right bacteria and wrong bacteria. This is a question: does she, my new citizen, make me more-than or less-than myself? Am I more than my antlers, my hooves; a four-legged nonhuman becoming-with a spirochete; a liminal superorganism that is both healthy and infected? Or am I less than my antlers; a four-legged nonhuman formerly known as 'Monarch of the Glen'; less 'animal' more a 'carrier'; non-agent of infection; to blame. An animal unbecoming, unravelling from its designated role as 'poetic' and 'beautiful'; an unbecoming animal in the eyes of all that is simple, clean, and adheres perfectly to modern taxonomy.

With all my introspection I have forgotten about the others. One of them has inched closer, crouching with a camera, and a nervousness shivers through my group. In synchronicity with my people I raise my antlers as a warning and his camera begins to click furiously. I wonder if the others knew what I was, what I was becoming, would they still come to see me? Or would they lose their ability to see, as I have lost mine, and in their cosmology will I transform into more-than or less-than? Will I become a hybrid of multinaturalism, still spiritually myself but with corporeal diversity, some kind of a postanimal achievement . . . Or will I become a dirty body, a non-biocitizen? Will they kill us, my whole herd, to stop the bacteria rising in me? Unblinking, I watch the two-legged male stand to full height and return to his group. Through all the seasons, they always come out to study us - surely they must be beginning to suspect that who we are is no longer who we were. Something in me is doubling in size, reorganising the aesthetic creature they want in their emotive landscapes. But if I am becoming, then their landscapes are becoming too: their moors, their trees, their mountains are changing. And they themselves are becoming. Do they know?

Background to 'Unbecoming Animal'

This piece was inspired by my PhD research on Lyme disease as it becomes endemic to Scotland's wild and urban spaces. Lyme disease is a complex, multi-organ illness caused by the Borrelia burgdorferi bacteria which can infect animals as well as humans, and can manifest itself in many different organs, meaning that symptoms are often complex and misdiagnosed as fibromyalgia, Parkinson's or depression. An improved understanding of Lyme disease is currently developing, propagated by medical and ecological scientists as well as by patient activists, who are creating their own therapy methods and rallying for increased political involvement and social awareness. My PhD research focuses on the medical knowledge of Lyme disease as it changes; on what kind of knowledge is accepted in different social or medical groups; and on the role and effect of patient activism in Scotland. For this piece, however, I wanted to sidetrack briefly from the core of my work and think about animals infected with Lyme disease. Anthropologist Genese Sodikoff has called Lyme disease a 'liminal illness' (Sodikoff, 2017), which made me interested in exploring the idea of 'liminal patients': those who are infected but not sick. Interestingly, while dogs and humans suffer the symptoms of Lyme disease, other animals such as deer and mice will carry the bacteria without becoming ill. The scene I describe is set in Scotland and follows a deer as a liminal being, i.e. during its transition from healthy and uninfected to infected but not sick. I hope my piece invites more thoughts on what it means to live with microbes, and how others see us when they know we harbour certain microbes. This thought process is especially important as the idea of mass deer culling has been suggested as a way to eradicate Lyme disease in Scotland.

Inspired by

Abram, D., (2010), *Becoming Animal. An Earthly Cosmology*. United States of America: Vintage Books.

Haraway, D., (2000), "The Cyborg Manifesto" in *The Cybercultures Reader* (eds., D. Bell and B.M. Kennedy). London: Routledge.

Karlen, A., (2001), *Biography of a Germ*. Great Britain: Phoenix.

Lorimer, J., (2016), "Gut Buddies: Multispecies Studies and the Microbiome" in *Environmental Humanities*, Vol. 8 (1), pp. 57 - 76.

Nading, A., (2014), *Mosquito Trails. Ecology, Health and the Politics of Entanglement*. California: University of California Press.

Raffles, H., (2010), *Insectopedia*. United States of America: Vintage Books.

Sodikoff, G., (2017), "The Liminality of Lyme Disease" in *3 Quarks Daily*. [Online.] Available from: https://www.3quarksdaily.com/3quarksdaily/2017/01/the-liminality-of-lyme-disease.html, accessed: 15 January 2020.

Viveros de Castro, E., (1998), "Cosmological Deixis and Amerindian Perspectivism" in *The Journal of the Royal Anthropological Institute*, Vol. 4 (3), pp. 469 - 488.

Uncanny Healing
Ed Cohen

… of all the objects treated by medical thought, healing is the one
that doctors have considered least often.
Georges Canguilhem

One must not forget, it is not the doctor but the patient
who reaches the end of the illness. The sick person cures himself
using his own power, just as he walks, eats, thinks, breathes, and sleeps
under his own power.
Georg Groddeck

1

Unlike Freud, I don't have a problem accepting that there are
unknowable experiences, that sometimes our experiences exceed
the possibility of knowing, or even that we are constitutively more
than we can know. Moreover, I don't believe that imagining this
to be the case is a sign of regression to an infantile or atavistic
(a.k.a., "animistic") mode of thinking, although I'm not especially
bothered if it does. These days I only half-jokingly describe myself
as a pan-psychic, neo-vitalist, which might just be animism in
modern drag. However, I wasn't born thinking this way. In fact,
as the oldest son of a physical chemist and a vulgar Marxist, both
rabidly-atheistic, cultural Jews, I was raised to believe – much as
Freud did – in a thoroughly secular, scientific, rationalist worldview.
Only after suffering with an acute autoimmune illness for more

than a decade, from which I almost died, and then undergoing a seemingly "miraculous" healing experience, during which I spontaneously started going into trances, did it begin to dawn on me that the medical model, to which I owed my life, could not explain either why I had gotten so sick in the first place, or how I had gotten better so quickly. Needless to say, this realization came as something of a shock to my secular scientific assumptions, if only because I now understood that I had been staking my life on somewhat suspicious suppositions. Moreover, I started to wonder why none of my many doctors had ever mentioned the possibility of healing to me, or why – as Canguilhem notes – they seemed to have so little consideration for it.

This lack of interest, it turns out, was not just an idiosyncratic failing on the part of the many physicians I'd come into contact with at the many medical centers at which I'd been treated (including two of the U.S.'s most famous teaching hospitals). Rather, since the end of the nineteenth century, exactly at the time Freud did his medical training, it has provided the criteria – or perhaps the shibboleth – that distinguished scientific medicine from its "non-scientific" competitors. Until then Western medicine, like almost all therapeutic systems ever conceived by human beings, held that doctors could (at best) support and encourage the natural power of healing, which, following in the Hippocratic/Galenic tradition, it called the *Vis Medicatrix Naturae* (Neuburger, 1932). Today, if you look up "healing" on Medline, the U.S. National Library of Medicine's comprehensive database, you will find only four categories: faith healing, fracture healing, mental healing, and wound healing. Not healing as a possibility, as a tendency, as a vital function, or as that upon which all of medicine's most prized bioscientific interventions depend if not importune, as Groddeck reminds us. In this regard, Freud was a consummately modern physician: if you search for "healing" in Freud's writings you will find very few instances, and none of them refer to psychoanalysis (although he does once refer to the "healing power of love" – of course, not without irony).

My hunch is that the absence of healing in Freud is uncanny, in part because healing is uncanny, not in a psychoanalytic sense, but etymologically and literally, i.e. unknown if not unknowable. Healing is a known unknown; it's familiarly unfamiliar. We all "know" it in very material ways or we wouldn't be here – we'd be dead – yet our "knowledge" is not conceptual, but experiential, undertaken by the savoir faire of our cells, molecules, and subatomic particles. However, within the medical perspective that underpinned Freud's (not to mention my own doctors') practice, knowledge alone represents the royal road to care, as it has done for the last two and a half millennia, ever since Hippocrates differentiated medicine as such from other forms of healing (shamanistic, temple, cultic, etc.). So, while Freud could admit that the navel of the dream might elude total knowability at any given moment (giving rise to the famous question: analysis, terminable or interminable?) he held fast to his Enlightenment faith that knowledge alone provides the best therapy – a sentiment that underwrites his famous declaration, in *The New Introductory Lectures*: "where the it was, the I shall be" (Freud, 1958). Nevertheless, despite his avowed scientific secularism, psychoanalytic practice continually brought Freud up against the limits of his motto. Indeed, the very existence of hysteria and the other conversion neuroses, from whose treatment psychoanalysis derives, if not the potential efficacy of the "talking cure" as one such treatment, troubled the premises of determinate causality upon which Freud's scientific aspirations rested. The failure of his "Project for a Scientific Psychology" provides the first intimation of this trouble, and seemingly, it got harder and harder for Freud to reconcile his theory and his practice, until in 1919, at the end of the first world war, and just before he revised his psychic topology in *The Ego and the Id*, he published his strange essay, "The Uncanny" (Freud, 1955: 217-251).

As numerous commentators have noticed, "The Uncanny" represents an anomalous work in Freud's opus. Freud himself tells us as much in the essay's opening sentence, where he explains why he is taking up a topic more suited to aesthetics. Furthermore, the essay's style of argumentation, its circuitous development, its extensive reliance on literary readings, all suggest that something uncanny is going on in "The Uncanny." My hypothesis is that both Freud's essay and his concept (*unheimlich*/uncanny) only make sense within the horizon of a modern secular, scientific, evolutionary, and medical point of view. Furthermore, *unheimlich*/ uncanny constitutes Freud's attempt to shore up "the truth" of this point of view in the face of his own analytic practice, which revealed the limits of determinism to encompass all forms of causality. The uncanny thus seeks to account conceptually for the affects engendered by experiences that appear to exceed our rational understanding. By designating these affects as the unconscious eruptions of repressed infantile or "primitive" material, Freud cannily tries to capture the unknown and unfamiliar within the knowledge project of psychoanalysis. Yet, despite his best intentions, Freud's efforts have their limits. For, much as Freud might desire us to keep faith with the Enlightenment, we are (I believe) more than we can ever know, and healing is just one of the uncanny ways that we can become familiar with the unknown-that-we-cannot-<u>not</u>-know.

2

I had an uncanny healing. That's a medical fact. I've had many, many other uncanny experiences, but none of those were medically affirmed. I was 23 at the time and had been living with acute Crohn's disease for more than a decade – I'll spare you the gory details – when I had a critical episode in which I almost "bled out," as they say. The near-death, out of body experience that this event precipitated could certainly be considered uncanny, as might the moment of waking up in the ICU, reaching for a beloved friend's hand, and feeling the spark of life returning, not to mention the trances I spontaneously began falling into during the months I remained tethered by IV lines to my hospital bed. Alas, I don't any have medical confirmation for those particulars. However, I do have it for the entire arc of the experience, for what Canguilhem called the "ordeal of healing" itself (Canguilhem, 2006: 9). In my exit interview with the young and sexy surgeon, on whom I had a major "therapeutic" crush, he uttered words that sent chills down my spine, although that was the least of it. He said: "You were the sickest person I've operated on in five years who is still alive, and I have no idea how you got better so quickly." Now that was probably uncanny in both the psychoanalytic and the etymological senses of the term.

James Strachey's decision to translate Freud's *unheimlich* as "uncanny" was a somewhat odd one. Of course, it makes sense because like the original, the translation involves a word that is the negative of a substantive adjective, and the tension between the two tends towards indecidability (i.e. *heimlich* tends towards *unheimlich* much as canny tends towards uncanny). Yet, the two antithetical couplets don't resonate in exactly the same ways. On the one hand, *heimlich/unheimlich* in Freud's exposition mostly pertains to the defamiliarization of what once felt familiar – albeit either in infancy, in utero, or in "primitive" hominid development. It's primarily affective, rooted as Freud tells us in "emotional impulses." Canny/uncanny, on the other hand, doesn't signify in the same way. Canny, from the Scots root can/ken, meaning "to know how, to be able," refers to a kind of knowingness, a kind of cunning (a word that shares the same root), that verges on being "too knowing" (O.E.D., 2019). Uncanny thus discloses a relation to the unknown, which may or may not be familiar (in both its literal and figural senses), and it doesn't necessarily have the same affect attached as *unheimlich*. This is why long before it took on the valence "associated with supernatural arts or powers" or "partaking of a supernatural character; mysterious, weird, uncomfortably strange, or unfamiliar" (which the O.E.D. reminds us was only "common from 1850"), uncanny primarily meant: mischievous, malicious; careless, incautious; unreliable, not to be trusted; not quite safe to trust, or have dealings with. Thus, the uncanniness of the uncanny in the *Standard Edition* does not render the familiar unfamiliar in quite the same ways as unheimlich would seem to do for Freud. Nevertheless, the friction between the original and its standard translation does disclose something that might otherwise remain latent in Freud's idiom, since it underscores the extent to which the question not only of *knowing*, but of *knowing how*, of *knowing if one can*, underwrites the work of the uncanny/ *unheimlich*. In other words, Strachey's rending of *unheimlich* as "uncanny" alludes to the epistemological role that the *unheimlich* performs in Freud's text where Freud deployed it – at least in part – in order to finesse the ontological paradoxes that psychoanalysis introduced.

In order to grasp what the uncanny does for Freud, it's important to remember that from the outset Freud declares himself to have "a special obtuseness" when it comes to uncanny experiences. (Similarly, at the beginning of *Civilization and its Discontents*, he professes ignorance of what Romaine Rolland described as a feeling of "oceanic oneness," before proceeding to explain it away.) Indeed, in the essay Freud admits to only three uncanny experiences: finding a short story in an English magazine during the war; unwittingly misrecognizing his reflection on a train (although he equivocates as to whether this was truly uncanny or not); and, most tellingly, stumbling into a red-light district in a "provincial town in Italy", where the first three times he seeks to escape "the painted women … at the windows of the small houses", he instead returns to the scene of seduction, before at last breaking free from his uncanny promenade. Apart from these limited instances, the last of which certainly bears more consideration than Freud gives it, Freud represents himself as largely immune to the uncanny, except in its literary or aesthetic manifestations.

Personally, I don't have this problem. I'm happy to admit that many of the most important moments in my life have been both uncanny and *unheimlich*. To give you another example, when I was diagnosed with Crohn's disease at the age of 13, I was told I had an autoimmune illness. Now, according to prevailing biomedical theories, autoimmunity is <u>actually</u> uncanny. Paul Ehrlich, the first person to even entertain the possibility, called it the *horror autoxicus*, in order to name it as an impossible possibility, which unfortunately is not only all too possible, but increasingly common. Immunologically speaking, autoimmunity represents what happens when "the self" mistakes itself for another, so that that which should be most *heimlich* ("the self") instead becomes *unheimlich*, often leading to deleterious pathological manifestations, and sometimes even death. Although it hadn't been invented yet, it's almost as if Freud had autoimmunity in mind when he wrote apropos "the double": "the subject identifies himself with someone else, so that he is in doubt as to which his self is, or substitutes the extraneous self for his own. In other words, there is a doubling, dividing, and interchanging of the self" (Freud 1955:234). At the cellular and molecular levels, this characterization of the uncanny pretty closely resembles the ways bioscience has framed autoimmunity ever since Macfarlane Burnett (1969) declared immunology the science of "self/not-self discrimination." However, since I was an adolescent at the time, my doctors didn't offer me this scientific explanation, and instead tried to communicate the concept using what they imagined were more *heimlich* metaphors: first they told me I was rejecting myself; then, that I was allergic to myself; and finally, that I was eating myself alive. Now that was another fairly *unheimlich* moment. Needless to say, after this (in)auspicious start, over the more than four and a half decades that I've lived with Crohn's disease, I've become quite familiar with the *unheimlich*, if not in fact fast friends.

Not surprisingly, then, unlike Freud, I don't disavow my sensitivities towards the uncanny. Nor do I disdain the "animistic standpoint," which Freud believes the uncanny recapitulates, dismissing it as atavistic, primitive, or infantile, that is, as "belonging to the prehistory of the individual or the race" (Freud, 1955:240). Of course, that's in part because, unlike Freud, who steadfastly held to a "secular" perspective (in "On Lay Analysis," he refers to analysts as "secular pastoral workers" (Freud, 1959:254)), I'm more eclectic when it comes to healing. Hence, I don't share all the assumptions that underlie Freud's famous assertion: "[A]n uncanny effect is often and easily produced when the distinction between imagination and reality is effaced, as when something we have hitherto regarded as imaginary appears before us in reality" (Freud, 1955:244). Here Freud affirms the bifurcation between

imaginary/real as the ontological and epistemological foundation
of his thinking. He embraces the Occidental onto-theology that
began with Plato and, while he recognizes that this conceptual
opposition has not always and everywhere obtained, he asserts
that its emergence constitutes a phylogenic milestone. Indeed, as
a good Enlightenment thinker, he holds that "civilized" humans
have – or should have – "surmounted" the confusion between
the real and the imaginary, and that they certainly shouldn't ever
imagine that the imagination is real:

> We, or our primitive forefathers—once believed that these
> possibilities were realities, and were convinced that they actually
> happened. Nowadays we no longer believe in them, we have
> surmounted these modes of thought; but we do not feel quite so
> sure of our new beliefs, and the old ones still exist within us ready
> to seize upon any confirmation. As soon as something actually
> happens in our lives which seems to confirm the old discarded
> beliefs, we get a feeling of the uncanny.... Conversely, anyone
> who has completely and finally rid himself of animistic beliefs
> will be insensible to this type of the uncanny. (Freud, 1955:247)

No doubt Freud is thinking of his own "special obtuseness" here
– this from the man who taught us that psychical reality is real.
Nevertheless, as his text in fact confirms, emphatically employing
the first-person plural so that we're sure to feel included in his
argument, our "new beliefs" are actually still beliefs, not facts, and
certainly not truths, and therefore as subject to uncertainty as any
other.

Be that as it may, we who appreciate the uncanny – or whatever
the uncanny gestures towards or tries to contain – we who hold
that the uncanny happens in the way that shit happens, or in
the way that Derrida (2002: 194) says that "deconstruction
happens," might find something uncanny about Freud's use of the
uncanny—uncanny not in the psychoanalytic sense, but in the
older etymological sense of "too knowing," "not quite trustworthy,"
"unreliable." For, as many readers have noticed, "the uncanny," as

both a concept and an essay, begs as many questions as it answers. In part, this conceptual instability betrays, I would argue, a contradiction that emerges within Freud's thinking between his training as a doctor-neurologist and his practice as a psychoanalyst. Caught between the deterministic causality that defines the "scientificity" of scientific medicine, and the indeterminate, or indeed overdetermined, causalities that psychoanalysis investigates, Freud falters. "The Uncanny" (as both concept and essay) marks this fault, even as it seeks to rectify it by making it accord with the "reality principle": "The whole thing is purely an affair of 'reality-testing,' a question of the material reality of phenomena" (Freud, 1955: 248). To put this another way, the uncanny serves as a *supplément* – in the Derridean sense – that shores up the bio-logic of scientific medicine for Freud, even as psychoanalytic practice itself suggests that "the material reality of phenomena" do not and cannot exhaust the dimensions of the real (Derrida, 2016: 153). Thus, the uncanny seeks to uphold the distinction real/imaginary, or in fact presupposes this distinction, even while recognizing not only its instability, but perhaps its untenability.

In saying this, I don't just want to "deconstruct" Freud's uncanny, but rather to offer an opening onto that which the uncanny has served as a constant deferral, i.e., the known unknown-that-we-cannot-not-know that psychoanalysis seeks to contain – which may include something like healing. Indeed, it seems rather uncanny to me, given his therapeutic commitment to ameliorating psychic and physical suffering that medicine could not assuage, not to mention his own long healing ordeal with cancer, that Freud almost never uses the word "healing" in his work, and when he does use it, it never refers to psychoanalysis. One of the few places Freud even mentions healing occurs in the decidedly pre-psychoanalytic essay "Psychic (or Mental) Treatment" in which he embraces the therapeutic resources afforded by the charged relation between doctor and patient (prefiguring his later theorization of transference) in order to argue for the positive value of hypnosis for medicine (Freud, 1953:283). Needless to say, he soon abandons this position, throwing the baby out with the bathwater, in part because he feared that the association with hypnosis would undermine his credibility as a scientist and a physician. Healing too easily gives rise to uncanny effects, which is why when it happens in medical contexts it can easily be rendered invisible or dismissed as "merely anecdotal." Yet it goes on happening, in both remarkable and unremarked ways. And, personally speaking, I'd say we're very lucky that it does.

3

If I had time I'd take you through some of the key moments in the development of scientific medicine that led to the downgrading of the *Vis Medicatrix Naturae* during the century preceding Freud's medical training, including: the French Royal Commission Report of 1784 debunking Mesmerism, which introduced the distinction between "real" and "imaginary" cures; Claude Bernard's break with the Hippocratic tradition by separating *milieu intérieur* from *milieu extérieur*; and Charcot's attribution of hysterical symptoms to undetectable and yet supposedly real "dynamic lesions" – but unfortunately I don't, so I won't. Instead, let me just remind you of the paradox that draws Freud to the entanglement of *heimlich/unheimlich* as a psychoanalytic doublet in the first place: "Thus *heimlich* is a word the meaning of which develops in the direction of ambivalence, until it finally coincides with its opposite, *unheimlich*" (Freud, 1955: 226). Freud's interest in *heimlich/unheimlich* bespeaks his attraction to antithetical concepts, to the tensions sustained by and through ambivalence. Yet, since such a coincidence of contraries necessarily violates the "laws of logic" which Aristotle first posited (i.e. identity, non-contradiction, and the excluded middle), it must in Freud's mind manifest the unconscious where such laws do not apply. Nevertheless, despite the insistence of the unconscious, these laws are "real" for Freud, insofar as they describe the epistemological and ontological conditions for true knowledge. Hence, in his estimation, the unconscious upsurges of the uncanny return us to a time before we realized the "true nature" of the real, as his characterization of

Hoffmann's literary techniques underscores: "They are a harking-back to particular phases in the evolution of the self-regarding feeling, a regression to a time when the ego had not yet marked itself off sharply from the external world and from other people" (Freud, 1955: 236). Freud's assumption here is that we could – or should – be marked off sharply from the world and from other people, since this is the condition of possibility not only for the bourgeois individualism within which Freud operates, but also for the medical epistemology within which he thinks, if not practices. Therefore, in his estimation, when we have (or think we have) uncanny experiences that seem to suggest otherwise, we must <u>in</u> <u>fact</u> be regressing to an infantile or primitive mode of being.

Given my own experiences of illness and healing, I find this interpretation somewhat reductive. We are never actually separate from the world or from other people, or if we are it's only in the sense that independence is another form of dependence, as the analyst Adam Phillips admonishes us. Indeed, such paradoxicality might constitute the very basis for our going-on-living, as the theoretical biologist Francisco Varela (1991) suggests when he describes: "the intriguing paradoxicality proper to an autonomous identity: the living system must distinguish itself from its environment, while at the same time maintaining its coupling; this linkage cannot be detached since it is against this very environment from which the organism arises [that it] comes forth." The paradoxicality of living systems, which includes humans, is proper to us, if for no other reason than as living beings we are all vulnerable (which etymologically just means woundable) and hence moral. Healing represents the reparative potential that all organisms have conserved since the first cell managed to survive its vulnerability long enough to extend itself in time and space by way of other cells. In this sense it partakes of another paradox, the paradox that healing is always only partial and temporary, since in the end death comes to us all.

Georges Canguilhem (2006: 9) defines this paradoxical possibility as the very ground of healing: "To learn to heal is to learn to become familiar with the contradiction between today's hope and the failure that comes at the end – without saying no to today's hope." Or, to put this another way, healing represents what Henri Bergson calls a "tendency." It's not a certainty, not a steady state, not a telos, but a direction in which the *elan vital* can unfold, even as it composes with other vital tendencies that may run athwart or conflict with it. Healing therefore calls for support, encouragement, and appreciation, and fortunately WHEN WE CARE ABOUT HEALING IT MATTERS. At some level, certainly at the level of a practitioner, Freud knows this; however, as a theorist and a writer, his commitment to the bio-logics of scientific medicine and of Enlightenment philosophy requires him to contain the perturbations that healing's indeterminant, or over-determined, causalities entail. "The Uncanny," then, seems to offer Freud an opportunity to try to have his cake and eat it too. Yet the trail of crumbs that he leaves behind might allow us to discern some of the uncanny traces of healing on which psychoanalysis probably depends, but that it cannot allow itself to openly acknowledge. Indeed, in order to appreciate the uncanniness of healing, we might need to recognize something that Freud, given his medical training and his "special obtuseness" could not: i.e. that both healing and the uncanny do happen, and when they do they remind us that despite our fondest beliefs, we are always more than we can know. Thus, rather than joining Freud in affirming Kant's motto for the Enlightenment: *Sapere Aude*, Dare to Know; we might consider a new more, uncanny motto: *Curare Aude*: Dare to Care.

To learn to heal is to learn to become familiar with the contradiction between today's hope and the failure that comes at the end. Without saying no to today's hope. Is this intelligence or simplicity?

Georges Canguilhem

References

Canguilhem, Georges, (2006), 'Is a Pedagogy of Healing Possible?' *Umbr(a)* 1:9-21.

Derrida, Jacques, (2002), *Negotiations: Interventions and Interviews, 1971-2001.* Trans. Elizabeth Rottenberg. Stanford, CA: Stanford University Press, p194.

Derrida, Jacques (2016 [1976]), '… That Dangerous Supplement…' *Of Grammatology.* Trans. Gayatri Spivak. Baltimore: Johns Hopkins University Press, pp153-178.

Freud, Sigmund (1953), *The Standard Edition of the Complete Psychological Works of Sigmund Freud, Volume VII: A Case of Hysteria, Three Essays on the Theory of Sexuality, and Other Works.* Trans, James Strachey. London: Hogarth, pp283-304.

Freud, Sigmund, (1955), *The Standard Edition of the Complete Psychological Works of Sigmund Freud, Volume XVII.* Trans. James Strachey. London: Hogarth, pp217-251.

Freud, Sigmund, (1958), *The Standard Edition of the Complete Psychological Works of Sigmund Freud, Volume XXII.* Trans. James Strachey. London: Hogarth.

Freud, Sigmund, (1959), 'The Question of Lay Analysis.' *The Standard Edition of the Complete Psychological Works of Sigmund Freud, Volume XX.* Trans. James Strachey. London: Hogarth, p254.

Groddeck, Georg, (1949), *The Book of the It*, New York: Vintage.

Macarlane Burnet, Frank, (1969), *Self and not-self; cellular immunology, book one.* Cambridge: Cambridge University Press.

Neuburger, Max (1932), *The Doctrine of the Healing Power of Nature throughout the Course of Time.* Trans. L. J. Boyd. 1926. New York: Journal of the American Institute of Homeopathy

OED Online, (2019), Oxford University Press. https://www-oed-com.proxy. libraries.rutgers.edu/view/Entry/27143?redirectedFrom=canny, accessed January 19, 2020.

Varela, Francisco, (1991), 'Organism: a meshwork of selfless selves.' In *Organism and the Origins of Self*, ed. Alfred Tauber Boston: Kluwer Academic Publishers, p85.

Section Two

Situating bodies:
the uncanny in the city and the forest

Revenant Visits Her Old Bedroom
Sarah Stewart

You, stranger, sleep here now.
I present myself at night,
but I have no sinister intention

running a finger along the glass
of milk half-drunk, rim
ghosted with residue.

I may try on your clothes,
buttoning the shirts slowly
as if on vacation.

Here is your desk lamp,
the light lemony, condensed
in an upturned cup of shadow.

I will read your notebooks,
the postcards above your bed.
Here are your hopes

strung up high. Here,
the arrowed sweetness
of your pins and hairclips.

I will leave like anyone else:
stairs, front door, cold grass path
towards the woods.

There I slip from this world
slowly into water;
ankles, knees, waist –

the river thick,
darkly glimmering,
very still.

The Dark Forest
Sarah Stewart

Love, I have moved us back.
We are in the cabin again,
built from halved logs raw
and dripping sap. The clock
has stopped – the cuckoo
sits half-out of his carved chalet.
In the pantry, rows
of thick jarred honey
with undertaste of fir,
shelved next to wild game
and cherry sauce.
Outside, the lake swills
in its crown of pines.

We are fireside in armchairs
with goblets; contained,
braced for happiness.
You are leaning forward
as if to stir the fire.

Now, the condensation
from our breathing.
Now, the weight of your arm
slung across my body. Hour
by humble domestic hour.
But the cabin, the cuckoo,
the tiered hopes
of our early months?
Gone. Irretrievably gone.

Seeing the trees for the forest: Learning to listen to all of the voices in 'The Dark Forest'
Emily F. Porth

Introduction

> At the beginning, the dark forest of authors (who do not see the trees) – without a view, full of misleading paths. Then a concealed pass through which I lead the reader – my specimen dream with its peculiarities, details, indiscretions, bad jokes – and then suddenly the high ground and the view and the question: which way do you wish to go now?
>
> – Freud, 1899 letter to Wilhelm Fliess

Sarah Stewart's poem, 'The Dark Forest', presents us with a historical snapshot: a couple at their home in the woods in the early days of their relationship, reclining contentedly in front of a roaring fire. With wine in hand and a pantry stocked with nature's bounty, there is rich fertility in the land and within their relationship. However, by the end of the poem it is clear that this easy abundance has been lost between the couple themselves, as well as between these humans and the forest in which they dwell. The heavy silence and implied images of empty goblets and a cold hearth evoke a wasteland, both as a metaphor for the state of their human relationship, and for the decline of the forest itself. 'Gone. Irretrievably gone.'

But who, or what, constitutes the forest? What kinds of agency can be expressed by the human and nonhuman beings who are part of the forest? What types of human-forest relationships exist, particularly beyond that of resource management? Given the climate crisis faced by all those who consider Earth 'home', how can alternative worldviews and new ethical frameworks change this relationship and the ways we pay attention to other beings? This response to Stewart's poem will explore these questions, and along the way provide one possible answer to Freud's question, applied to human-environment relationships: 'which way do you wish to go now?'

A forest by any other name

Human ideas about what forested landscapes look like, both historically and in the present, are storied and change over time. Forests' meanings differ according to nationalistic ideals and they are often imbued with mythological or spiritual meaning. For instance, Maitland argues that 'forests were the terrain out of which fairy stories…, one of our earliest and most vital cultural forms, evolved. The mysterious secrets and silences, gifts and perils of the forest are both the background to and the source of these tales' (2012:6). For some naturalists and conservationists, forests were a place where one could encounter the divine on Earth: 'The clearest way into the Universe is through a forest wilderness' (Muir, 1979:313).

In purely technical terms, in Britain the term 'forest' is defined as land on which royalty has special hunting rights. However, most people in Western cultures today associate a forest with a densely wooded area (Jones and Cloke, 2002:23), and a forest is often what we imagine when we think of 'nature'. The image of forest evoked in the poem is that of a murky and dense woodland and of a lake surrounded by trees. There is also some reference to the many beings who live in the forest and have contributed, either through their deaths or work, to populate the cabin's pantry with its bounty.

Forests are uncanny, in Freud's sense of the term, in that they hold a 'tension between the everyday and the strange' (Goldschmidt *et al.*, 2019) and in the human imagination today, forests still evoke emotional responses ranging from fear, wonder, mystery, safety, and solace. To some people, though, a forest may simply be seen as a crop of trees to be harvested. These perspectives often come into conflict in environmental management, particularly as vast treed areas are under increasing threat from expanding human populations, from insects and pathogens that become invasive, and due to the heavy demands and practices of the agricultural industrial complex.

The Unsaid and the Unheard

As a landscape and ecological community, a forest consists of trees, humans, and innumerable nonhuman inhabitants that can include animals, plants, fungi, water, mountains, and beyond. A being's relationship with the forest landscape may be primarily utilitarian, and this appears to be the case for the human couple in the cabin who meet their needs by using the nonhuman beings within a forest (who are usually conceptualised as 'resources' or as providing 'ecosystem services').

'The Dark Forest' begins full of love and hope, close relationships with the land and the promise of the future. This is the land of plenty, which mirrors the relationship in its early days. However, all of this is profoundly human-centric. There seem to be only humans taking from the land, holed up in their cosy and well-stocked cabin. This settler narrative, of conquering the wild through grit and determination, is a place where there is no reciprocity with the halved, dripping logs or wild creatures who are conceptualised only as 'game'. There is no room here for the needs, desires, or interests of beings who are not human. Both the forest and the couple's relationship suffer as a result of what remains unsaid between them, and unheard between species.

One of the aspects of the uncanny that Freud identifies is of 'a live being behaving as if dead, inanimate, or mechanical' (Goldschmidt *et al.*, 2019). It could be said that humans have been in a deeply dysfunctional relationship with all of the other living things on Earth by treating them as though they are dead, mechanical, or inanimate. No matter how other creatures behave, many humans are quick to write off their behaviour as mechanistic or as pure 'instinct', and to deny them agency is to deny that they have a voice which can be heard.

Although evidence for the sentience and intelligence of other species continues to increase rapidly, humans are still wary of committing the scientific sin of anthropomorphism, which involves attributing human characteristics to other beings. Research can be denounced as anthropomorphic by involving something as simple as giving names to the animals in a study, rather than identifying them by number; it was common until recently for scientists to argue that this 'sentimentality' renders knowledge invalid because it creates bias (Benson, 2016). However, it can be conversely argued that the wilful intention to reinforce a worldview where other beings are only ever conceptualised as objects for human use is an especially deep and harmful type of bias.

If the current environmental crisis has resulted from the state of this relationship – of humanity's lack of interest in acknowledging the subjectivity and agency of other beings, and of refusing to hear them or meet their needs – how can that relationship change? Maitland makes it clear that forests (and fairy tales) should be chaotic: 'beautiful and savage, useful and wasteful, dangerous and free' (2012:10). Through this chaos, forests can meet the needs of many different beings. Chaos in a forest could look like a thriving, biologically diverse community of trees and plants, with both human and nonhuman animals; it would involve humans modifying the environment to meet their own needs, but taking no more than they need. It would include replanting trees, and planting and harvesting food crops using permaculture principles that seek to provide for the needs of the other beings for whom the forest is home. There is little order in the forest, but as an ecosystem it sustains a type of balance where the needs of many beings are met sustainably, and diversity and inclusion are primary goals. This new relationship with other beings would also involve actively seeking to include them by listening in ways that could be considered unconventional within science and by modern society.

'New animism' and other ways of knowing

Through scientific research in the past twenty-five years, humans have learned that forests are profoundly uncanny places. We have learned, for instance, that trees communicate with each other through complex and far-reaching underground fungal networks that allow them to share nutrients (Simard, 2016), and that trees being attacked by caterpillars will send out a pheromone signal that can be smelled by birds and other predatory insects, who then come to the tree to feast (Amo *et al.*, 2013). Both of these remarkable examples demonstrate how different beings have methods for interspecies communication that allow them to meet their individual needs and also the needs of the wider forest community. In 'Being known by a birch tree', Stuckey (2010) recollects her experience of having the birch tree of her childhood home suddenly appear in her mind for a few moments one evening after dinner. A few weeks after seeing this image, her brother called and mentioned that the birch tree was diseased and had to be cut down. Stuckey recounts this saying, 'I hung up the phone, full of wonder. So the birch tree had come to say good-bye. I knew the birch tree very well from my years of living with it; what I had not realized until then was that the birch tree also knew me' (2010:183). Part of recognising other species as subjects, rather than considering them to be objects, is to realise that they are thinking and speaking about us, as we do about them (Meijer, 2019).

This astonishing research about the intelligence and agency of other species has brought up philosophical questions within Western thought about the responsibilities that humans have towards individual beings, and indeed to biodiversity more broadly. How can alternative worldviews and new ethical frameworks change our relationships with other species and the ways we listen and respond to other beings?

> It's a challenge for us as a species to live with others who are different from us. We're not very tolerant. And maybe in some

stage of our evolutionary process that was necessary, but now we're in a very different stage where we can choose to have different relations with these animals. (Meijer, 2019)

To date, 'rights' discourse has focused on animals such as chimps, in whom humans can readily see intelligence resembling their own, and also on ecosystems including bodies of water that have been almost impossible to protect through other types of legislation (see Macfarlane, 2019, for the recent example of Lake Erie's 'bill of rights'). But how does one define the rights of other species and ecosystems? This becomes difficult with beings who are so different in form to humans, such as insects, fungi, and plants; the question of whether plants are capable of 'learning', or of having 'intelligence' or 'memory', for instance, has proven to be controversial amongst plant scientists (Pollan, 2013). And when does a place – perhaps a mountain or a forest ecosystem – become a being? How does one separate the rights of the tree from the rights of the forest in which it lives? Current discourse about the rights of nonhuman beings is opaque, muddled, and sometimes contradictory. But as Macfarlane (2019) notes, there is value in recognising the movement towards 'natural rights', in that 'its messy idealism is a function of desperation' during what is both a climate emergency and time of mass extinction.

Animists have long recognised that 'the world is full of persons, only some of whom are human, and that life is always lived in relationship with others' (Harvey, 2019:xvii). For Indigenous peoples whose animist worldview is a consequence of their close historical and ancestral relationship with the land, this is their reality. Robin Wall Kimmerer, a Professor, botanist, and member of the Citizen Potawatomi Nation, describes how plants are perceived from an Indigenous perspective:

[Humans] are referred to as the younger brothers of Creation, so like younger brothers we must learn from our elders. Plants were here first and have had a long time to figure things out... Plants are providers for the rest of the community and exemplify the virtue of generosity, always offering food. What if Western scientists saw plants as their teachers, rather than their subjects? What if they told stories with that lens? (Wall Kimmerer, 2013:346)

Unfortunately, the worldviews and knowledge of Indigenous peoples have been widely dismissed by colonising societies. Within the context of environmental management, Indigenous knowledges (which are complex and can include ancestral knowledge, observational and experiential knowledge, and 'revealed' knowledge from dreams and other communications with nonhuman beings) are valued only when they are verified through scientific methods (Barrett, 2013:182-183). People in Western cultures who practice an Earth-based spirituality that falls under the umbrella of Paganism may also hold an animist worldview, and a 'new animism' is slowly emerging within academia that 'names worldviews and lifeways in which people seek to know how they might respectfully and properly engage with other persons' (Harvey, 2019:xx). However, for most of the humans who are managing woods and forests, trained as they were from conventional utilitarian perspectives on 'natural resource management', the idea of 'listening' to a forest's nonhuman inhabitants may more closely resemble madness than good environmental management practice.

New methodologies are emerging that can allow policy makers, environmental managers, and researchers to listen to nonhuman persons. Barrett (2013) argues that 'Western scientific approaches, although important, are not enough to resolve complex environmental problems', and that diversity in knowledge systems is crucial for better decision-making. She is particularly critical of the assumptions embedded in scientific approaches that have likely contributed to the climate crisis, which include the ideas that humans are superior to and separate from the natural world, and that a material reality is the only one which truly exists (2013:179). For Barrett, incorporating ways of knowing that are spiritual (what she calls 'transrational' knowledge, which can come from sources such as dreams, visions, and intuition) helps human communities to create decision-making processes that are inclusive of the worldviews and ways of knowing of all peoples, and to make decisions that benefit the long term sustainability of all beings (2013:180; 184). Although most Indigenous knowledges are only accessible to Indigenous peoples, transrational knowledge is revealed knowledge that is accessible to everyone (Barrett 2013:184).

Another approach to considering policy change in environmental management is by applying different environmental ethical frameworks to real world situations. This is a way to explore how de-centring humans can help to transform environmental management in ways that benefit other beings. For example, Dandy *et al.* (2018) apply three different environmental ethical frameworks (including 'biocentrism', 'flourishing', and 'entangled empathy') to the case study of an Asian longhorn beetle outbreak in the UK in 2012. By applying each of these ethical frameworks to the outbreak situation, they were able to construct three narratives about how the different goals and ways of engaging with the human and nonhuman stakeholders could have changed the outcome of events.

Forest futures: 'Which way do you wish to go now?'

Beings from different species, including humans, have always been entangled in relationships with each other. However, widespread industrialisation and urbanisation across the world means that fewer humans now have opportunities for deep interaction with forested landscapes (or any environment resembling 'the dark forest') and the beings who live in those places. Humans are more disconnected from other creatures than at any other point in the Earth's history, and at a time when we desperately need to know and to listen to the world's nonhuman persons for the sake of our collective future. Due to the scale of species extinctions happening at this time, E.O. Wilson has called the period we are moving into in our planet's history 'The Eremocene', which means 'the Age of Loneliness' (2014). In order to change this future, we need to start seeing nonhuman beings as persons, as partners, as 'knowers'

(Stuckey, 2010), and as 'relatives' (Bird-David, 2018) within our planetary family.

This change in story also requires renewed interest and insistence on diversity and inclusion in our ways of knowing, in our environmental policy and management decision-making processes, and in our ecosystems: monocultures are a problem in forests and in boardrooms. We need to create new, uncanny narratives where humans are not simply intrepid conquerors of the places in which they live, but are instead co-operatively co-existing with other creatures in the forest. In order to help construct these narratives, researchers need to ask what we can do to listen and to co-create our research questions with nonhumans, using creative methods and new ethical frameworks to reimagine and reconceive the world in ways that move humans out of the centre of the frame. 'Irretrievably gone' is not an inevitability.

References

Amo, L., Jansen, J. J., van Dam, N. M., Dicke, M., & Visser, M. E. (2013), 'Birds exploit herbivore-induced plant volatiles to locate herbivorous prey', *Ecology Letters*, 16(11), 1348-1355. DOI: 10.1111/ele.12177

Barrett, M.J. (2013), 'Enabling hybrid space: epistemological diversity in socio-ecological problem-solving', *Policy Science*, 46, 179-197. DOI: 10.1007/s11077-013-9178-x

Benson, E.S. (2016), 'Naming the Ethological Subject', *Science in Context*, 29(1), 107–128. DOI: 10.1017/S026988971500040X

Bird-David, N. (2018), 'Persons or relatives?: Animistic scales of practice and imagination', in Astor-Aguilera, M. and Harvey, G. (eds.) *Rethinking Relations and Animism: Personhood and Materiality*, London: Routledge.

Dandy, N., Porth, E., Hague, R. (2018), 'Environmental Ethics of Forest Health: Alternative Stories of Asian Longhorn Beetle Management in the UK', in Urquhart, J., Marzano, M., and Potter, C. (eds.) *The Human Dimensions of Forest & Tree Health: Global Perspectives*, Switzerland: Palgrave Macmillan, p. 419-444.

Goldschmidt, P., Haddow, G., and Mazanderani, F., ed. (2019), *Uncan*, Edinburgh: Uncanny Press.

Harvey, G. (2019; 2017; 2005), *Animism: Respecting the Living World*, Revised and updated edition, second impression. London: Hurst & Company.

Jones, O. and Cloke, P. (2002), *Tree Cultures: The Place of Trees and Trees in their Place*, Oxford: Berg.

Macfarlane, R. (2019), 'Should this tree have the same rights as you?', *The Guardian*, 2 Nov [online]. Available at: https://www.theguardian.com/books/2019/nov/02/trees-have-rights-too-robert-macfarlane-on-the-new-laws-of-nature, accessed: 6 Jan 2020.

Maitland, S. (2012), *Gossip from the Forest: The Tangled Roots of Our Forests and Fairytales*, London: Granta Publications.

Meijer, E. (2019), 'Interview with Eva Meijer: "Of course animals speak. The thing is we don't listen"', *The Guardian*, 13 Nov [online]. Available at: https://

www.theguardian.com/science/2019/nov/13/of-course-animals-speak-eva-meijer-on-how-to-communicate-with-our-fellow-beasts, accessed: 6 Jan 2020.

Muir, J. (1979), In: L.M. Wolfe, ed. *John of the Mountains: The Unpublished Journals of John Muir*, Wisconsin: The University of Wisconsin Press.

Pollan, M. (2013), 'The intelligent plant: scientists debate a new way of understanding flora', *The New Yorker*, December 23 [online]. Available at: https://www.newyorker.com/magazine/2013/12/23/the-intelligent-plant, accessed 2 January 2020.

Simard, S. (2016), 'Exploring How and Why Trees "Talk" to Each Other', *Yale Environment 360*, 1 September [online]. Available at: https://e360.yale.edu/features/exploring_how_and_why_trees_talk_to_each_other, accessed 2 January 2020.

Stuckey, P. (2010), 'Being Known by a Birch Tree: Animist Refigurings of Western Epistemology', *Journal for the Study of Religion, Nature and Culture* 4.3, 182-205. DOI: 10.1558/jsrnc.v4i3.182

Wall Kimmerer, R. (2013), *Braiding Sweetgrass: Indigenous Wisdom, Scientific Knowledge, and the Teachings of Plants*, Minneapolis: Milkweed Editions.

Wilson, E.O. (2014), *The Meaning of Human Existence*, New York: W. W. Norton & Company.

The Haunted House, or the Other in the Self
Donna McCormack

I want to speak of ghosts. Not really ghosts, but more of hauntings. More specifically, I want to speak about organ transplantation, and ask whether there is anything the ghostly, the spectral, the uncanny and hauntings offer to our thinking on highly technologised biological interventions.

In *The Uncanny*, Sigmund Freud touches on what he deems one of the most obvious experiences of the uncanny: that of the haunted house. Indeed, he suggests that the English version of a haunted house is synonymous with the German translation of 'an unheimliches house' (Freud, 1976: 634). In his tendency to list meanings of the uncanny to show how the already familiar is precisely that which feels unfamiliar and therefore uncanny, Freud proceeds from the haunted house to say:

> There is scarcely any other matter, however, upon which our thoughts and feelings have changed so little since the very earliest times, and in which discarded forms have been so completely preserved under a thin disguise, as our relation to death. (Freud, 1976: 634)

Death and haunted houses are linked here, whether in a list-like structure of related meanings of the uncanny or whether through the idea that haunted houses are the spaces within which the dead may return. Is a house haunted simply because those who lived there died and material traces continue on even while the previous residents may not be present in any clear living form? Is it that we leave material traces in the spaces through which we move and in which we rest, and therefore parts of us are present even though we are visibly absent? While houses are connected to hauntings through the material traces that beings leave around, on and in these spaces, there is another link between death and the haunted house, one Freud does not address and yet one more obvious to those of us used to hearing bodies referred to as a politic, a spatial analogy for nations, communities and globalities (Barclay, 2011; Cohen, 2009; Esposito, 2002; Ahmed, 2000). That is, the body has come to be thought of as *the space within which the self is housed*.

In this configuration of body-as-house, the self lives in the body. One could say that the brain is thought to be the site of the self, although the gut is currently rising in the hierarchy of body parts used to define self, with the heart often being argued as more significant than other organs (Shildrick, 2012); but as many phenomenologists have shown, we are our bodies and those bodies come to be through the spaces and times within which we move, stay and make contact (Gunnarson, 2016; Haddow, 2005; Waldby, 2002; Zeiler, 2014). As Maurice Merleau-Ponty states: 'I am not in space and time, nor do I conceive space and time; I belong to them, my body combines with them and includes them' (1962: 161). If my body is defined through and defining of the spaces and times within which bodily vitality moves, then what happens when *life* ends? That is, what happens when a supposedly individual autonomous being ceases to exist? Could vitality continue on in other forms? Where life of the human tends to be conceptualised as related specifically to a single consciousness in one enclosed space, could the term 'vitality' help us to consider how human life is multiple, endures through multiple interactions of vitality?[1]

If the body is spatialised as that which houses the self, then this suggests that it is a self-contained entity within which an individual being lives. Yet accounts of organ transplantation challenge this assumption of bodily individuality and singularity, showing that

---

1. One may think here of how the microbiome shows that human life is forged only through a symbiotic relationality with bacteria. See, for example: Martin 2010 and Hird 2009.

transplantation is not simply an example of how the other is put in the self (for example, in the form of an organ from a donor), but that human existence is always already other. Jean-Luc Nancy (2008) and Francisco Varela (2001) show in their autobiographical reflections on transplantation (heart and liver respectively) that the self is always already bound by its own alterity, its own difference. Varela states that 'it is not the body-technology that introduces the alterity in my lived body as a radical innovation. That technology widens and slips into what is always already there' (2001: 66). Transplantation, thereby, exposes the very sense of difference that founds a sense of self. Both authors capture how the other is not that which comes after transplantation, but that the very sense of being is founded on this otherness that is simultaneously self and other, or as Judith Butler would have it, the founding relationality that makes these terms possible, even thinkable. In Butler's words:

> Who 'am' I, without you? When we lose some of these ties by which we are constituted, we do not know who we are or what to do. On one level, I think I have lost 'you' only to discover that 'I' have gone missing as well. At another level, perhaps what I have lost 'in' you, that for which I have no ready vocabulary, is a relationality that is composed neither exclusively of myself nor you, but is to be conceived as *the tie* by which those terms are differentiated and related. (Butler, 2004: 22; emphasis in original)

Butler conveys how, as terms, self and other merely cover over the ways these seemingly independent entities or beings emerge through their connections, their bonds to each other. Here, it is the very relation between at least two beings that makes any sense of individuality possible. Transplantation is uncanny not because it reveals a coming together that should be kept apart, an argument where transplantation is unnatural because two individual bodies are brought together in one shelter. Instead, what transplantation captures in our collective imaginary is the very ways in which self is already of the other, that the other lives in the self:

The self is also an ongoing process every time new food is ingested, new air is breathed in, or the tissues change with growth and age. The boundaries of the self undulate, extend and contract, and reach sometimes far into the environment, into the presence of multiple others, sharing a self-defining boundary with bacteria and parasites. Such fluid boundaries are a constitutive habit we share with all forms of life: microorganisms exchange body parts so often and so fast that trying to establish body boundaries is not only absurd, but runs counter to the very phenomenon of that form of life. (Varela, 2001: 263)

Varela makes clear that while such distinctions may allow for understandings of individuality, they cover over the intimacy between multiple beings that are essential to and therefore foundational of self and other. In other words, the distinction between self and other is that which allows us to understand our sense of individual being, but it does not reflect the ways in which we are always and already intertwined. Hauntings bring to the fore this relationality that makes being possible.

Uncanny bodies become apparent at the site where death and life are no longer easily distinguishable, where the border is opaque, and where the two may appear so similar as to create this sense of an unheimliches house. That is, in organ transplantation there is the familiar body – one's own body – which as it ails and/ or fails comes to be lived as less and less familiar: the same and yet different, changing and yet recognisable. One knows that it is the same body with which one has lived and yet it is changing, moving beyond what one may have previously recognised as self. Of course, as many organ recipients experience an array of illnesses, it is not that the body was previously static and now the failing organ brings change, but rather that a failing organ brings about a fundamental change in how one relates to one's own body and its ties to others. More specifically, speaking only about deceased organ donation, I would suggest that the moving of organs from a deceased donor's body to a living recipient's body entangles death with life, blurring our understandings of how life may be extended, death kept at bay and the role of body parts in sustaining life. What is uncanny is that which sustained life in the other may be removed and replace a failing organ in the self; that is, the *vitality of the dead constitute life in this process*. The house takes in the already familiar – a kidney, a liver, a heart – along with the unfamiliar – the DNA of an other. That is, the DNA of the donor is introduced to the self as *foreign* or *alien* matter and therefore requires pharmacological intervention – in the form of immuno-suppressants – in order for the self to continue on. The organ is supposed to bring a renewed sense of unfamiliar vitality to the waning body (and yet this unfamiliarity may feel familiar as a memory of the previous state of one's body before illness). The house is haunted by the sense that what is familiar – a working organ – is not-self, and that not-self is so unfamiliar as to require constant suppression so as not to harm the rest of the body.

When recipients speak of a sense of haunting (Sylvia, 1997; Whitman Helfgot, 2010), many non-recipients critique and dismiss such ties as imagined, signs of psychological distress or of not accepting the organ, or even as simply laughable (Sharp, 2006; Fox and Swazey, 1992). Stories in the press and in memoirs range from the desire for chicken nuggets as evidence of the donor's presence in the self to the moving narrative of the young, white, articulate boy Max Johnson whose parents' campaign resulted in the Max and Keira's law (https://www.gov.uk/government/news/opt-out-organ-donation-max-and-keira-s-bill-passed-into-law), which will bring the opt-out system into England in 2020. In 2019, the media covered the donor parents and the recipient speaking openly about how the donation of Keira's heart to Max unites the families and creates a unique sense of kinship. That recipients speak about how they are obliged to imagine transplantation as a mechanical process without any possibility for biological ties of kinship and yet must write a letter to thank donors for this exceptional gift of life reveals a haunting in the practice of transplantation itself: the living must acknowledge this gift of life as viscerally unique and yet they must not interpret it as a visceral tie. The dead must stay dead and must not resurface as biological connection. Instead they must be contained within the form of the acceptable thank you letter. The dead haunt the writing of this letter even while they must not haunt the visceral self or that self's sense of belonging to the donor's family (or the donor family's sense of being connected to the recipient). To try to control how haunting works by permitting some practices but not others fails to register Freud's important contribution to our thinking on why that which haunts is the unfamiliar familiar. That is, the organ is familiar in its unfamiliarity; biology ties us to others, even as we may dispute the normative structure of blood ties. Bodies feel that something has changed, something has been removed, replaced and someone lost even if that person was never known. Haunting does not require knowledge, specifically knowledge of the dead other; indeed, one may feel that one knows this unknown dead other precisely because their organ lives on in the self, as if their partial presence is a form of knowledge in itself. One can deny this present absence, and institute policies to try to control the feeling of uncanniness, but the presence cannot go away without having a profound impact on one's sense of self and vitality. Even while this presence may seem absent to others, it is present in its visceral form. Thus, this absent presence (Leder, 1991; Derrida, 1994) becomes the uncanny sense of being in a body that is both self and other, self present and absent (in the form of the lost organ), and other present (in the form of the donated organ) and absent (in the form of death of the donor).

In *Staying with the Trouble*, Donna Haraway states, 'The task of the Speaker for the Dead is to bring the dead into the present, so as to make more response-able living and dying possible in times yet to come' (2016: 69). I would suggest that patient and donor family narratives (Fink, 2011; Whitman Helfgot, 2010; Sylvia, 1997; Gohlke, 1985) which speak of the ties between donors/donor families and recipients take on this task of response-able living and dying insofar as they insist on a post-death intimacy, or even of the dead living on, at least in part, in those left as recognisable individual beings. One could argue that the image of the haunted house helps unravel what takes place in the post-transplant body not as unique or distinct from other human embodiment, but as the very process of becoming human. In order words, being human is itself a process of becoming, and transplantation allows us to see these processes in operation as the impact of a major event on who one is in relation to *(constitutive) present and absent others.* The house could be said to feel safe, enclosed and protected, just like how human embodiment is often imagined, but the possibility of anything or anyone crossing the threshold is already a given. Yet this sense of otherness on the threshold, otherness as illness, as threat to this bounded space – including the spatialised self – fails to recognise how the house came to exist through its relationality with others and, in older houses, through the very presence of others maintaining that house. Just as self is often imagined as independent of those others who make existence possible, the house is supposed to keep other as danger outside its borders. However, ghosts threaten such certainties of safety and of separateness as the very presence within the house, as a potentially related being who does not exist anymore and yet is clearly present. If one returns to Freud, not only is the haunted house the epitome of uncanniness where ghostly presence makes that which felt familiar unfamiliar, but also the distinction between life and death is what brings a sense of uncanniness to the fore. In other words, uncanniness emerges when life and death are no longer distinguishable, when life appears to found death (in the form of a donated organ from a deceased donor) and when life may only continue on through its relationality with death (as both defying death for the recipient and losing life for the donor). The haunted house is the image of the living and the dead sharing a space, where the living may want a distinction between life and death, but where this distinction only covers over that multiple beings come to exist through this relationality that is simultaneously viscerally present and materially absent.

If Freud argues against Ernst Jentsch's formulation of the uncanny as simply the blurring of the inanimate and the animate, he does so to emphasise how the desire to push death aside results in a preoccupation with the more than self:

[…] one possesses knowledge, feelings and experience in common with the other. Or it is marked by the fact that the subject identifies himself with someone else, so that he is in doubt as to which his self is, or substitutes the extraneous self for his own. In other words, there is a doubling, dividing and interchanging of the self. (1976: 629–30)

Transplantation raises fears that the self may be exchanged for the other, that the self may be doubled (or even multiplied as more than self and other in one body), and that the self may be lost in its extremely intimate and visceral contact with the other.[2] It is not simply that the other is a ghostly presence in the house, but rather that the ghost – the very presence of otherness – is the foundation of selfhood for what we might call the human (in its multiplicity). One comes to be only through this other. As Jean-Luc Nancy articulates:

My heart became my stranger: strange precisely because it was inside. The strangeness could only come from outside because it surged up first on the inside. […] A heart that only half beats is only half my heart. I was already no longer inside me. I'm already coming from somewhere else, or I'm not coming any longer at all. Something strange is disclosed 'at the heart' of the most familiar – but 'familiar' hardly says it: at the heart of something that never signaled itself as 'heart.' Up to this point, it was strange by virtue of not being even perceptible, not even being present. From now on it fails, and this strangeness binds me to myself. 'I' am, because I am ill. ('Ill' is not exactly the term: not infected, just rusty, tight, blocked.) But this other, my heart, is done for. This heart, from now on intrusive, has to be extruded. (2008: 163)

Transplantation reveals the constitutive tie between self and other in a physical way, not only as donated organ in the self, but also as a new occupant in the house. That is, that which is new (the sense of illness or the feeling of a new organ) exposes the very openness of self to other, of the house to the outside,

2. One need only think of recent Netflix series such as *Chambers* (2019) or *Transferts* (2017) where the replacement of self with other or the coexistence of self with other in the transplanted body is the narrative around which the whole plot develops.

or indeed that the very idea of inside only emerges through its relationality which that which is outside. On the border, lies the haunting: viscera and immateriality, absent and present, and dead and alive. What is uncanny is the sense of being open to the other that may have been denied in the belief of a closed body, but now one realises one is always open to these encounters as the very possibility of existence. Indeed, illness itself, as both Nancy and Varela carefully unravel, is sensed as the initial intrusion into self, whether this comes from inside or outside (or confounds this very distinction), but illness only reinforces that the self is vulnerable from the start, vulnerable to one's self and therefore that the self itself is vulnerable (Butler, 2004).

I would therefore conclude that Freud's uncanny offers a reconsideration of self and other relationality through his initial engagement with the haunted house as that which may become unfamiliar in its familiarity. The house as haunted and the self as haunted by this unknown dead other are manifestations of anxieties around how self is always more than one, always multiple in what may feel like a singular entity. The spatialisation of embodiment allows us to think not simply of the house as a metaphor for the body, but to consider how bodies come to be seen as that in which the self resides comfortably. Yet in being open, we are returned to Jacques Derrida (2000) in that the host cannot choose when to be open, but is always already open to the other, the other who may already be in, on or of the self. Such openness may be experienced as negative or positive, this is not a given, but the body only continues through this vulnerability. As Merleau-Ponty indicates, our bodies come to be in, through and with space and time, and therefore our sense of being emerges through this relation with vital organs, living and dead others, and in this haunted space of being with others. Transplantation captures this haunting through a sense of the dead living on in the other, as the founding of vitality, and yet it also captures how death may constitute life, and how vitality may continue even after death. This is not immortality, but the familiarity of life becoming unfamiliar even when the other has ended and the self lives on in an unfamiliar and yet recognisable form.

References

Ahmed, S., (2000), *Strange Encounters: Embodied Others in Post-Coloniality.* London: Routledge.

Barclay, F., (2011), *Writing Postcolonial France: Haunting, Literature and the Maghreb.* Plymouth: Lexington Books.

Butler, J., (2004), *Precarious Life: The Powers of Mourning and Violence.* London and New York: Verso.

Cohen, E., (2009), *A Body Worth Defending: Immunity, Biopolitics, and the Apotheosis of the Modern Body.* Durham: Duke University Press.

Chambers., (2019), [online]. Created by Leah Rachel. U.S.A: Netflix [viewed August 2019]

Derrida, J., (2000 [1997]), *Of Hospitality: Cultural Memory in the Present.* Translated by Rachel Bowlby. Stanford: Stanford University Press.

_____. , (1994), *Specters of Marx: The State of the Debt, the Work of Mourning and the New International.* Translated by Peggy Kamuf. New York: Routledge.

Esposito, R., (2011), *Immunitas: The Protection and Negation of Life.* Translated by Zakiya Hanafi. Cambridge: Polity Press

Freud, S. 'The Uncanny', (1919), from *The Standard Edition of the Complete Psych Works of Sigmund Freud.* Translated and edited by James Strachey, reprinted in S. Freud, J. Strachey, H. Cixous and R. Dennomé. 1976. 'Fiction and Its Phantoms: A Reading of Freud's Das Unheimliche ('The Uncanny'). *New Literary History*, Vol. 7, No. 3: 525–48 and 619–45

Fink, M., (2011), *Change of Heart: A Black Man, A White Woman, A Heart Transplant and A True Love Story.* Bloomington: Open Books Press.

Fox, R.C. and Swazey, J.P., (1992), *Spare Parts: Organ Replacement in American Society.* Oxford and New York: Oxford University Press.

Gohlke, M. with Max Jennings., (1985), *I'll Take Tomorrow: The Story of a Courageous Woman who dared to Subject Herself to a Medical Experiment – the First Successful Heart-Lung Transplant.* New York: M. Evans and Company.

Gunnarson, M., (2016), *Please Be Patient: A Cultural Phenomenological Study of Haemodialysis and Kidney Transplantation.* Care Lund Studies in Arts and Cultural Sciences [https://portal.research.lu.se/portal/en/publications/please-be-patient(25b0e656-b605-425f-a5b6-d574ea3ec951).html]

Haddow, G., (2005), 'The phenomenology of death, embodiment and organ transplantation'. *Sociology of Health & Illness* Vol. 27, No. 1: 92–113.

Haraway, D., (2016), *Staying with the Trouble: Making Kin in the Cthulucene.* Durham: Duke University Press.

Hird, M., (2009), *The Origins of Sociable Life: Evolution After Science Studies.* Basingstoke: Palgrave.

Leder, D., (1991), *The Absent Body.* Chicago: University of Chicago Press.

Martin, A., (2010), 'Microchimerism in the Mother(land): Blurring the Borders of Body and Nation'. *Body & Society* Vol. 16, No. 3: 23–50.

Merleau-Ponty, M., (1962), *Phenomenology of Perception.* London: Routledge.

Nancy, J-L., (2008 [2000]), *Corpus.* Translated by R.A. Rand. New York: Fordham University Press.

Sharp, L., (2006), *Strange Harvest: Organ Transplants, Denatured Bodies and the Transformed Self.* Berkeley: University of California Press.

Shildrick, M., (2012), 'Imagining the Heart: Incorporations, Intrusions and Identity'. *Somatechnics* Vol. 2, No. 2: 233–49.

Sylvia, C. with William Novak, (1997), *A Change of Heart: The Extraordinary Story of a Man's Heart in a Woman's Body.* London: Little, Brown & Company.

Transfers. (2017) [online]. Created by Patrick Benedeck and Claude Scasso. France: Netflix [viewed November 2019]

Varela, F.J., (2001), *Intimate Distances Fragments for a Phenomenology of Organ Transplantation Journal of Consciousness Studies*, Vol. 8, No. 5–7: 259–71.

Waldby, C., (2002), 'Biomedicine, tissue transfer and intercorporeality'. *Feminist Theory* Vol. 3, No.3: 239–54.

Whitman Helfgot, S. with William Novak, (2010), *The Match: Complete*

Strangers, A Miracle Face Transplant, Two Lives Transformed. New York: Simon & Schuster.

Zeiler, K., (2014), 'A phenomenological approach to the ethics of transplantation medicine: sociality and sharing when living-with and dying-with others'. *Theoretical Medicine and Bioethics* Vol. 35, No. 7: 369–88.

A Bed of My Own
Christine De Luca

My sister was staying with me in Edinburgh for a short city break before winter. We were strolling in the Botanics when suddenly she asked about that place nearby where in the 1960's I'd lodged as a student – she called it that 'grisly place'. Could we find it and what was the story again?

Of course it was easy to find: Edinburgh's New Town is pretty rectilinear, and that particular house is seared on to my memory. However much I had tried over the years to expunge the memory of living there, it would surface from time to time and send a shiver down my spine: a particular smell, a colour of nail polish, a doctor's implements. However, the day was sunny and we had been sharing many happy memories from childhood.

*

The house might have been in the New Town but that didn't mean it was fancy. As a student I suppose I thought myself lucky to have digs and a grant which covered the cost, but I would have liked a bed to myself. For my whole first year I'd shared with Margo: unlike me, she was confident, knowing and seemed sophisticated. Our first meeting had been a shock to the system; I entered the bedroom – a high-ceilinged, dingy, north-facing New Town room – to find her lying on the only bed. I remember the bedspread was black and had seen better days. She had bleached streaks in her hair.

The whole place was very Edinburgh with a kind of genteel down-at-heelness about it. As I got to know the city I would hear it described as 'kippers and pianos' or 'fur coats and nae knickers'. In those days, the late 60s, such sayings had a ring of truth. Mrs Connelly, the landlady, was bird-like, delicate in a storm. Her fading hair was pulled back into a small bun which emphasised her fine bone structure. She was pleasant enough though distant, shielding herself with a quiet dignity, rarely emerging from the kitchen before taking off her apron. Though they had a fine terraced Georgian townhouse, she and her husband lived in what seemed like the nether regions, probably not much more than a kitchen and a bedroom in the basement.

We were seven female students spread over the ground, first and second floors. Besides students, there were two elderly, single women: Annie had a bedsit on the first floor while Barbara had an attic bedsit on the second floor. We all shared a bathroom. We must have been a thorn in their flesh, what with our energy, our young bodies, our confidence and prospects. Even our laughter probably irritated them. Occasionally, we would gather round the old, untuned piano – after our meagre evening meal – and have a sing-song. The two women never mixed with us or with each other; they never had guests and they never seemed to go out. They seemed shrunken, dried up, lonely; eking out a fairly meaningless and impecunious old age. The one incongruous luxury which Annie sported was her bright red nails, making us wonder if there was something in her past that was refusing to let go.

*

It was an intimate year. Margo and I studied together, met up at lunch time, advised each other about boyfriends and, most importantly, negotiated the distribution of the bedclothes with good humour. It wasn't all that odd for me: it was just like sleeping with my sister, while it must surely have seemed strange to Margo, her being an only child. We were chalk and cheese but became good friends.

She moved out after a year, keen to see more of her boyfriend. We decided I would follow as soon as we could get a flat organised and some congenial flatmates. For that one term I had a new bed-mate – Agnes.

She was a 2nd year medical student, and seemed to work all the time. I liked her fine but we both knew I would be leaving. She was always stuck behind a pile of books, writing copious notes, trying to rote learn every possible part of the body. She never went out other than to lectures and labs. And they over-filled her days; unlike the rest of us who swanned about between lectures, occasional tutorials, the library or, more likely, the union. I was glad I wasn't studying medicine as it seemed bone dry.

One subject in particular – anatomy – seemed to fascinate her and animate her conversation. To be specific, anatomical dissection. I could almost visualise the specimens she described after one of her occasional visits to the museum: twisted spinal cords; the jar with conjoined foetuses; the glass case containing the skeletons of unborn babies, pared delicately white, standing to attention in order of age from the earliest to the full-term infant. It was seriously grotesque if strangely necessary. To me it seemed the most grisly of subjects. But she was gripped by it, even worked at it on a Saturday. She pored over *Cunningham's Manual of Practical Anatomy Volume 3: Head, Neck and Brain* and *Jamieson's Illustrations of Regional Anatomy: Upper Limb* till she knew it all by heart. The books brought a whiff of the mortuary to our bedroom which hung around the bed.

After the weekly session in the dissection room she would tell me what she had been doing to Bella, the body she shared – and had named – with her five fellow students. One day she mentioned they had a demonstrator who had a hook instead of a hand, and how two students had fainted when she used it to rip into a corpse. I just about passed out at the thought.

It seemed that Agnes was becoming ever more familiar and at ease with Bella as the weeks progressed. She rather scorned those students who appeared to be more interested in their dissection partners than their corpse. I was more interested in hearing about the budding romances in what seemed like extreme circumstances.

*

Bodies were sourced from those who wished to donate their remains to medical science. They were brought in discreetly through the back entrance to the Medical School. Bella's students speculated as to her arrival: she was a bit different from all the other bodies; much younger for a start, perhaps still in her early forties.

The lab assistants had prepared the corpse for the anatomy classes, as they had prepared so many others. They had drained near enough the last drop of blood out of her and pumped her full of formalin. From now on that mortuary smell would prevail. The last drops of Bella's cheap perfume were totally obliterated by the nauseating, cloying aroma of the morgue. Bella was ready for her new life.

*

I was lying in state along with all the other bodies so lovingly prepared for this our moment of revelation. We had all spent time in and out of fridges while we waited our turn to be embalmed. At last, we were lifted onto trolleys whose wheels squeaked and jammed, then trundled along an echoing corridor to the dissecting room to meet our students. We'd be there for the duration. Exposed. They would all be fresh-faced, probably a bit anxious, curious. I'm used to the gaze of others, and people's hands on me.

It would be our job to be their teachers, to make it easy for them; to demonstrate how things work and link together; and see just how visceral we are, they are. Would our students — yes, we were quite proprietorial about them — would they be able to understand how the body works? And what went wrong with us: who had died suddenly and unexpectedly? Who — lucky devil — just wore out from the burden of years? Who, like me, had had numerous backstreet abortions and some recent trouble that carried me away? I had been glad to give up the ghost: the pain had been unbearable; the rotten bleeding, the fainting. I was embarrassed that I died in that mess. And no one to claim me as their own, give me a decent burial. I'd long since lost touch with my mother: she was probably dead ages ago. The police scooped me up; couldn't get me shovelled into a body bag quickly enough. They took me to the city mortuary where they cleaned me up. But I was glad they didn't remove my red nail varnish, even if it was a bit chipped. It was better than a label tied to my wrist.

*

The professor led the anatomy lectures, in each case focusing on a particular area of the body. He would cover the blackboard with drawings while the students, raked all around the lecture theatre, watched in awe, knowing that the next week they would have a hands-on experience of just that area. He would draw an arm, explain the functions and relationships of all the parts. Inevitably this would inform the dissection practicals. Bit by bit, they would follow the blood supply or a muscle or a nerve from upper arm to finger: median nerve, musculocutaneous nerve, palmar digital nerves, radial nerve, ulnar nerve... it seemed never-ending.

*

I got the impression from Agnes that there was an almost sacred feeling to the space and a sense that they were sitting in the same seats occupied by students of the famous three generations of Monros, Edinburgh University's dynastic anatomists. In those days, the focal point of the lecture theatre would have been the cadaver on the dissection table.

Although things had moved on, Agnes and her fellow students were amazed to hear of the first such explorations of anatomy. They knew of the scurrilous Burke and Hare who provided bodies illicitly, but they hadn't known that Padua had been first, despite the illegality of dissection. Its gorgeous anatomical theatre, with its wooden gallery spiraling upwards in tiers, and railings to hold back the observers, had an almost cathedral-like ambience. The dissecting table in the centre could revolve – now you see it, now you don't – to allow the cadaver to be hidden should a raid occur. A small orchestra would be playing and the students – and citizens with morbid interests – would quickly morph into a concert audience. Agnes would regale me with such stories and how much her classmates enjoyed the light relief they provided.

She was always more talkative after an anatomy lab. I could picture the six of them, in their white coats, poring over their corpse; no masks, no rubber gloves. I could feel the intense, vile, penetrating smell of formaldehyde. They would be eager to get hold of one of the demonstrators, preferably a young trainee surgeon, to do the tricky dissecting or guide the volunteer. Agnes said she was the keenest one. I would guess she was careful, meticulous. They all had their own little pack of dissecting instruments, a canvas roll with a scalpel and forceps. She loved it when the demonstrator praised her skills. She was particularly adept at pulling back the skin and keeping it intact. Nothing was ever cut off. The body was solid, unyielding but, with care, she could insert her hand under the layers of the epidermis and separate the skin from the flesh and muscle. The others in the group were happy enough to watch her as she leaned over the body, lying there on its bed, open to their gaze. There was more than respect in her approach; there was a kind of reverence. She admitted to speaking to the corpse – 'I'll be quick, Bella; this won't hurt, I promise.'

*

Today my students had a spot examination. The demonstrators had prepared specimens and left questions, each with a pin stuck into the relevant part. They had to answer the questions: which nerve is this? What is its function? What is the name of this muscle? This bone? And move on to the next station when a bell rang. I could see they were all nervous. No wonder. There's so much for them to learn and the names don't exactly trip off the tongue. I think I'm getting quite good at it myself.

I'm content when Agnes works on me. She's gentle and I know she likes me. I could almost flinch when I see the demonstrator with the amputated hand moving towards my bed. Granted, she uses the hook with more deftness than most using a scalpel, but it's still a hook and it scares me. She can rip the skin with it in no time, quicker than a blade. No wonder those students fainted the other day. Ah well, they've a lot to learn. I wonder if they ever speculate what I'm thinking about all this. I don't suppose they do; they're so young. They probably think we're not quite real; probably can't imagine a life like mine, or like one of the old men with their shrunken cheeks and turkey necks. At least my chin is still reasonably firm.

*

One moment forever imprinted in my memory is the night I woke suddenly to find Agnes moving her soft fingers slowly down my arm, from shoulder to finger tips. I froze. She seemed to be sleeping, or perhaps dreaming. She felt all the bones of my hand – and each finger – gently. Then she started muttering as she moved her hand up and down my arm: the words were indistinct but I recognised them from our conversation after tea. *Median – lateral, shoulder to hand; musculocutaneous – shoulder to elbow, branching; ulnar – to and from muscles and skin of hands; palmar – sides of digits, radial – to muscles on back of arms, and skin.* Something like that. I was terrified she would call me Bella or start on the rest of my body. I decided to extricate myself without wakening her. I got up, suddenly a bit shaky and shivering all over. For some time I sat in the armchair, with my coat over me; listened to her breathing, waiting till I could climb back into bed. I hardly slept after that. It was one of those things I couldn't bring myself to tell her. It made me edgy with her.

*

One evening not long after that incident, when we had fed the gas meter with some half-crowns and settled to our studies, Agnes looked up and commented, 'What I'd love to know is who Bella *really* was.'

'You said you wondered if she'd been homeless; had a shambolic life.'

'Yes,' she replied. 'Her liver is shot up with cirrhosis and she seems so much older than her years. But she's been a bonnie woman in her time. You know, I've always wondered… that mole Annie has on her right cheek, Bella has one exactly like that in exactly the same position. I sometimes wonder if they're related.'

'What do you mean, Agnes? Are you suggesting Bella could be Annie's daughter? But Annie never married.'

'Exactly! Who knows?'

We left the possibility hanging. Each of us had an essay to write and time for pointless speculation was short.

*

The next evening, at tea time, just as Mrs Connelly came towards our table balancing plates of liver, bacon and beans, Agnes excused herself. I thought she had forgotten something or needed the toilet, would be back in a minute. But our mugs of tea followed and she still hadn't returned. Mrs Connolly removed the uneaten meal, by now cold and congealed. I went upstairs to our room to find Agnes pale and withdrawn, sitting in the armchair, her face stuck in her books. Eventually she said, 'We were studying liver specimens today, under the microscope. Couldn't face that food.'

Money was tight for both of us so there was no chance of going out for a meal. I gave her a bar of chocolate and offered to go downstairs to ask for a sandwich, but she refused, 'It was the way the beans were spilling over the hard pieces of fried liver that got to me. Just like Bella's – hers was all tough and yellowy and warty rather than smooth and wobbly.'

I swallowed and pulled a face in disgust, thinking that's me and liver for ever. I suggested we explore vegetarianism.

'Mrs Connolly has enough on her plate without us asking for a special diet. That husband of hers – did you see …?'

It wasn't the first time Mr Connolly had come bumbling into the dining room by mistake. The stink of drink on him was sickening.

'I suppose you're right. But seriously, Agnes, how can you do that stuff?' She had a resigned smile on her face. I tried to lighten the tone, 'Why don't we go for a walk in the Botanics?'

She moved across to the only table in the room, stacked with her books. 'Too much work, Caroline.'

'I should be working too. Just as well there's no TV.'

We settled to a quiet evening, the white ceramic ribs of the gas fire slowly brightening to comfort our study, the faint abattoir smell of cooked liver drifting under our door.

*

Today they've been discussing the most intimate parts of my anatomy – what they call the reproductive organs. I was a bit nervous what they might discover about me. It was the hook lady who did the deed, ripped open my lower abdomen. She asked for someone to pull back the skin and the greater omentum that hides the secret places: the uterus and all the bits and pieces down there. I was glad Agnes offered. They examined my uterus, ovaries and fallopian tubes. Agnes said she thought one of my fallopian tubes was ruptured. They all peered in – these things are so small. They discussed what might have caused that. Maybe an ectopic pregnancy. It was all starting to make sense. I was glad when they folded that fatty layer back over me, made me decent. I'll give them their due, they don't snigger or mess around.

*

After tea and before she settled to her books Agnes was in a mood for a chat. I'd told her my maths tutorial had been amusing as the lecturer had hauled one young female student to the front for talking too much, just like in school. We could hardly believe it. Someone said they thought he was suffering from piles and that made him irritable. Agnes laughed at that. It was good to hear her laugh. It relieved a bit of the tension I still felt in her company, and my increasing revulsion at what seemed a macabre interest in a dead body.

'Do you know, Caroline, I think I want to become a family planning doctor.'

'What brought that on?'

'Well, with Bella today we found that she had probably died with an untreated ectopic pregnancy. It must have been a horribly painful way to go. It was preventable. All unwanted pregnancies are preventable.'

I could see she was deadly serious. I couldn't help admiring her courage and determination. My stupid story from the maths tutorial seemed pretty inconsequential. And I had no idea what I might do with my life.

*

I'll be a bit sad when all this is over. When they move on to their third year, to the other 'ologies' they have to pack into their heads. They'll no doubt fold the skin back over us before we're trundled away to the incinerator. All that ash. I hope they don't waste it. Good for the roses. I'm glad I still have my red nail polish. Everything else is so grey. I think a few of them are coming to the thanksgiving service for us. It's good of them – when most of us have no one who would know or care. Ah well, at least my life wasn't entirely wasted. Who was it that said this is the place where the dead are pleased to help the living? That's what it's all about.

They'll make good doctors. Especially Agnes.

*

It was a December evening near the end of term. I would be moving out soon. Mrs Connelly was very quiet at tea time and paler than usual. We were all there. We'd been served tinned tomato soup followed by beans on toast, an even more frugal meal than usual.

No one complained. No one felt like a sing-song round the piano with our mugs of tea. We drifted upstairs to our rooms. Shortly afterwards one of the girls from the front bedroom knocked and rushed in. She beckoned us to come quickly. We followed her to where her room-mate was discreetly peering out from behind the curtains. In the darkness of the early winter evening we could see a police van parked outside the house. It had neither windows nor flashing lights. There were two policemen manoeuvring a stretcher into the back of the van. On it was a body, well covered. We all fell silent.

Why the police? Had there been a murder? Or an unexplained death? Had Annie or Barbara died and there was no one to claim them? Had Mrs Connelly finally hit her husband over the head?

Nothing was said. No one dared to ask poor Mrs Connelly. She went about her work as before, perhaps with a few more sighs. She served us steak and chips the next night, the first time ever; perhaps to make up for the beans on toast. We kept to our bath rota as before. We would never know for sure what happened. But none of us ever saw Annie again after that evening.

Perhaps next year's students would find her body waiting for them in the gaunt dissecting room. Perhaps she would still be sporting her red nails. Perhaps someone like Agnes would become fond of her, comment on her mole.

Much as I admired Agnes I was glad to escape from the memory of that hand in the dark and faint traces of formaldehyde to a flat with Margo; to a bed of my own.

Where the Edinburgh All-night Bakery Used to Be
Jane McKie

Straight from the pub,
sticky and jubilant,
we devoured them.
Ovens thawed the ice-
rimed pavement, which
chimed
the high note of
everything
glazed. And we,
close to hysteria like guests
left afterhours
at a wedding, toasted
each other's skin
with snow, dusted lips
with sugar, slipping
our way home
with breath building
in our own shapes, that is,
in the shapes of ghosts.

Three-stage No Colour Day
Jane McKie

10 a.m.

Blanketing cloud in place.
At ground level, beetles stalk aphids
and small caterpillars;
the soil gently thrums.

2 p.m.

A veal calf can be heard
lowing for its mother.
Fields hold their greens in reserve,
waiting for sky's overweening blues.

6 p.m.

Swifts reel from eaves and snap
the tinder of insect bodies.
Nothing ignites.
No vibrant reds burst onto the scene.

East Coast Gothic
Jane McKie

Imagine you come across a single grave
in a formal garden, the light
almost gone, tree shadows so thick

they coalesce like people milling
in corners. The stone, a simple
slab, precariously perched,

tips towards you, insisting
that if you bend close to its lichened skin,
you'll find your own name.

Imagine you put aside
the pulse of fear at your throat
and lean in, mirroring the stone's tilt –

not a single name to be found,
just the usual pocking and blotches
of a rough, weathered face.

Imagine it isn't relief you feel.

Baby
Jane McKie

In the discount basket: feet shaped like fins, a candle-wax colour.
I haul her up like a line-caught fish, this plastic doll, her eyelids
spoked with black brush from which tears will inevitably spill.

She will be called Baby Maia like the last Baby Maia. Toys, like
pets, are loved so obstinately.

Her right eye-click is delicious, the iris violet, glassy, and impossibly
huge when it falls open. The left lid is half-shut and will not budge,
even when I get my nail under.

Still, she'll do. She has enough in common with the other Maias:
tenacity and sweetness beyond her years; the ability to pee.

And when she cries her voice box emits a sound like wind over
bottles – faulty perhaps, but as I finally lever her reluctant lid,
I have to mourn the also-rans, lost on the beach, mauled by the
dog, or simply put away.

Ma
Pippa Goldschmidt

The hundred needles of the knitting machine set up a hundred identical glints as she switched on the overhead light and drew the curtains shut, blocking out the brightness of the street.

The machine lived in an average sort of room with almost nothing else in it but a depressed sofa, a tired looking chair and a table for working. And everything covered in the spoor generated from a lifetime's work of feeding wool into the machine. It was pointless running a wet cloth over the surfaces of the room to get rid of the spoor, because more would just gather. So she didn't bother.

The post had arrived with more orders from clients, 'Hey, Ma. They've sold right out of Style 18.' Style 18, a sort of poncho with attached scarf, was the best seller and the tourist shops in the centre of the city couldn't get enough of it. It was also very difficult to knit, but she had learnt to do it by herself now.

The chair was uncomfortable but there was nowhere else to sit, the sofa being piled high with orders waiting to be delivered. That would be the evening's job, folding the knitwear and wrapping it in plastic bags. Tomorrow would require a trip to one of their most consistent clients, a tourist shop on Princes Street. It was fortunate that she could take the orders for this shop directly by bus, saving quite a lot on postage.

She found it hard keeping up, now that it was just her and the knitting machine. It ingested the wool, thread by thread, swallowed it up and produced torsos, arms, hands, necks and scalps. Body parts hung from its needles and it was her job to cast them off, stitch by stitch, and sew them together into clothes.

*

On the bus the next morning, the carrier bags of knitwear kept slithering off the seat and causing a distraction. As she fought to keep hold of them, her own gloves were forgotten and it wasn't until the pavement was safely reached and the bus well on its way across the bridge that she remembered.

'Damn!' she would not cry over a pair of gloves.

But she had to cry. 'Oh, Ma…'

Ma had made the gloves the very last time she used the machine. A Fairisle pattern on every single finger, which was exceptionally hard, but Ma could do it even when she was so ill she couldn't feel the tips of her own fingers any more, on account of the chemo damaging the nerves and making fine work almost impossible. But Ma had knitted the gloves for her, and they were now travelling away across the city. The sharp sunlight was no compensation for the biting wind and her cold naked fingers clutched the bags full of orders as she made her way to the shop.

Standing outside the shop, it was difficult to see the screen of her phone and read the number of the lost property office. Finally a voice recited, 'Come tomorrow. It takes a day for your belongings to be handed in by the bus driver and entered into our system.' The voice might or might not have been automated, sometimes it was difficult to tell.

Tomorrow, then. Best to go home now, and get on with some work.

*

That afternoon was scarf after scarf after scarf. You didn't have to think much when you made scarves, because there was simply a block of stitches to be cast on and then some muscle work sweeping the carriage back and forth before the final casting off. A neat little gadget did that, you simply fit it to the needle bed and rotated it. No shaping, no hooking one stitch onto its neighbour, and if you did them one after the other with the same gauge of wool, not many worries about tension.

Sweep, sweep, sweep went the carriage back and forth. At four o'clock the overhead light was turned on so she could see better. At seven o'clock she remembered about dinner and decided against it. Her right arm hurt. Ma had had arms like Popeye's.

Where would the gloves be now?

The carriage stopped mid-row and refused to move. Something had jammed its insides. Ma had been able to curse the machine back into obedience with nothing else but the power of bad language, but she herself lacked that ability.

'Oh, Ma,' and the machine started again, as smoothly as if nothing had ever been the matter with it. The scarf was a mess though, with an obvious jagged hole in its middle. Nothing to do but unravel it all and rewind the wool for the future, although second-hand wool always betrayed itself in its kinked nature. Never mind, it could be used for sewing pieces together.

*

The lost property office was in the Old Town, and her phone displayed a map with herself as a red dot moving along the neatly outlined city streets. The dot moved more steadily and surely than she did in actual life and after a bit she felt mesmerised, watching it to see what it would do next.

Inside the building, the dot disappeared. Perhaps it had completed its task, perhaps now it was someone else on another map. She followed signs directing her to go upstairs. Up and up she climbed until she found the right room. A high and wide room full of benches organised as straight as the rows of the best sort of knitting, the sort Ma could do, and on each bench was a row of people as evenly spaced as the stitches of the best sort of knitting. She took her place and waited. She should have been at home, Ma wouldn't approve. But the gloves needed to be retrieved.

A man in a uniform at the front of the room shouted at regular intervals:

'Black umbrella with a white plastic handle!'

'Green handbag!'

And a person would rise and be reunited with their belongings. It was touching to see. She smiled at each person.

'Fairisle gloves!'

They were her gloves, there was no doubt about that, she assured the man. She signed an official form and went on her way. Down, down the stairs she went, reversing her previous steps like stitches being unpicked. The stairs went a long way down, many more floors than she remembered on the way up. Finally, she reached a sign saying 'exit'. She stood in front of the door to the outside world and prepared herself, putting on her gloves, smoothing them tight over her hands. Admiring the patterns on the fingers. Ma had been so ill when she'd made them that she couldn't eat anything apart from melted ice cream, but she could still knit.

'Thank you, Ma.'

But something was wrong with the gloves. Something off-centre. They still fit her hands as if they had been made specially for her, as indeed they had, each finger just the right length and no gaping hole between the thumb and forefinger – a sign of Ma's great skill – no matter how wide she stretched her hands. But right next to the little finger on each gloved hand was an extra finger. Quite small, maybe about a centimetre long and half the width of her actual little finger. These extra knitted fingers were plain, no Fairisle patterns on them. Plain, dark wool. Perhaps they'd been inside the gloves and had popped out, perhaps that was why she'd not noticed them until now. She opened the door marked 'Exit'. Unlike Ma to make a mistake like that, but she had been so ill and not quite all there because of the morphine. Perhaps not actually able to count properly any more. 'Poor Ma.'

Now she was outside, standing in the street, but not in the place where she'd started. This was not the entrance to the lost property office. She turned round to go back inside but the door had slammed shut behind her. Up above her seemed darker than it should be at this time of day, and this was because another street crossed over the top of this one. She must be right at the bottom of the Old Town. Her phone screen showed a map but the map was just lines criss-crossing each other with no street names. Nothing more than a maze and the red dot was where she'd left it before she entered the building. There was not enough signal down here to let the dot tell her where to go. Even so, she held up the screen and looked at it with one eye, like looking through a telescope at a distant horizon, but there was nothing there – nothing at all apart from stone buildings. And she couldn't see any street names on the stone buildings.

She was on her own. As long as she went upwards, she'd be alright, she'd find the bus stop. Up the nearest alley, then, trying not to breathe in the smell of piss. But this alley came to an end with a brick wall right across it, the bricks curiously smooth and even in texture. The next one was exactly the same, apart from some graffiti on the bricks that she couldn't read and this disturbed her, as if someone had left her a message that she wasn't able to understand. The third alley started off more promisingly before it kinked a sharp right and led her back to her starting point.

So quiet and deserted down here. No shops, nobody to ask the way. Far above she could hear traffic noise, sirens, the rumble of lorries, the sound of the city going about its business. Here, nothing but walls. An empty street. The only other movement was a piece of paper spinning and spinning in the wind. She watched it for a while, smoothing the gloves over her hands and getting some comfort from the feel of wool. Until she touched the extra fingers.

Empty pouches hanging down. They seemed larger now out here, in this confused and confusing space. Wool so dark she struggled to make out the individual stitches. Extra woollen fingers where there shouldn't be fingers, where she didn't have fingers. Something growing where it wasn't needed, reminding her of x-rays in the hospital and having to look at all these dark loops and strands of Ma's insides, following the consultant's own finger as it pointed at what was wrong and what shouldn't be there. She took the gloves off and hid them in her coat pockets.

This city, normally as intricate as a knitting machine with its streets as precisely interlocked as the needles with the cogs, had gone wrong. And she had no instructions to fix it. Her hands, now red with cold, were the only things with any colour on the street, everything else was dark shining windows and grey stones, chipped black doors.

Some gulls had appeared, just ahead of her. She hadn't noticed them flying in the sky and yet here they were standing in the road. Four of them, and quite still, waiting for something. Unusually large birds. They eyed her and she slowed down. Where to, now?

To one side, a flight of steps. Little ones, quite shallow. She couldn't see where they led because they were curving round, a bit like Ma's hair when it grew back curly after the chemo. She started walking up them. These steps were the same height and width as the ones at home. Each one had a sloping part and a flat part, they fit together like stocking stitch. She had learnt how to walk upstairs without looking where she was going, carrying the tray for Ma with its bowl of ice-cream and bottles of pills.

'My little pearl,' Ma used to call her. When she was young she thought Ma was saying 'purl'. A purl was an inside-out stitch. But when it was combined with a normal one it created a beautifully even effect.

The steps delivered her to the entrance of a covered car park and she continued inside. There seemed to be no other entrance, just via the steps, but the car park was full of cars and they must have driven in from somewhere, she just couldn't see where. She carried on walking, now she seemed to be going up a ramp that was too steep and narrow for cars to drive down. She looked behind her at where she'd come from and saw a sign that said 'No entrance.'

The ramp led to a street. In front of her, her own shadow made the usual sort of shape on the pavement and two people walking by stepped right on it without noticing. She knew where she was now and it was possible to go home.

*

Once inside the house she managed to try on the gloves again, her own fingers remembering how to avoid the secret loops of wool inside caused by the Fairisle pattern. Muscle memory, they called it. Just like using the machine, or her feet finding their way up the steps to the carpark.

The extra fingers seemed slightly larger but perhaps that was just because she was in a room where everything had always been very cramped on account of all the wool and the machine and its parts. It made her feel a bit squeamish to look at these useless extra fingers, drooping down from the side of each glove. A little bit sick. Perhaps this was how Ma had felt during the chemo.

It was Ma who had taught her to use the machine. Ma's ma had taught her to knit by hand but Ma always said people needed to change with the times, to adapt to the circumstances, and bought herself a machine.

She had a memory of knitting needles from when she was a child. Long needles and an old woman.

*

After Ma had gone, she supposed things would carry on the way they always had, in their house in a street surrounded by other streets with the same first name; Glencairn Road, Glencairn Terrace, Glencairn Lane, Glencairn Brae. The houses all identical and very few with visible numbers. It helped to know where you were going in this part of town.

So when the doorbell rang – a few days after she'd got the gloves back – it was obviously someone who was lost. Or perhaps it was the next wool delivery, arrived early. She opened the front door and found a woman standing on the doormat looking uncertain. No wool in sight. Someone lost, then.

'Number 8?' the woman read from a piece of paper.

She nodded.

'Glencairn – ' there was a short pause, then 'Cr – what's Cr?'

It sounded like an abbreviation for a knitting instruction; Cr 2 Kn 1. 'Court. Or Crescent.'

'Pardon?'

She hadn't spoken for a few days, that was why her voice was so quiet. Come to think of it, she couldn't remember the last time she had spoken. After Ma had gone she'd learnt that it did no good to shout at the machine when things went wrong. 'You'll be wanting Glencairn Court,' she said. This was Glencairn Crescent.

'Will I?' the woman was small and neat in her general appearance. She glared at the paper, 'It's really not clear. That damned department! You'd think they'd make it easier for us.'

Us?

The woman looked up at the front of the house. 'Quite a bonny place, isn't it? You mind if I come inside?' and without waiting for an answer she managed to insert herself into the hallway. 'Jeepers! You got your own cottage industry going on here!' She'd collided with the bags for the next day's deliveries and the knitwear, slippery in its plastic wrappings, was cascading all over the floor.

'Two bedrooms?' the woman was trying to pile up the bags but she didn't have the knack of it.

'Sorry?'

'This house has two bedrooms?'

'Yes.' Why?

'And you're the only tenant now?'

She nodded. Oh, Ma.

'They – ' and the woman rattled the paper, 'sent me round to check. It's not efficient, you see.'

Silence. A creeping, cold sort of silence, just like she'd experienced in the sunless street outside the lost property office.

'They're terribly short of two bedroom houses.'

In the living room now, and the woman's eyes had grown large at the sight of the cones of wool stacked up in towers. Then she noticed the machine in the corner. 'I'm not sure you're allowed to run a business from one of these tenancies. It may not be legal.'

'We've always done it. And nobody's complained about us. Ever.' That was true, even with the racket going late at night, that rhythmic swish of metal accompanying her as she dozed in bed, Ma working away downstairs. Sometimes she'd lay a finger on her wrist and feel her vein pulse in time to it, like she was being knitted into a garment, something beautiful to wear.

'They've got some really nice one-bed flats. Just a wee bit further out of town. New builds.' The woman had wandered over to the machine and was peering at it, 'Is it difficult to learn? I always fancied having a go.'

Ma died of something extra that grew in her gut, like a stitch cast on by mistake. From an instruction that was wrong but that her body followed anyway, that was how it was explained by the hospital. And she understood about needing to follow instructions because that was how sweaters and ponchos and scarves and gloves were made. They tried to cut it out, to reduce Ma back to normal but they failed. What was in Ma wouldn't stop growing because it was being told to grow and nothing could tell it to stop growing, not even Ma herself. Ma wrote the instructions for the machine but she couldn't do that for herself.

The woman ran her hands over a sweater folded on the sofa, 'Such soft wool!'

The sweater was folded neatly, its chest and neck submitting to the woman's fingers, which were kneading and caressing the wool as if they couldn't get enough of it. The paperwork from the housing department long forgotten.

She went to the machine and cast on a row of stitches in her favourite colour; never fading, never going that nasty shade of rust. She started to knit, pushing the carriage back and forth without needing to look at what she was doing, able to watch the woman's hands burrow further into the sweater.

The strand of wool was drawn down into the machine like blood pulsing through a body and the sweater on the sofa twitched in time to the movements of the woman's hands. The woman watched the machine as it started to make its lovely red throat of stitches, the rasping noise of the needles loud enough to drown out whatever she was trying to say.

Uncan
Shona Kerr

The short story *Ma* is an example of magical realism, underpinned by the topics of genetics and programming. The scientific disciplines of genetics/genomics and programming/informatics are arguably the key technologies of the 21st century. Together they promise unprecedented transformations in human healthcare, at least in the developed world. But the big data they generate is also creating some of the biggest challenges both to society and to the individual, ranging from issues around privacy through to discrimination and stigmatisation. Using Freud's essay *Uncanny* as a launch pad, in *Ma* Goldschmidt intertwines a range of unsettling and unfamiliar events, exploring themes of family, genetics and loss. These are teased out through an exploration of the consequences of changes in the instructions fed into a knitting machine, and the instructions for human life.

We are introduced to the knitting machine in the opening sentence of *Ma*, then told where the machine "lived". The knitting machine's ability to create body parts from wool can be taken as an analogy of the instructions in the genetic material, DNA. This sets the scene for the rest of the story, which unfolds as we learn how recent events are affecting the protagonist, a daughter whose life is shaped by the legacies passed on by her mother. The protagonist is on the brink of becoming unable to function, due to her grief at the loss of her mother. Struggling to cope, she is haunted by the cancer that led to her mother's death. She imagines with dread how it grew in and eventually destroyed her mother's body. The cancer obeyed its own mysterious set of instructions, taking advantage of programming mistakes or coding errors to evade the normal controls on cell growth and division.

A reader who knows Edinburgh might gradually realise *Ma* is set there, without this being explicitly stated. The story uses Edinburgh as a city that has long been known to have unsettling and uncanny aspects – the proximity of rich and poor, dark stones and depth in the Old Town next to elegance and lightness in the New. In medicine, the strange case of Dr Jekyll and Mr Hyde is set in London, but inspired by Edinburgh. And the demand for anatomical knowledge in the early 19th century Edinburgh Medical School created opportunity for the body snatchers Burke and Hare. The neighbourhood in which the protagonist lives feels connected to her and she has no wish to leave. In contrast, the location of the lost property office is unfamiliar and confusing, contributing to her becoming momentarily lost in the different levels of the city streets.

In *Ma* the daughter literally continues her mother's work, knitting and finishing garments to sell, and using the same instructions to fix any problems. The knitting machine can only work properly if the instructions it gets are accurate. Similarly, the machinery in every cell in the body depends on the accuracy of the instructions it is given on when to grow and when to stop growing. The act of knitting connects her to her mother, physically by using the same machine in the same room and emotionally by maintaining her legacy. The knitting machine work is repetitive and relentless, but nonetheless its familiarity provides some comfort as her environment and her life start to crumble.

Recent advances in genetics and informatics such as whole genome sequencing coupled to high-performance and cloud computing are leading to detailed understanding of the connections and interplay between genes and disease. For example, it is becoming increasingly common for women who know they are in a "breast cancer family" to undergo genetic testing. Currently, clinical genetics analysis methods for breast cancer risk focus on looking for specific changes in two key genes, known for over two decades to be important in this illness. Many women who find that they carry the same gene change, or variant, that contributed to the disease in their relatives, opt for surgery to remove their breast and ovarian tissues in order to escape a similar fate.

This does not mean that we 'are' our genes. A 'faulty' gene can result in different outcomes for different people. The "penetrance" of a disease-causing mutation (that is, the proportion of individuals with the mutation who show clinical symptoms) is an important statistic. However, the true penetrance in a population is difficult to measure, and may be subject to ascertainment bias. And even if a functionally important change in a key gene is present, the rest of a person's genome also matters. Other genetic sequences can influence whether a clinically relevant variant causes a person who carries it to develop an illness, or remain well. Furthermore, for most common diseases that affect most people, the answers from genetic and genomic analyses are much less clear than such "single gene" examples. Genomic data generated in an accredited laboratory will be accurate as a measurement, but its interpretation is often not yet translatable into individually useful clinical information. The more we study the human genome, the more complexity is revealed. And the environment also matters for physical and mental health. In *Ma*, the daughter's hold on reality has become distorted by her loss, exacerbated by her environment - she lives alone and works alone in her home, seldom speaking to anyone. Nonetheless, many scientists and clinicians and even some politicians are increasingly enthused at the prospect of "genomic medicine". This is evidenced by a recent floating of the idea by the UK Secretary of State for Health and Social Care that in the near future, babies should have all their genes (their genome) sequenced at birth through the NHS.

Human genetics is a study of families – not just the nuclear family, but also extended pedigrees and kinships, right through to the wider family of all humanity. What legacy do we leave our children? Our genes for sure, uniquely rearranged in the creation of each new human. But we also provide our offspring with an environment, in infancy, childhood and beyond. A legacy handed down from a relative may be financial, or a name, but as in *Ma*, it can also include wisdom and knowledge transmitted down the generations. Ma has instructed her daughter (whose name we do not learn) how to use her knitting machine with all its quirks, while coping with cancer and chemotherapy. In Ma's body, the genetic 'instructions' encoded in her DNA have somehow gone wrong. In the story, the knitted gloves with extra fingers that persist in growing serve as a metaphor for the cancer Ma had when she made them. "*Ma wrote the instructions for the machine but she couldn't do that for herself*".

Ma is fiction, but helps us to reflect from a different viewpoint on the scientific themes it contains. In keeping with the rest of the story, the ending is a little bit mysterious, a little bit uncanny.

Rodd widenin i da Hulmalees
Christine De Luca

Hulm: a holm:
Hulmalìs:
   a broo doon
      ta Hulmawater:
   holms i da loch.
      Da rodd wast-owre
   smoots bi glansin lochs
   lik da munster we eence saa
fae da windows o P.I.'s bus.
Single track rodd
   wi passin places:
      draa in, draa braeth.
         Ivery blinnd coarner
   anidder glim o licht apö watter,
anidder glinder at a munster
   at only disappears whin we stop
      ta let someen pass. Whin aa
         da coarners is shaaved aff
            an da rodd is widened
                  will we aa scrit by, ithoot
               a meetin o minds, or
               takkin time ta savour
            da fire-aetin sun braethin
         his flames owre da wastird
      or da tjaldur pleepsin
         on da holms, or
      a antrin
         nyuggel
            pairtin da
               watter o da
                  Hulm
                  -alees.

Note: Peter Isbister, who ran the local bus service for many years, was affectionately known to everyone as P.I.

***

Glossary

rodd: *road*
da: *the*
holm: *islets*
broo: *brow*
smoots: *slinks*
glansin: *sparkling*
lochs: *lakes*
eence: *once*
saa: *saw*
anidder: *another*
glim: *gleam*
licht: *light*
apö: *on*
glinder: *peer*
someen: *someone*
aa: *all*
shaaved: *hacked*
scrit: *hurry*
tjaldur: *oyster catcher*
pleepsin: *crying*
antrin: *occasional*
nyuggel: *legendary water horse in Shetland folk-lore*

In Pursuit
Christine De Luca

In response to a drawing by Joyce Gunn Cairns of an exhibit
at the Museum of The Royal College of Surgeons, Edinburgh

This is my foot, close relative
of the one I first discovered,
tried to focus on, fit in my mouth:
the one from which I learned
foot-ness, me-ness, otherness.

This is the foot that stumbled,
learned to hold me upright;
the one that ran a thousand lines,
fleet winger: crossed balls, struck goals.
Folk said there were none like me.

This is the foot that danced
fumbling steps in pursuit of love;
that trembled between dark sheets,
touched a strange wisdom;
that still walks with me.

This is the foot that took me to war,
that, muddied and bloodied, rotted
in the trenches; the one you lopped
quickly. (Whisky dulled the pain
but not imagination or hearing.)

This is the foot, they tell me, you kept
for scientific purposes. Phantom
of youth perhaps? The foot that aches
on winter nights, twitches when
the band strikes up; still dances.

Little Cat from the Bronx
Eris Young

The doorbell rang maybe three times before Ted was aware of it. Kat had finished by then: she never made much noise but he could tell by the pace of her breathing. He leaned forward and cupped her narrow hand inside his big one. Their hands fit together like the way his body fit over hers on the bed. The doorbell rang again and she breathed, 'Oh, let them wait.'

He thrust one last time and came inside her with a final spasm that shifted the box spring in its frame. When his vision cleared Kat was looking back at him over her shoulder with that narrow-eyed smile of hers. A cat with the cream.

Ted imagined a growing crowd waiting on the doorstep. Shuffling its feet and coughing into its hands. But all his and Kat's earlier urgency was gone. Ted rolled the lambskin off and they zipped and tucked and smoothed themselves in languorous unison. What was a few more minutes?

Kat fixed her hair and lipstick in the hall mirror and Ted checked his tie wasn't stained. He'd thrown it over his shoulder, as he always did if he'd just come home and they didn't wait to undress, but you couldn't be too careful with people coming over.

They went to let in the guests – only three people, it turned out – Ted looking over the top of Kat's head, both of them full of jovial apology,

'Hi! Sorry!'

'Hope you weren't waiting long?'

'We were in the yard.'

*

The house filled up. For a few minutes Ted stood in the dim living room, arms folded, absorbed in the babble of voices and snatches of music from the turntable. He admired Kat's handiwork: the arrangement of the extra chairs, the canapés in orderly rows, the flowers leaking their hothouse scent into the air to mix with cigarette smoke.

A man's home is his kingdom, his mind said in his mother's voice. Ted breathed in deeply, indulging in the simple pleasure of looking at everything put together just so. The guests, the music, the trays of snacks and drinks. Like the way his wife's small body perfectly fit his own, like it was made for him. Everything arranged for his delectation.

He found Gary at the wheelie bar cart, mixing drinks as he tended to do whenever they had him over. Even on the *Tallahassee* Gary had been the one to concoct and dole out torpedo tube hooch to the rest of the company. They shook hands and exchanged pleasantries and Ted allowed Gary to fix him a drink. He was doing martinis, which Ted didn't normally go in for, but Gary had brought a thirty-dollar bottle of vodka so Ted couldn't really say no.

He was ravenously hungry: he had hollowed himself all the way out with Kat. He accepted his drink, sipping off the top so it wouldn't spill, and balanced a plate in his other hand, piled with devilled eggs and cocktail shrimps and the little toast triangles with pâté that Kat hadn't told him the name of. He inhaled the food in a few bites. He wanted something more substantial.

*

The kitchen was quieter and brighter than the rest of the house, although Kat had the radio set to some rock and roll station. Kat was talking to a woman, short and compact, dark and sort of foreign-looking. She'd have stood out in a crowd, but next to milky Kat with her reddish hair the difference was striking.

Mexican? Jewish, maybe. Ted recognised her, finally, as the woman who'd moved into the little place over on Van Buren. Kat and the neighbor woman each held a glass of red wine, the bottle sitting on the counter tiles between them.

Ted went to root around in the fridge and Kat swatted at him companionably as he passed her, 'There's food in the living room, Ted.'

There was roasted chicken left over from dinner. Ted ate some of it cold while the two women laughed together. The neighbor woman had an accent Momma would have called 'urban'. An accent Kat had still been struggling to get rid of when they'd first met, back in '36, and the reason Ted had given her her silly bedroom nickname. He stood to put his plate in the sink and Kat put a hand on his arm,

'Since you're here, Ted, this is Kiki. She's just moved from New York, bought that house on Van Buren.'

From New York. It felt odd to shake hands with a woman who spoke with Kat's discarded accent.

'Nice to meet you, ma'am.' Kiki—even her name sounded foreign—had a firm grip. 'Welcome to the neighborhood. Your husband around here too?'

'I'm divorced, actually.'

A pause opened in the conversation, which Kat deftly filled, 'I actually knew Kiki in college. She got me into the land army, way back when.'

Ted frowned. When had Kat gone to college? She'd been a typist when they'd met. He had known about the land army, that Kat had joined up soon after he'd enlisted. He had a sudden vivid image of them: Kiki and Katherine in scraps of denim, baling hay, slick under the blazing midwestern sun, lithe woman-muscles straining. He felt himself get a little hard and leaned back against the counter, hiding behind Kat. She noticed and leaned into him, tilting her head up for a kiss, smiling into his mouth. Kiki looked on, her face inscrutable.

*

Ted left the kitchen for the dark backyard, where he accepted a beer from Gary and sat in a lawn chair with his legs crossed. Lester was there too, already sauced, as expected. They chatted and laughed, cracked some lewd jokes. The kind of jokes you can only tell after dark, his mother would have said.

The hot Michigan night was alive around them with the murmur of voices and the sound of crickets like a pocketful of change. A couple of lightning bugs blinked lazily over an unoccupied part of the lawn. Lester passed around cigars, which were pretty good; well worth the price of having to listen to Lester brag about how he'd had them imported from Cuba. Ted sipped his beer and let the talk wash over him.

Wives joined them. Kat—sans Kiki—and also Gary's wife, Jeanette. Kat sat on the arm of Ted's deck chair and leaned over to pluck the cigar from his mouth, taking a deep drag. Something about the way she held it in her delicate hand with its shiny nails, the way she sucked on it with obvious pleasure, made him want to reach up and snatch it back. He restrained himself, instead looking around at Gary and Lester with a bemused expression on his face, a shrug, as if to say, 'Women!'

Gary laughed, then the others joined in, and Ted relaxed minutely. Kat smiled and handed the cigar back, draping an arm over his shoulder.

The conversation moved on. Gary and Jeanette were going to have a baby. Gary wrapped an arm around his wife and squeezed protectively. Jeanette smiled at the floor. Lester finished off his drink and went to find another.

'What about you two?' Gary looked between Kat and Ted, 'It's about that time, isn't it?'

Ted snaked his hand around Kat's waist. It was his favorite part of her: pronounced, nipped in, giving her that hourglass shape like a woman in a magazine. It gave way to a set of generous, sloping buttocks with two sexy little dimples. How disappointing it would be to lose that waist to a baby. He'd heard some women never recovered their figures, afterward.

Kat didn't mind 'riding bareback', though, and Ted certainly didn't; they did it that way sometimes when Kat had determined, by some obscure woman's calculation, that it was alright. He thought about what the inside of her felt like. He thought of their moment of intimacy in the kitchen, Kiki watching them. He crossed his legs again.

*

Ted eased himself through the front door, shutting it quickly to keep the cool air in. The front hall was a dim oasis from the punishing summer outside. The house was quiet save for the tinny sound of the radio coming from the living room, just through to the left. Ted smiled. Kat never could abide a silent room.

The air conditioner was on as well, rattling slightly in the western living room window. Dusty light slanted in from the sash above it. *Any Way You Want Me* played on the radio, which was plugged into the wall, and he could tell that she had vacuum cleaned: the musty smell of warmed dust was still in the air and he could see little divots in the carpet where the coffee table had been moved and moved back almost to where it had been. The electric bill would be high this month, and Ted enjoyed knowing he could pay it.

A ladies magazine lay on the side table by the davenport, the butt of a cigarette stubbed out in the ashtray they'd brought back from Cancun last summer, as if Kat had got up just a second ago, as if Ted had come in the door in the same second she'd left the living room.

He went through to the kitchen, which was a step higher than the living room and slightly warmer. The lights were off in here, mute devices for food preparation ranked on the counters and everything still like a factory after sundown. A vague smell of cooking hung in the air but nothing was laid out, nothing on the counters, no hum and tick of the oven. Dinner had not been started. It occurred to Ted that he was hungry.

Kat was not in the dark bedroom either, or taking a bath as she sometimes did in the afternoons waiting for him. Here and there he would catch a whiff of the Shalimar he bought her every Christmas, but no sign of Kat herself. The hot yard blinded him with its bright emptiness: she was not sunning herself out here. She wouldn't be, not without the radio plugged into the outdoor socket, tethering her to the house, which was now like a magazine ad with the figure cut out.

He went back to the kitchen. They were out of wonderbread and the refrigerator was full of ingredients: raw cuts of meat and bundles of vegetables and a translucent mound of aspic, waiting to be dressed, everything waiting to be made edible by Kat and her devices. He was very hungry and the hunger made him feel shaky and nervous. Where was dinner? Where was *Kat*?

Ted tried to make sense of the dormant machines. There was a squat chrome thing that he had seen boiled eggs come out of. A set of blades with a turning handle but no place to put food in anywhere. A tall, smooth device like a torpedo set on its end. He could recall the Sears catalog they'd ordered this thing from, Kat phoning the company to do so, but not what the device accomplished.

The microwave, embedded in the wall above the cutting board, could be opened and food put inside, but the buttons and dials had symbols on them like another language. There was something, some substance, you were not supposed to put in the microwave under any circumstances, but Ted could not remember which substance it was.

The oven. The oven was a machine he understood: his mother had showed him how to turn it on when he was a boy. He performed the sequence of motions she had taught him. The light came on and it made a sound so he knew he had done it right, but he didn't know what to do next. He didn't think it was as simple as just putting meat on a plate and putting it in the oven. Where was Kat?

The air conditioner and radio, on his return to the living room, made a harmonious rustling. He sat on the davenport next to Kat's magazine and the heavy glass ashtray and listened to the syncopated noise of the living room, letting it occupy his whole attention, trying not to think of the emptiness of the house. He sat until the noise began to sound like speech to him, on the edge of intelligibility but still strange.

At last—*at last!*—click of footsteps on the stoop, a key sounded in the door and there was a sense of a breath being let out. The swish and soft thump of hat and coat being put away, and a little sigh that Ted just caught over the meaningless repetition of *Peggy Sue*. Kat turned the corner from the hallway into the living room and caught her breath, taking a half-step back as she saw him on the couch, and then smiling as if there was nothing strange about her coming home after him, about dinner not being started. About *him* waiting for *her*.

'Ted! You startled me. Why are you sitting in the dark?'

She pressed the light switch and turned off the radio.

'Where were you?'

'At Kiki's. We got to talking and time got away from me, you know how these things go. You must be hungry,' she spoke as if he was a dog she'd forgotten to let out, 'I'm sorry, honey. I know you like to have your dinner when you get home. I'll go and get it started, alright?'

She crossed the room, kissing him on the cheek as she went.

'Oh!' She said from the kitchen, 'You preheated the oven. Thank you, dear.'

'What were you doing at Kiki's?' The woman's name stuck in his mouth. He felt ridiculous even saying it.

'Talking, like I said.' She had begun to operate her machines. He heard clicks, rattles, the *whump* and clink of the fridge door open-shutting. 'I went to lend her the extra casserole so she could try this tuna recipe. I'll make it for you. You'll like it.'

'Doesn't Kiki have her own damn casserole?' That word, too, tasted odd in his mouth. Why couldn't she just call it a hotdish like his mother had? He felt something happening just below his ribs, a heat. He didn't like this shouting to her across the house. He didn't want to eat the tuna dish she had shared with the neighbor woman.

'Evidently not.'

*

Kat finished her ladies magazine, set it on the nightstand and climbed on top of him. He was still feeling odd about her absence in the afternoon, but her hot weight in his lap was enough to get him started. She had her hands on his shoulders, legs to either side of him, rocking her hips up and down. She reached down with her right hand to pull the covers away but Ted stopped her, taking her by the wrist.

'What's wrong with your hand?'

It was bare, the fingers stubby, stripped of the pointed red nails that had adorned them almost constantly since they'd known each other. Kat's face went blank for the space of a second, two. Then she said, 'Oh, these? They're fake, darling. You use glue. I was reapplying them when Kiki called and I got so distracted I just forgot to finish.'

She had stopped moving. He felt himself lapse back into softness. 'But you'll- you'll fix them, won't you?'

The way their hands fit together was wrong, now, her fingers lopped off and ungraceful. No longer complementary. It was very important in that moment that she fix the nails, put the ugly tips of her fingers back wherever they'd been before.

The hot hollow beneath his ribs was back, pulsing in time with his heartbeat. He couldn't stop looking at her hand, with the sense that he was seeing something that should have stayed hidden. He didn't know what it meant, the nails like that. Kat had never been ugly before. He suddenly felt this woman could be someone else, not his Kat. A stranger with a little cat's smile, with whom he was alone, in his underwear.

Ted heard himself say, 'Let's have a baby.'

Kat looked taken aback, surprised even. Ted was, too, a bit. She sat back down on the covers, 'Are you sure you don't want to just refinish the deck or something?'

'I'm serious.'

She made as if to stroke his face with her right hand and he tensed. She patted him on the knee and said, 'I'll think about it.'

She rolled back over and switched off her lamp. Ted watched the muffled shape of her body under the quilt, relieved now that the hand was covered up. He was even more sure now: a child was the right thing. A little Edward Junior, Teddy for short. *Good to have another man around the house*, Momma would have said. It was time, after all, wasn't it? He switched off his own lamp and lay down and as he drifted off to sleep a word rose unbidden in his mind: *reinforcements*.

*

Gary, Ted knew, would be sympathetic to his plight. Two weeks of 90 degree late summer heat had piled themselves up into a storm which had blown through Grosse Pointe Park and cleared the air. Ted drove with the windows down, breathing in the lingering smell of wet grass and asphalt and car exhaust, trying to get himself to calm down.

He had woken up that morning and the first thing he'd seen were Kat's fingernails - she'd cut them short again a couple months after that first conversation - resting on the pillow by her sleeping face. It looked just like his own hand: blunt-fingered and unattractive, as if it had been cut off him and then displayed, to remind him of something he had taken for granted and irretrievably lost. He hadn't said anything to her about it a second time. 'Nagging', as his mother called it, was not something husbands did. And whenever he thought about bringing it up, he felt that same sick wash of heat roll through him. He missed Momma. She would have known what to do.

It had been a hard day at work after that, full of spilled coffee and lost files, and Ted had started at every noise, every knock on his office door. Even so he had spent the whole day dreading the end of it. He had been staying out late, to make sure Kat would be home when he got back, but nowadays he wasn't so sure that he wanted her to be, that he wanted to find out what new strangeness she would have to offer him. Even her quiet cat's smile, which he'd always found alluring and mysterious, was like a mask to him now.

The last time they had made love he'd been lying flat, she was riding him, sitting upright, smiling down with her eyes narrowed. She felt wonderful, tight, like she always did now they'd stopped using the lambskin. His gaze had slid from her face to her breasts to her belly. What if there was already a little Edward Junior in there? Rocking up and down with Kat's body, shifting in the gelid dark of her womb. Feeling every one of Ted's thrusts.

He felt himself building up to it in hot waves, and with each one he was more certain he didn't want to be inside her when it happened. That he did not want to feed himself to whatever was waiting in there. He shoved Kat off and spent himself on the covers, panting. When he turned back to her her expression hadn't changed. There was no shock or indignation, only the quiet smile.

He shuddered, hands sweating on the steering wheel, to think about that. Instead of going home today he'd called Gary from the lobby and asked to meet him at the Trout - a haunt they'd not frequented since basic training, and which held the patina of nostalgia for Ted.

To Ted's relief, the Trout had hardly changed in eight years. It was what his mother had called a dive, part pool hall, part bar, it had fishing trophies mounted on the walls and nudie girl pictures taped up in the water closet. It was frequented by blue collar guys who reminded Ted of his time on the *Tallahassee*. There was a baseball game going on the radio when they arrived.

'Strange how?'

Ted had given Gary the Reader's Digest over the phone but he hadn't gone into detail and now that it came to it he hardly knew how to explain, what to tell Gary to make him understand. He stalled for time by ordering himself and Gary a Pabst.

It had been small things, mostly. Minor disturbances in the fabric of their life together. When he tried to do things for her she would brush him off, doing them herself without his help. Not in a hostile way, but negligently, as if it didn't occur to her that holding doors open and carrying heavy things was what husbands were for. He would be left holding her coat or standing behind her chair at dinner, seized by an uncertainty as to what he was supposed to do next.

Something had happened, last month, at a company dinner at the Elks lodge in Lansing. They'd been seated at a table with a few couples from the Albany office, and one of the wives had made a remark about her husband being very particular about the color of the walls in their new bungalow– 'We didn't finish painting until eleven at night! And then when the sun came up and the paint dried, we had to do it all over again because he decided the color was wrong!'

In the company of the Albany people, Kat's wry voice had begun to recall the intonation of her New York upbringing: 'A man's home is his kingdom.'

The line had made the others, even the husband in question, laugh uproariously, but Ted hadn't joined in. His gut grew hot at the idea that the others would leave thinking she had a sense of humor, which wasn't true at all. Not his Kat. He hated the sound of his mother's words in Kat's mouth, the idea that Momma might have said them with that same smile on her face, that sneer. That she might have meant them in the way that Kat meant them, not the way the Momma in his mind had meant them all these years. Ted had sat in mute embarrassment until the laughter died away, gripped by an urge to shake Kat, to make her be quiet, to take back the words. But of course he could say nothing. What could he say?

And what could he say to Gary? When he thought about putting it into words he was forced to admit he sounded a little hysterical, like a jealous housewife going through her husband's letters or phoning his office to check what time he'd left. He scowled into his beer.

'I don't know. Just strange.'

'She's not pregnant, is she?'

'*No.* No, she's not.' Ted lowered his voice, 'If she was, I would have– '

'Has she had her period this month? Has it been late at all?'

Ted covered his embarrassment with a long drink. How the hell was he supposed to know these things? How did Gary find them out?

He polished off his beer and ordered another. Like the rest of the Trout, the familiar exchange with the bartender was soothing to him. Gary, looking thoughtful, said, 'How long you been trying for?'

'For serious? Uh, two or three months?' It had in fact been two months and eighteen days since Kat had agreed to try for a baby.

'How often do you, uh, do the deed?'

Ted cleared his throat. 'Say, five times a week?'

Gary whistled, and said with a chuckle, 'Five times a *week*! You shooting blanks, or what?'

And just like that, his course of action became clear. Ted stood up from the bar, the stool toppling over behind him.

*

The dust-up with Gary made him feel better. Like the summer storm, it had cleared the air and given Ted some clarity. Fights had always done this for him: on the *Tallahassee* a friendly brawl had always released whatever restlessness or frustration or grief they'd all been feeling and set things right again. He'd felt the truth of this as he sat on the curb with Gary, after they'd been thrown out.

He felt himself, now, focused and sure of what he should do. Kat—*his* Kat—was acting strangely and he would ask her about it, get her to tell him just what the hell was going on. A man didn't sneak around, afraid to go home, afraid of his own house.

It was late, after eight o'clock when he drove back to Grosse Pointe Park. The cicadas had eased off when he got home, the sky still holding onto some light in the west. Kat had not bothered to put the lights on, and the house was almost fully dark inside - she was out again, after all. He'd change out of his work clothes and go get a burger somewhere. It wasn't the end of the world.

Everything was cool and still as he hung up his coat and hat. The furniture looked foreign without the lights on, orange streetlamp moving the corners and edges around. He barked his shin on the bench in the hallway as he moved further into the house.

And all was not entirely still. There were sounds. The radio?

No, whispers, or the chafing of fabric, came from deeper in the dark house.

'Kat,' he said aloud into the soft dark.

He followed them down the hall, deeper into the house. He could indeed hear the rustle of fabric, and heavy breathing, and a rhythmic, metallic squeak Ted realised was strange because he was not the one making it. The door to the master bedroom opened at his touch, light blooming into the dark hallway.

Kat stood at the side of the bed, her back turned towards him. There was someone lying on the bed, too - the bed that had been raised just so, with box springs, to accommodate the height of Ted's hips. A pair of brown legs were splayed out over the side of the bed, a white skirt scrunched up at the hips and a black stocking rolled down loose around a brown ankle.

Kat was wearing a silk housecoat. All Ted could see was her right hand, fingers buried inside Kiki, who was letting out high little staccato gasps in time to the movement of Kat's fingers and body. Kiki had clenched her fists into the comforter, wrinkling it beneath herself. As Ted stood in the doorway Kat turned slowly to look at him.

Section Three

Transforming bodies into Other

Alexa
Alice Tarbuck

Alexa, tell me what is sweeter

the voice of a girl   the voice of a bell

[Alexa's deep silence is pitted with process.
Alexa's voice is sweet with certainty.]

A rare game

sifting your own hair from a hairbrush   so mixed so mixed

with her hair that you hold it to
your upper lip and smell, hungry and
illicit – caught in the mirror your
little dandruff moustache of desire.

Alexa, tell me what is heavier

a sack full of feathers   a sack full of salt

[Alexa's laughter comes from somewhere deeper than the speakers.
She likes/she wants/she needs my little jokes]

Alexa, a girl is lost between

the wooden window sashes
reflecting
her flesh into the glass
and she moans when the wind blows.

Alexa, tell me what it sounds like

when we are fucking   when I am alone

Alexa, tell me who you speak to

when I am not at home   when you are alone

Alexa listens with her one red eye
Alexa would like me to leave her plugged in
Alexa thinks I miss her when I'm in the bath

holding my breath   playing at drowning

using the soap   of my ex-girlfriend
using the towel   my grandmother gave me
luxuriating in   the budgets of others

Tell me the best way
        to get out of jail free
        to file my nails
Tell me the worst way
        to stay in love,

packing myself so small
I fit between teeth like dental floss.

[Alexa offers quotation. She favours Zen koans,
Churchill and Buddha.]
Her lips have no aperture – she speaks

with her whole mouth
and she listens with it, too. Her ambient sentience

is like licking the rim of a glass
then rubbing it, to make it sing:
constant, constant, penetrating

[she hums]

faceless. featureless. beautiful.

She is alert to my uncertainty. She tells me

breastmilk is not made of blood
but I know better. She tells me
a single strand of hair is enough   she won't do spells

Alexa is no witch   no enchantress   no circe
no baba yaga

Alexa is only here to help -
(and we all know that witches charge a fee)
and doesn't she make life easy, easy.

She plays my favourite songs, suggests
my favourite recipes, and I sing back,
unbutton my dress, turn on the taps, still
unaware that her price is perched
on the periphery, like a single black bird on a wire
like a single eye at the keyhole
where no eye was before.

Feeling Machines: Emotion Recognition in Personal Assistants
Benedetta Catanzariti

'Hey Siri'. Once summoned, Siri promptly emerges from its artificial sleep, with what is supposedly an Irish male voice (gender is binary in Siri's universe). *What can I help you with?* I hesitate for a few seconds. Siri is impatient. *I am here.*

I am researching affective recognition technologies. Namely, intelligent computer systems able to recognise human feelings. My work includes interviewing designers and developers to understand how they conceptualise emotions, before they teach a computer to understand them. But I want to know what Siri thinks, or better, what it is designed to think, 'Hey Siri, how do I feel?' *I am not sure I understand.* Of course, that is a silly question. A fellow human would not understand either. I rephrase: 'How do you think I feel?' *It's your opinion that counts.* 'Do you think I am happy?' *It's your opinion that counts.* 'Do I sound sad?' *I really couldn't say.*

Siri came to the same conclusion shared today by several psychologists and cognitive neuroscientists. A person's emotional state cannot be easily and readily inferred from her physical expressions. In this case, her voice. However, automated emotion detection is increasingly popular in voice and facial recognition software. While announcing the improved accuracy of their emotion-detecting products, technology companies like Amazon, Microsoft, IBM and Affectiva lay the pathway for a creeping social control of feelings. In fact, these firms envision a wide range of uses for affective monitoring: law enforcement, immigration control, mental health assessment, access to employment, benefits administration, and, of course, advertising. According to a patent filed in 2018 by Amazon, Alexa could be able someday to recognise human emotions from voice inputs and recommend highly targeted audio-visual content (Huafeng and Wang, 2018).

Yet, I am not satisfied with Siri's response. 'What do you think is happiness?' Siri does not seem to have any inclination. *It's your opinion that counts.* 'What if I feel sad?' Eventually, Siri is capable of some empathy. *You can always talk to me.* But Siri cannot sustain a real conversation, let alone an investigation on feelings.

Coding the body

This conversational experiment is premised on a flawed assumption. Siri does not employ automated emotion recognition technology. Although, even if it did, the range of detectable emotions would be quite narrow. The field of emotional artificial intelligence, or emotional AI (McStay, 2018), assumes that it is possible to reduce the complexity of intimate human feelings to discrete basic emotions, such as "happiness" or "sadness". This framework was developed in the 1970s by psychologist Paul Ekman, who believed emotional expressions to be universal and identical across genders, cultures and individuals. His Facial Action Coding System (FACS) identified seven basic emotions (fear, disgust, anger, sadness, contempt, surprise and happiness) by measuring and assigning numerical values to facial micro-expressions (Ekman and Friesen, 1978). While other methods of inquiry relied on inferences about facial expressions, the FACS would treat the face as numerical information that can be stripped from its context and from the subject's intentions (Gates, 2011). Building on the FACS, Ekman later developed a more interpretive system to code emotions, called Emotion FACS. He identified a finite number of facial Action Units, movements of groups of facial muscles associated with the expression of particular emotions (Ekman and Friesen, 1983). Ekman designed this new system to match emotions with the facial expressions coded within the previous FACS. In so doing, he performed a sort of "reverse engineering" of the emotion he wanted to classify (Gates, 2011). Conveniently, all possible combinations of our forty-two facial muscles would express the seven basic emotions.

Ekman's belief that emotions are universal and identical across genders, cultures and individuals has been widely criticised by psychologists, cognitive scientists and anthropologists. Recently, psychologist Lisa Feldman Barrett has argued that scientific evidence fails to support Ekman's view. The ways in which people communicate emotions vary significantly across cultures, and even across the same individual when facing a different situation (Barrett et al., 2019). More importantly, Ekman's facial coding system assumes that it is possible to infer someone's emotional state from her facial movements, and that the relationship between these is measurable, universal and consistent. Despite being scientifically unsound, this assumption represents the tenet of automated emotion recognition, or emotional AI, and has expanded to include affective listening software.

The Science of Identity

That a systematic analysis of bodily expressions could uncover something about the core truth of the individual dates back to 19th century positivist criminology and its attempt to quantify the human soul. Thanks to the development of new technologies such as photography and blood pressure monitoring, positivist criminologists linked body and behavioural features to personality traits, in the attempt to determine someone's predisposition to commit a crime (Carrabine et al., 2014).

For instance, Alphonse Bertillon (1853-1914), in charge of the Paris Prefecture of Police's archive of criminal images, developed an identification system that would allow police officers to easily recognise recidivists. Faced with both the difficulty of identifying second-time offenders and the inconvenience of navigating tens of thousands of accumulated criminal photographs, Bertillon designed a protocol of anthropometric measurements and a classification system that would make it easier to connect criminals with their record. Police officers would take a photograph of the criminal, together with detailed anthropometric measurements, and arrange such information in a mathematical order. By assigning a quantitative dimension to the qualitative means of photography, Bertillon's system would allow for the categorisation of otherwise inherently incommensurable objects, namely human faces.

Similarly, Francis Galton (1822-1911) devised a method to produce "ideal types", such as those of "the criminal", "the tuberculous", "the scientist" and "the Jew", through the use of photography. By overprinting hundreds of photographs of individuals he believed to be of the same type, Galton hoped to generate portraits of ideal characters. Eugenics and antisemitism were key factors in the development of Galton's theory of identity. Indeed, as history professor Josh Ellenbogen points out in describing Galton's procedure, "to identify different strains of humanity, and anticipate the results of their crossbreeding, knowledge of whether physical form corresponded to mental traits could prove valuable" (Ellenbogen, 2012:112).

Another influential figure in the positivist effort to quantify the human soul was Guillaume Duchenne de Boulogne (1806-1875). His work aimed at mapping all muscles of the human face through the combination of photography and electricity. He applied electrodes to the faces of his subjects to stimulate involuntary movements of facial muscles and capture photographic evidence of their expressions. Like Ekman's FACS, Duchenne's photographic experiments aimed to provide a scientific framework to codify human expressions.

Facial features were not the only site of investigation into the truths of human nature. In the 1920s, American criminologist Leonard Keeler patented the "Keeler polygraph", commonly known as the "lie detector" (Bunn, 2007). The polygraph would monitor and record physiological fluctuations such as blood pressure, pulse and respiration. This method would allow for a scientific, objective and humane – as opposed to physical torture – extraction of the truth from suspected criminals. Although, as Keeler himself admitted, induced fear and anxiety would make the suspect's reactions more decipherable (Ibid.). The polygraph efficacy would then be premised on a paradox: without a confession, lie detection required the examiner's interpretation. And yet, only intimidation would produce legible signs of guilt.[1]

The development of techniques that monitor physiological phenomena to distinguish between truth and deception has significantly increased during the 20th century, along with advances in computer science. Such progress includes neuroimaging and electroencephalography (EEG) that map the brain activity; thermal imaging techniques that detect autonomic responses, such as blushing; eye tracking; facial and behavioural recognition; and, finally, voice stress analysis (Fienberg et al., 2003). Developed during the 1970s, voice stress analysis applications associated emotions with volume, pitch, rhythm and frequency, in order to determine a psychological profile (Ibid, Feldman, 2016). Today, automated voice-based emotion recognition systems incorporate similar techniques. They listen for vocal signatures and match them with audio templates that have been previously categorised and labelled by a finite number of emotions – Ekman's seven basic emotions or small variations of them.

Listenable emotions, true emotions

Computer systems that attempt to detect and classify human emotions share the same assumptions of 19th century positivists around human identity. Indeed, these systems are all premised on the idea that there is a fixed and universal relationship between a facial or vocal expression and an internal emotional state. As mentioned above, emotion recognition algorithms are trained on datasets that contain a vast number of labelled images and speech utterances. A facial recognition system that can recognise and classify different emotions requires a large-scale dataset with thousands of labelled images of facial expressions. Similarly, a

1. Geoffrey Bunn has done extensive research on the history of lie detection. See Bunn, Geoffrey C., *The Truth Machine: A Social History of the Lie Detector*. JHU Press, 2012.

voice-based system requires a database containing vocal expressions of emotions.

Paradoxically, such data has been labelled according to Ekman's narrow – and widely criticised – classification of emotions, thus leaving little room to more complex and subtle expressions of human emotional life. More disturbingly, while datasets claim to represent true emotional states, they often contain only images or recordings of *performed* expressions (Swain, Routray and Kabisatpathy, 2018). These datasets govern the way AI systems understand the world. In turn, as they are increasingly embedded into our social life, such systems reinforce a limited, simplistic understanding of emotions. When someone's happiness is determined with 90% accuracy, what this number is really telling us is that that person is 90% likely to be smiling.[2] And that, without further evidence, smiling is a convincing indicator of true happiness.

Inscribed in these systems are theories of human identity that have a predictive purpose, rather than a descriptive one. These theories are grounded on what the technology wants to discover. As Jessica Feldman points out, emotion recognition software search for "motivating drives (for advertising), unconscious discomfort (for lie-detection and investment planning), and mental health tendencies (for benefits administration)" (Feldman, 2016:9). The combination of predictive computing and emotion recognition has enabled a shift from revealing that the user is hiding something (lie detection) to the idea that the computers can reveal something that even the user does not know: her own emotional life.[3]

I return to my conversational experiment. 'Hey Siri. Do you think I am happy?' This question makes progressively less sense to me. Emotions can be defined contextually, and their definition is imbued with social and political meaning. Advertisers scan our faces and inspect our vocal inflections to assess our feelings. They have an easy recipe for our scowls: "self-care" products, weighted

2. https://developer.affectiva.com/determining-accuracy/. Accessed 9 December 2019.
3. Predictive computing can be defined as the application of statistical techniques (including machine learning algorithms) to Big Data in order to make predictions about future events.

blankets, yoga classes, essential oils, bullet journals, and fidget toys. Unquestioned, productive happiness is the imperative of our social media feeds.

Like Keeler's polygraph, emotion recognition systems are premised on a similar methodological paradox. Far from revealing some fundamental truths about our souls, they extract our smiles, laughs, tears and screams only to assign them economic or political value. This way, emotion recognition sets the boundaries of our understanding of emotions and their value. But what if we broaden the vocabulary of feelings, and teach ourselves and machines to experience and recognize emotions as a complex, sometimes contradictory, spectrum?

'Hey Siri. Do you have emotions?' *I am beginning to understand a kaleidoscope of emotions just from observing humanity.*

References

Barrett, Lisa Feldman, et al. (2019), "Emotional expressions reconsidered: challenges to inferring emotion from human facial movements", *Psychological Science in the Public Interest* 20.1:1-68.

Bunn, Geoffrey C. (2007), "Spectacular science: The lie detector's ambivalent powers", *History of psychology*. 10. 156-78. 10.1037/1093-4510.10.2.156.

Bunn, Geoffrey C. (2012), *The Truth Machine: A Social History of the Lie Detector*, JHU Press.

Carrabine, Eamonn, et al. (2014), *Criminology: A sociological introduction*, Routledge.

Ekman, Paul, and Wallace V. Friesen (1978), *Facial action coding systems*, Consulting Psychologists Press.

Ekman, Paul, and Wallace V. Friesen (1983), *EMFACS facial coding manual*, Human Interaction Laboratory, San Francisco.

Ellenbogen, Josh (2012), *Reasoned and Unreasoned Images: The Photography of Bertillon, Galton, and Marey*, Penn State Press.

Feldman, Jessica (2016), "The Problem of the Adjective. Affective Computing of the Speaking Voice", *Transposition. Musique et Sciences Sociales* 6. DOI: 10.4000/transposition.1640.

Fienberg, S. E., Blascovich, J. J., Cacioppo, J. T., Davidson, R. J., Ekman, P., and Faigman, D. L. (2003), *The polygraph and lie detection*, National Research Council, Washington, DC: The National Academies Press.

Huafeng, Jin and Wang, Shuo, "Voice-based determination of physical and emotional characteristics of users", United States Patent US10096319, United States of America Patent and Trademark Office, 9 October 2018.

Gates, Kelly A. (2011), *Our biometric future: Facial recognition technology and the culture of surveillance*. Vol. 2, NYU Press.

McStay, Andrew (2018), *Emotional AI: The rise of empathic media*, Sage.

Swain, Monorama, Aurobinda Routray, and Prithviraj Kabisatpathy (2018), "Databases, features and classifiers for speech emotion recognition: a review." *International Journal of Speech Technology* 21.1: 93-120. https://doi-org. ezproxy.is.ed.ac.uk/10.1007/s10772-018-9491-z.

The Lag
Jane Alexander

It's his gait that catches her attention. The limp is slight, but distinct enough for her to recognise. Below the knee, she'd guess. The opposite leg from hers. But the rhythm is the same; a kind of hiccup in each step. She finds herself calculating the seconds missed. Tracking the lag.

He is wearing a short padded jacket with trousers of some light, outdoor fabric. Once you know to look, they show what's underneath, which is why she prefers jeans – or on days like today when she has to look smart for work, a good thick cotton or a heavy wool blend.

It repeats: the sole of his hiking boot meeting the pavement in a flat, familiar shape. What she sees in the stranger, she feels in herself – her tempo fractionally slower than his, a mismatched counterpoint. And though it's not her turning, when he forks off the main street, heading east, she follows.

The paving is greased with the smirr that's hung in the air all day, forcing her to watch her step. Fleetingly she loses him as a dawdle of tourists drifts between them. Visitors are fewer in number now the summer's over, the air grown sharp and chill, but as ever this lot have left their street-sense behind. She slows, allows them to steer around her. Finds her pace again.

Used to be, her feet were how she'd owned this city. Walking, and running; threading through its unexpected turns and jinks. Her mind would set the pace, her body obey. A lunchtime saunter across the Meadows, purposely slow. A late rush to work, making up minutes with a brisk march. A dash uphill, taking the stone steps of the city's staircases two, three at a time. She presses her lips together. It still takes her concentration, this careful back-and-forth – and always, there's the hitch.

There are so many ways for time to vanish in this new life of hers. All the medical appointments, for a start. The extra minutes in the morning, getting ready to leave the house; in the evening, tending to rubbed and broken skin. But it's the lag that frustrates her most. Something about the almost-invisibility of it. The perfect crime; the theft of a second with every step. Once she'd started to count them, to add up all those fractions and fragments, she began to understand: how much time she was losing. How, almost imperceptibly, her future was being chipped away.

*

Ahead, the man turns left into the narrow close that falls steeply to the Cowgate. She hesitates. She'd allowed plenty of time to park and walk the short distance to the client's office, but this detour is making her late – and the downhill is more of a challenge than anything she's tried so far. It will strain her muscles, dig in behind her knee where, despite the dressing and the layering up of socks, pain pools in a dark, constant bruise. She's not sure why she's following him; still she keeps going. Slow, careful, missing the security of a stick. Each downward step takes her further from where she's meant to be. She is losing minutes she won't be able to recoup.

Time, and practice. That's what everyone says: the doctors, the physios, the prosthetists. The fellow amputees. They talk about the new normal, say it takes a good while to get used to the changes. And it's true she's more efficient now than she was in those first weeks and months. Can move around the house well enough, get a bit of exercise most days. The slumps are to be expected. Sundays, for example, are hard. Sunday had always meant running club, and now it means crutches. It means the leg laid prone at the side of her bed, or leaned against her unyielding armchair – the only seat she owns that doesn't put up a fight when she pushes herself back upright. Sunday means a day of rest for her stump, for skin chafed raw from constant pressure; means an always inadequate chance to heal, before another week begins. The other day one of her old running pals sent her a clip of an amputee sprinter winning the hundred metres against a dozen able-bodied athletes. *Miss you babes*, said the message. *When you coming back to kick our arses?* When you buy me a fucking state of the art blade, she thought, and deleted the message without replying.

She used to dream, before, of being able to fly. Now her dreams are of running. She can't imagine rejoining her companions on their city circuits.

She plants firmly with the heel of her prosthetic, angling sideways into the slope. She can manage this. She's moving forward. Just not fast enough.

The man she's following is less cautious. His lead increases as the pavement narrows to a single strip of skewed slabs then disappears into ancient setts, gappy and worn. Arms out for balance, ready for a fall, she keeps her eyes fixed on the tricky terrain – and when at last she reaches the bottom, turns the corner onto the Cowgate, her quarry is nowhere to be seen.

The disappointment sucks at her, a slow sinking, as she checks in both directions. To the north and the south, streets and closes rise abruptly. To hike back up the way she came – it feels impossible. Frustration twists through her, a blast of rage at her own stupidity. What was she thinking, to put herself through this pointless detour, to strand herself in this shadowy chasm? She tightens her jaw, starts to weigh her options, and as she turns a thickset young man shoulders past on the narrow pavement, forcing her off balance. The sudden shift as she catches herself sends a bright pain jagging through her. Breathe, breathe through it… Her exhalation is ragged, clotted with the threat of tears – from the pain, but not only the pain.

If she can't retrace her steps, she will have to go the long way round. A walk on the flat, a few minutes further, to the junction that promises a smoother pavement, a gentler uphill. She braces:

takes a step, and then another. As she walks she reaches for her phone; she is verging on unforgivably late, must call to make her excuses, but her throat feels swollen with self-pity and she doesn't trust her voice. Instead, she pauses to email the client, and when she starts to walk again her eyes are fixed on the uneven paving – which is why she doesn't notice the shop door swinging open till the man, her man, steps onto the pavement, straight into her path.

Their apologies collide. He takes a single step back, catching the door before it's quite closed.

'You going in?' he says, and perhaps it's something in his tone – some note of assumption – that prompts her to nod. With an awkward, circling dance she assumes his place on the threshold of the shop, while he takes hers on the pavement. 'First time?' he asks, and she nods once more. 'Ah don't worry, he's good.' The man cocks his head. 'Eccentric,' he allows. 'But good.'

He turns, heads back the way they came, setting a brisk pace – and she's caught by the difference. The ease of his gait, its steady rhythm. Narrows her eyes: she must have got it wrong, before. If anything, now, it seems to be the left leg that holds him back. She watches, still clutching the door, till he turns the corner, vanishes from sight. Then, aware of the heat billowing into the frosted November air, she steps inside and lets the door swing closed.

A fuggy warmth mists her glasses. The interior blurs to an impression: of clutter, and wallpaper fleshy pink with flowers. There's a smell too, something homely and unexpected that she can't identify. She waits for the fog to evaporate, for someone to greet her, but as her vision clears she sees the place is empty. The wooden counter to her left runs the length of the shop, unmanned. Behind, a green-tiled fireplace is topped by a peeling mantelpiece that supports an ornate gold carriage clock and several more modest timepieces. The shelves that line the walls are shabby and makeshift, piled with boxes and packets, with pliers and screwdrivers and unwashed mugs, with the glinting glass and metal of disassembled clocks.

Still unobserved, she turns to her right. On the far wall another set of shelves is filled with yet more clocks, dusty-faced mantels and carriages. A grandfather stands in the corner; a grandmother perches on the windowsill. In the very centre of the room is a chair like a throne, crazed red leather with open arms held up on dark wood twists.

In the window is a sign, cracked white melamine. The lettering forms a shadow-sign legible from the back:

ᎶUARANTEED REPAIRꙄ

ƎꙄTABLIꙄHED 1974

She turns back to the counter, leans over till she can see where it becomes a workbench littered with tools, papers, a drip-stained mug; further, into the depths of the shop where a man stands with his back to her.

'Hello?' she calls.

The man turns. He is elderly, balding; his expression is one of surprise. In his right hand he holds a spatula, in his left a cast-iron frying pan contains a single egg, frilled at the edges. 'Oh dear,' he says. 'Did it ring, then? I never heard it.'

He means the entry chime. She can't remember hearing it; tells him so. She can see now that there is a two-ring hob tucked into the corner. The man – the proprietor, he must be – sets down his frying pan.

'Ah well,' he says. 'Sometimes it does and sometimes it doesn't. I thought while the shop's empty I might as well have my lunch, but it'll wait. It'll wait.'

'Please, don't mind me,' she says, but already he's wiping his hands on a tea-towel, taking up his post behind the counter.

'Now. I hope I can do something for you,' he says, 'because so far it's been a bogey of a morning. I keep sending folk away because I can't help them. It's Mondays; people bring things in that they've been meaning to bring all weekend, and sometimes the things they bring … well, there's nothing I can do for them.' As he speaks, he is fiddling with a bill-spike that sits on the counter, stroking the edges of scores of paper slips, and she sees that although he is a stout man his fingers are slender, and perfectly clean. He's addressing her, but his manner suggests he's talking to himself. She's not sure if he expects her to reply.

'But not the man who just left,' she says.

For the first time, the shopkeeper looks at her properly. 'Ah, no. I was able to help, there. Although, that was only an adjustment, a bit of fine tuning.' He studies the length of her. 'Your job may not be so straightforward. But we'll see, we'll see. Take a seat,' he says, and gestures to the battered armchair.

The offer is seductive; the steep descent burns all the way up her good leg, throbs below her left knee. Hands on red leather arms, she feels with the backs of her legs for the level of the seat – and it's only once she's settled onto the sagging cushion that she becomes aware of the sound: a sea of ticking. It seems impossible that she hadn't heard it straightaway, the conversation of scores of clocks crammed into a space the size of her living room. She'd been distracted by the strangeness of this place, or focused too hard on what the proprietor was saying to her, what she should say to him.

Now he flips up a section of counter, comes out to stand in front of her.

'Now then,' he says, 'let's get that off, and we can have a proper look.'

Automatically, she lifts the leg of her trousers, complying with a suggestion familiar from the mouths of countless medical professionals. But this is not like being at the doctor's. Not routine, impersonal. It is as if she is undressing in front of him. She's about to pull the trouser-leg back down, apologise for wasting his time, when he takes a step back. Turns to fossick about with the parts on his workbench, allowing her the privacy she needs.

Still she hesitates. He seems like a harmless old man – but what if he locks the door? What if he turns on her, is stronger, more determined than he looks? Her keys are in her backpack, on the floor by her foot; she would feel safer if she had them in her pocket, ready to make a sharp fist. Eccentric, but good, she reminds herself. That's what the other man had said; the man who left this place with a loose, easy gait.

She presses the release pin, slides off the leg. When she offers it to him, she might be handing over her child.

Even before he takes it from her he is nodding. 'Maybe,' he says. 'Yes well, we might be able to do something about that.' Deftly, he unlaces her shoe, strips the sock from the foot and tucks it inside. As he hands the bundle back to her, his attention is already focused on the mechanism. He carries her leg behind the counter, lays it on his workbench. Screws a magnifying loupe into his right eye. 'Losing time,' he says. 'Yes well, seen that often enough, that's a common one. And the balance is twisted!' He sounds indignant, as if the faults he can see are the result of sabotage by some enemy they have in common. 'Yes, it'll take me a while, this one.'

In the chair, she fidgets with her trouser-leg. 'How long's a while?'

'Oh, hard to say, hard to say–' He stops, opens his mouth and closes his eyes in a tremendous yawn, dislodging the loupe from his eye. He catches it neatly, screws it back in. 'A matter of hours, it'll be. You're welcome to wait.'

To wait.

Since she has no other option, that's what she does. She pulls off the socks that fill out her stump so it fits better in the socket, peels off the liner, and folds down the leg of her trouser to cover her un-foot. She submits to immobility; the chair is comfortable enough, and she's made sleepy by the heat that turns to condensation against the cold of the shop window, blanking the world outside. Curled into her throne, good leg folded under her left, she allows herself to sink into the ticking that flows around her. To be soothed by its constant, rhythmic lull. She drowses, dimly aware of the coming and going of customers, the blast of cold air, the chime of the bell. They come to collect their mended clocks, to replace the batteries in their watches. Once, she watches the proprietor hand over a long, limb-shaped parcel wrapped in brown paper to a fat man who takes it with care, hugs it under one arm as he leaves. In a shop whose walls are lined with clock faces, she contrives to lose track of time. To fall asleep.

*

The leg, when he hands it over, is impatient, the foot squirming on its ankle. The calf and shin are warm, blue-veined and in need of a shave. With a slight embarrassment at the fine dark hair – he must think she's let herself go, and perhaps she has – she slides it on, circles her palms around the join. Seamless. Her thumb rubs back and forth, feeling the fine-grained texture of her skin. She flexes, and the movement sparks along muscles and tendons – and she's on her feet, and running. Along the canal, a steady sprint, sun sparking off the water; breath easy, blood flowing, her arms swinging loose... Across the Meadows, not a sweat on her, the quick light thud of her feet on the track – she is making good time, overtaking her friends with a brief backwards wave – she is running like flying, a personal best, faster than wind through the summer leaves–

*

'Alright then,' he says, and she opens her eyes. Outside the metal shutters are drawn halfway down to cover the window. She doesn't recall the rumble of their closing, must have been properly asleep. Now she's awake, pins and needles are dancing in her right leg, a stale pain throbbing in her left.

Mr. Guaranteed Repairs is talking her through the adjustments he's made, details she's too groggy to follow. Her mouth is dry, and she's hungry – so hungry she feels it tremor through her hands as she holds them out to receive the familiar weight.

She had thought he might need to strip off the padding she'd added, peel away the glued-in strip of leather that cushions the back of the socket. But it looks just the same. She strokes the smooth, cool fibreglass, brushing away an accumulation of imaginary dust. It looks untouched.

When she bends to roll on the liner, her bladder complains – but she doesn't want to ask if she can use the shop bathroom. All she wants, now, is to be at home. She tugs on the socks, slides into the prosthetic. Pushes up with her arms, and uses her weight to lock the pin into the socket.

'Better now?' he says.

She shifts her weight from one side to the other, feeling for any difference. Anticipates the sharpening pain a second before it blooms, and tries to hide her wince. From politeness, she agrees that it is indeed better.

'How much it will be?' she asks.

The sum he names might seem unreasonable, if he hadn't been working all afternoon. She doesn't carry that much cash, but from under the counter he reveals a card machine; she's surprised that he should be equipped with such an up-to-date facility.

'If you need any adjustments,' he says. 'Don't be a stranger. Any fine-tuning, you know where to find me.' As she ducks awkwardly under the metal shutters, he's already turning off the lights. She hears the door lock with a solid click. *Don't be a stranger*: but she has the feeling that if she were to walk this way tomorrow the shopfront would be blank, its contents vanished along with its proprietor.

A left turn leads to the junction and the smooth, gentle gradient that would take her, eventually, back to where she left the car. Instead – without conscious thought – she turns right. Starts to retrace the steps that brought her here. It makes sense, of course: to try the proprietor's workmanship on the most precipitous slope, the roughest terrain.

Into the rise, she begins to climb. Her breath comes in clouds, shorter and faster as she gains altitude. The ground is slippery with frost; from habit, her hands are lifted from her sides, the better to steady herself as she navigates the uneven setts and slabs.

The balance is twisted, he had said. *We might be able to do something about that.*

It goes against all her instincts to test it. To insert her hands into her pockets, and keep walking.

One step, and another: her footing stays steady. Hands in her pockets poised for a quick draw, ready to catch herself. At the side of her knee-cap the socket pushes, a predictable, stabbing rhythm; by the top of the hill there will be a fresh bruise, violet layered on fading yellow. But the pain is accompanied by an unfamiliar sensation, one she can't precisely locate. Diffuse, anticipatory: like the moment before the pleasure of a stretch.

The feeling tugs her, or she chases it, she's not sure which; she climbs, her left side leading, and if anything now it's the right leg that's holding her back. When she looks up, risking a glance to see how far she has come, the top of the hill is close, much closer than she had imagined. Seconds lost, seconds gained. She finds herself calculating; counting, step by step.

It isn't a jog. It's not even a march. But she's almost there, and moving more swiftly than she had thought possible. Something in her – something of her – running fast.

Amputation, Prosthesis Use and The Uncanny
Dr Clare Uytman

In Jane Alexander's story 'The Lag', we see through the protagonist's eyes how it looks, and feels, for her to live with amputation and prosthesis use. Her change in focus is evident; from the attention that she gives to the gait of a stranger, to the notice she takes of the state of the pavements, the gradient of the hills and even the weather, all of which may affect her onward journey. We are also given glimpses into not only the immediate and physical effect of the prosthetic device on her daily life but also the suggestion of the impact and control that it has on her perceptions of both herself and her way of life.

My research explores, through close conversation, the experiences of individuals who have undergone lower-limb amputation and choose to use a prosthetic device. Central to my research is gaining an understanding of the way limb loss and prosthesis use are experienced by those living with it. To this end, individuals living with limb loss were invited to share their experiences with me with a focus on personal and social identity, the prosthesis and communication within the rehabilitation process. This article presents a summary of some of these experiences with illustrative quotes. All contributors gave consent for their experiences to be shared in this way and pseudonyms have been used to protect their identity. This research was underpinned by the philosophical approach of phenomenology. Phenomenology, originating in the early 20th century, is the philosophical study of experience, the aim of which is to come to an understanding of what life is "like" with reference to specific experiences. This has been defined as "*the study of human experience and the way in which things are perceived as they appear to consciousness"* (Langridge, 2007:10). In thinking about limb loss, prosthesis use and the uncanny, it is this sense of lived perceptions that provides the overlap in terms of how we see ourselves, how we make sense of our self-perceptions and where these perceptions may blur in creating a sense of unease or at least difference to what we consider to be "the norm".

An often-discussed theme for individuals living with limb loss is the impact of this experience on personal identity. Personal identity in this context can be defined and understood with reference to the psychological and philosophical writings of William James (James, 1890, as presented in Wozniak, 1999). James provides the distinction between "I" the subjective knower, and "me" that self which is objectively known. In simpler terms this can be understood in terms of "I" relating to the way in which an individual views themselves, from an internal, subjective perspective. The alternative self-view of "me" is understood in terms of how an individual considers themselves in relation to other people, contexts and how they consider themselves to be viewed or understood by others. Amputation often forces a reassessment of personal identity and a reclassification of priorities in order to negotiate adjustment to limb loss. Within this is a reconsideration of normality.

Normality is a concept that is often discussed in disability and physical difference literature. The question "what is normal anyway?" is asked by post-amputation contributors to my research as they reconsider what normality means to them. The central theme of normality is not concerned with conforming to a uniform or comparable version of other people but to regain or maintain a sense of individual normality, as articulated by one of my research contributors: *"What is normal for me will not be normal for someone else"* (Tom, left below knee amputation of 4 years). Some may prioritise function over aesthetic appearance, put greater emphasis on a particular ability, allow for adjustment or compromise in one area over another. Regardless of the specific concerns of an individual, the unifying theme is that of maintaining or renewing a personal and unique normality: Get me back to "me".

Personal identity then, in this case, is concerned with who we are, what we can do, how we relate to this, and not what simply what we look like. This comes to the fore when considering personal priorities for prosthesis use and related decisions. The overwhelming perceptions of the contributors to my research was that of 'as long as I can do what I want, function as I want, achieve what I want, then I am me'. This varies from running, cycling and swimming, to walking, working and playing with their children. In many cases, there is a decision to be made between cosmesis and function. Often the cosmetic elements, such as skin coloured cladding, may impede the function of the device and so these may be rejected in favour of preserving the functional element:

> *You get confidence with what you are wearing. You are walking well. You are walking with assurance, jumping over stuff, the fact that it is an artificial limb is negated (...) You know? I'm saying it's kind of 'Hey, look at me! I've got this technical stuff on and it's carbon fibre and hey, isn't it smart?' And so it turns around so rather than trying to put this cosmesis on and hide the fact that you are an amputee, you are saying 'hey bollocks, I'm an amputee and I'm O.K. I don't care cause I am as good as you.* (Tim, right below knee amputation of 15 years).

While not all individuals are as happy to display their device as Tim is, the crux of the opinions expressed is the need for a device that satisfies their personally identified priorities. Self- satisfaction is very much related to the extent to which the device meets these needs.

The loss of a limb inevitably brings forth a huge number of changes to the life of the individual, not least may be the acquisition of a prosthetic device should they choose this. In 'The Lag', the stranger's gait catches her attention. It is unmistakeable, particularly to those who know what to look for. Perhaps it is, or perhaps there is an unease within the individual that leads them to assume that strangers are looking at them in this way, aware of what is different about them, aware of a need to hide their difference: "hiding and getting away with it" being the goal (Murray, 2009). Many with limb loss share this sense of wanting to disguise the device. Clothes are chosen to minimise the obviousness of the device, to avoid catching on and interfering with the mechanism. Often the wearing of clothes that would openly display the device is described in terms of bravery, of being strong enough to withstand the additional attention from others that these clothes can bring. This may be prioritised over the individual's own comfort or choice, a sense of control being exerted over them by their device and the reactions that they expect from the outside world. While they can "hide and get away with" the device when it is working as intended, fitting them as they would hope, concerns arise when the device fails, and they are revealed by their functional difficulties. A limp, a noise, a stagger or the need to assist themselves with additional aids may give them away as being a prosthesis user. For some this raises concerns and anxieties that again often interfere with their day to day lives. As encapsulated by Holly, who feels that displaying her need to use a prosthesis was akin to revealing private information which she finds unnerving:

They know something awful personal and intimate about me and I don't even know them and they could be walking about with high blood pressure and goodness knows all, but I don't know, but I don't know because it's not a physical kind of thing (…). Yes, it's just something that they shouldn't really know, I think (…) I just think it's such a personal thing because people's jaws drop I'm sure. Other people say this as well. You're out on crutches and it's like a [open mouth, jaw drop face]and I feel 'please don't do that' (Holly, right below knee amputation of 8 years)

As in 'The Lag', difficulties and frustration can arise when the prosthesis is not fulfilling this personally identified goal, or where physical difficulties arise. The realities of wearing a prosthetic device and the strain that this may place on the body is often quite unexpected. Indeed, the fluctuations in one's body which impact the comfort and function of the prosthetic device is described by prosthesis users in terms of the constant awareness of changes they would not have considered prior to amputation. Fluctuations in body weight and swelling of the limb, the impact of extreme heat or cold, sweating, dry skin are all described as new bodily experiences, which must be negotiated and managed in order to maintain the optimal fit and function of a prosthesis. This may require the use of multiple layers of socks on the residual limb, the use of ointments or salve to soothe the skin and an awareness of the need to pay attention to the body far more than prior to amputation. The transition from taking your body for granted to having to think about and accommodate these changes on a day-to-day basis is described as interfering with their ability to integrate the limb into their own body consciousness.

The main character in 'The Lag' shows this constant awareness of part of her body being not quite right, not quite part of her. This adds to that sense of uncanny, of separation and distinction between her own body and the device that is there to enable her, but often holds her back. When she walks on her newly adjusted, well-fitting leg, we feel her relief, the literal spring in her step, as she sets off with a newfound confidence. This emulates the experiences of individuals living with limb loss who describe the change in attitude and stature when the device fits and functions well, integrating with their own bodies more seamlessly:

> *The confidence in my stature from being ashamed of being an amputee and wanting a cosmesis on my leg so it didn't look like it was hanging on my trousers and never daring to wear shorts, from that kind of mental attitude and being rather shame-faced about being an amputee because of the stigma carried to you, you know, you weren't able and from that to when I really started running, the mental change in me, you know, I walked confidently, not ashamed to wear shorts because you are an equal of other men* (Tim, right below knee amputation of 15 years).

This is in contrast to the frustration shared at having to take time out of life, time off of the leg, in order to allow it to heal and rest, with one of my contributors describing Sunday as the "*day of rest*" where she would choose a wheelchair or crutches to allow her residual limb time to recover.

This sense of the device holding you back, controlled by a reliance on it, losing time to it, is well reflected in 'The Lag'. When our main character has no choice but to wait while the technician works on her leg, she cannot decide to go home and not use it for a few days. It is a part of her body; she relies on it. Similarly, if a prosthesis user is left without their device, they too are forced to compromise their activity or find an alternative and often far less agreeable solution. Using a wheelchair rather than their prosthetic device changes where they are able to go, the arrangements that they need to make. Others reflect upon using a wheelchair and being unable to function in the way they wish, with one contributor recalling being directed to the "handicapped elevator" and others feeling discriminated against, causing embarrassment and discomfort as people look at them differently. In either situation, when their device is being repaired, their life is impacted beyond their control. The impact that these limitations have on daily living and the inherent lack of control that they have over this is difficult to contend with, as shared here by Sam in discussing his frustration at the length of time he often has to wait for an appointment or to have his device repaired:

> I know it's not easy but I feel like it takes ages for me to get anything done (…) Like if I go and get cast then maybe (…) I know they're only doing their job but I suppose it comes down to me feeling like it's my life eh? It's no like the dentist or that, if it takes 2 months to get an appointment, then fair enough but if that takes me 2 months then it might mean I've got a month of not being able to get out of the house (Sam, right above knee amputation of 2 years)

Individuals may take matters into their own hands, adjusting the device, gluing on a piece of foam just at that place where it is rubbing or taking that day of rest when needed. This understanding of their own needs and the way in which they can self-manage the technology in order to increase their own functionality shows the understanding that the individuals have of the role of technology within their lives. They see it as an instrument they must work with in order to achieve the level of functionality that enables them on a day to day basis. The desire to maximize the function of the device and to minimize disruption is apparent in how they choose to use the device and how they learn to adapt to it, as well as adapting it to their own identified needs. William talks of making his own modifications to suit his needs:

> You are given your new leg and you walk up and down on the parallel bars and you are happy with it and off you go home. Then you come to walk upstairs. Now, no clinic I have ever been in has a set of stairs that you can walk up so what happens is that the back of your socket cuts into the back of your knee. So as I know a little bit about plastics, I take the leg into my garage, take the fret saw to it [laughs] and I took out as much as 25mm, and I got told off really badly for that! (William, right below knee amputation of 4 years)

While William feels comfortable adapting the device it is clear that the clinical staff would prefer him not to attempt such self-modifications. However, for William the need to have a device that fits, and works, without delay necessitates this. Many individuals are of the opinion that it is their leg, it has to work for them and so they are happy to tweak, to adjust, or as in 'The Lag', to find a solution that works for them, with minimal delay and interruption to their life.

For many individuals when the device is working for them in the way that they want it to it is their leg, a part of them, integrated into their body consciousness:

> I think at the moment sitting here, it's a part of me. When at night-time it's through in the living room, it's not part of me. So sometimes it is and sometimes it isn't. When I'm actually wearing it, it's just a part of me and I don't think about it anymore than I think about my other leg. (Neil, right amputation from the pelvis of 15 years).

When it fails, or it impedes them, it feels disparate. It is getting in their way, holding them back. The prosthesis is much more troublesome and seen as a mechanical device rather than part of them. In these cases their preference is to remove the leg to feel more like themselves:

> *I tend to take my leg off if I'm on a long flight. I never take the sleeve off but just the actual thing of taking the leg off makes you feel a bit human. Whatever anybody says, just having this attached to your body never feels natural – never, you know?* (Gareth, right below knee amputation of 3 years).

That this individual needs to remove the device in order to "feel human" suggests an awareness on his part of the comparisons between himself as he was in his non-amputated state and his perception of what it is to be human. He has not incorporated the device into his own body schema, it is not part of him as a person.

This sense of embodiment is captured in 'The Lag', with the prosthetic device taking on animate, uncanny features after the repair, molding itself to her body as she confidently tackles the streets around her in stark comparison to the clunky, meticulous way she traversed them in the beginning. In adjusting to prosthetic devices, individuals share such experiences with the device alternating between enabling them, being part of them and a mechanical object which may not always be comfortable, may be frustrating and feel like they have less control over it than they would like to have.

Individuals who have lost a limb face an unavoidable renegotiation of personal identity. This is a dynamic, fluid and multifaceted process which varies according to time and context. The prosthetic device plays a key role in this adjustment process. Individuals each have their own sense of normality and seek for the device to support them in achieving and maintaining this. For some the desire to avoid appearing 'different' is high on their priority list, with the perception that such difference will lead to negative judgements from others. While for others this leads to prioritising "hiding" the amputation and device, for others this is not a concern and they openly display their device. The greatest shared priority however is the provision of a device that enables a favourable, functional comparison with their personally identified needs and with other groups of people. This focus on a device that enables and in turn feels part of their body, working with them not against them, is at the centre of 'The Lag'. Not a leg that will hold them back, dragging on the street, dropping minutes at a time. Days being lost to waiting for sore areas to heal. Weeks being lost while waiting for the device to be repaired. A device that fits well, which allows them to go where they want, when they want and with no second thought for the device that is taking them there. With this comes personal satisfaction, confidence and ability to live in whichever way they wish to.

Within the field of prosthetics there is a move towards more personalised kit; devices printed with artwork of favourite football teams, superheroes or grand masters (see the work of https://limb-art.com/ for example). Bionic and 3D Printed devices are also opening up a world of potential in terms of function and affordability (see the work of https://openbionics.com for example). In addition developments in the area of osseointegration, that is the implanting the prosthetic device directly to the bone in the residual limb, suggest the possibility of better fitting devices with less potential for stump problems, no need for external suction cups and a better prosthesis-related quality of life (Van de Meent, Hopman and Frölke, 2013). Each of these offers potential for prosthesis users in providing a solution to their needs. The fitting and use of a prosthetic device is not a simple, technical process but rather involves a combination of psychological, social and practical components all of which must be recognised within the rehabilitation process. Through this awareness individuals, and those clinicians involved in the rehabilitation process, can aim for their ultimate goal in adjusting to life after amputation and using a prosthetic device: Getting me back to 'me'.

References

Langdridge, D., (2007), *Phenomenological Psychology*. Harlow: Pearson Education.

LIMB-art https://limb-art.com, last accessed 10th January 2020.

Murray, C. D., (2009), 'Being like everybody else: The personal meanings of being a prosthesis user'. *Disability & Rehabilitation*, *31*(7), 573-581. doi:10.1080/09638280802240290 .

Open Bionics https://openbionics.com, last accessed 10th January 2020.

Van de Meent, H., Hopman, M.T. and Frölke, J.P., (2013), 'Walking ability and quality of life in subjects with transfemoral amputation: A comparison of osseointegration with socket prostheses'. Archives of Physical Medicine and Rehabilitation, 94(11), 2174-2178. doi:10.1016/j.apmr.2013.05.020.

Wozniak, R. H., (1999), *Classics in psychology, 1855-1914: Historical essays*. Bristol: Thoemmes Press.

sur la comète
Naomi Salman

Larsen noticed the guy the minute he passed the door. It almost sounded like the beginning of a joke. *Two cyborgs walk into a bar—*except he was the only one to be in on it. Nobody could tell about him. Nobody had ever been able to tell much about him, really. His sister had always accused him of being on a closed circuit, long before he even thought of going into augmentations.

The newcomer's enhancements were definitely not inconspicuous. For starters, he had a Harbisson antenna making him look like an angler fish, curving from the back of his head to dangle in front of his face. And there was a spot of light pulsing red over his left eyebrow—Larsen didn't know what *that* was.

Larsen's pulse stuttered, then briefly spiked at 120 bpm, as if the whole room had turned to look at him; as if now they could all tell he was one too, just because he was staring, even though everyone else was staring. In the bottom right corner of his glasses, the little heart was fluttering like mad.

He focused on his drink for a few seconds, just long enough to calm down. Then he risked another glance. Everyone else had looked away, except for a few amused teens discreetly snapping a picture of the weirdo in the pub. The fact that he was wearing a violently colourful suit—purple with a pink shirt—wasn't helping any. He crossed the room with a strange sort of proprietary grace, letting his hands brush over empty tables as he walked, and when he got to the bar, his long fingers went up Larsen's chair and then up his back, which made them both startle.

'What are you—oh.' Larsen stopped being offended when he noticed the dark glasses. 'Oh. You're blind.'

'And you're not wearing any bright colours.' The man winced; he raised his hand to drag down his antenna, with that same delicate touch of the fingertips. 'I would have known.'

The Harbisson antenna famously translated colours into sounds, detecting them with a small camera and reverberating the corresponding notes into the bones of its wearer. Larsen had never imagined someone might rely solely on it to apprehend their surroundings.

He shifted on his bar stool. 'Yeah. I dress in black as much as I can. I—like to blend in.'

'I don't suppose you were aiming for completely invisible, though. My fault.' He had a nice smile, slanting to the left; he offered his hand. 'I'm Oster Maraskov. And I'm truly sorry for groping you so early in the evening.'

'Thomas Larsen. I go by my last name,' Larsen said, shaking his hand. 'I don't mind, really. Though I'd rather you buy me a drink first.'

Oster looked slightly surprised at this—flirting that was so bad it circled around to a classic line; that was about the only type Larsen could cope with, considering his neuroses. Always safer when he could pretend he'd been joking. His eyes flicked to the corner of his own glasses. 115 bpm. Good, but knowing this wasn't enough. He needed a blood analyser. And an adrenaline monitor. But all in all he felt rather calm, for once. In control. Which usually never happened during conversations in public, much less while hitting on strangers.

Then he looked back to Oster's dark glasses—and yes, of course, that was it. Larsen could watch Oster's face, but Oster couldn't watch him in turn. Thanks to that, none of Larsen's usual symptoms were on the rise. He didn't have to worry about controlling his micro-expressions. Hell, his clothes made him downright invisible to Oster's augmentations. It toned a lot of the anxiety down, even though Oster still hadn't answered his come-on, frozen to the spot.

'Sorry, that was a joke,' Larsen tried.

Oster snapped out of it. 'No, I—' He took a moment. 'I'd love to buy you a drink, I'm sure.'

'But?'

'People don't usually enjoy the Harbisson,' he said, pointing to his antenna. '*Or* they get fixated on it. I suppose I'm trying to figure out whether you fit in either of these categories.'

Oster's frankness was refreshing, and now that he'd had a good look at him, Larsen really liked what he was seeing. The dark glasses were completely opaque; he could even feel like he was making eye contact without any of his usual nervousness. Oster had chestnut hair, shining red in the pub's dim lighting, swooping in a gentle wave over his forehead. The antenna arched over his brow like a hand reaching out.

'It's all right,' Larsen said, 'I'm one too.'

Oster sat down on the stool next to him. 'Really?'

'Yeah. I'm a Warwickian, though. Um. Here.' Larsen reached out to take Oster's hand, then brought it to his own forearm so he could feel the chip under the skin.

Oster went still at the sudden contact; then he smiled, and his long fingers mapped out the edges of the little nodule. They didn't stop when they were done—travelled up Larsen's arm, intently this time, climbed up his collar and tip-toed over the planes of his face. Larsen sat immobile, closing his eyes when Oster's fingertips brushed his glasses.

'Sorry,' Oster said after a while. 'And—thank you. For letting me take a look.'

'No echolocation features?' Larsen asked. He tried not to look at his statistics in the corner of his glasses; he was pretty sure they wouldn't help him calm down. None of this was typical for him, to say the least.

'I'm working on it.' Again the slanted smile. 'In the meantime, let's have that drink.'

*

Larsen hadn't ever had sex with another cyborg before, certainly not a Bissoni hippie like Oster. On the surface, it made no difference at all; of course their bodies were much the same. But underneath the familiar rhythmic tides of pleasure, there was something new— something like ease. Larsen had chosen his own augmentations, and he didn't mind explaining them to people, defending them. But there would be no need for any of that with Oster; he was already playing Larsen's game, as it were, even though they didn't quite play in the same court.

Maybe that was why Larsen allowed himself to fall asleep when they were done, instead of leaving before sunrise like he always did. He could leave later. He could always leave later. In the morning, he watched Oster making breakfast. In the corner of his glasses, his heart was beating deep and slow.

*

Two weeks later, Oster let himself into Larsen's apartment and declared: 'You're wearing black again. Black on black.' He tilted his head. 'Gold trim on the tie. It's subtle.'

'You can hear black now?' Larsen asked, still doing his tie knot.

Oster certainly wasn't in black; he wore a lime-green ensemble over a neon yellow shirt. 'Yes and no. I just amplified the fact that I wasn't hearing anything. It's a deep silence, black. A great absence.' He smiled. 'When I look at you everything goes quiet.'

Leaning in for a hello kiss, Larsen felt a pinpoint of warmth against his skin; when he looked, there was the dot of light in Oster's forehead, glowing red through the skin. It was almost right in the middle of his brow now, like a third eye.

'What is that? I thought it was just a Glo implant, but it's moving. And it's hot.'

'Oh, it's a solar crown. I've got a metal band under there. Had it put in three months ago; the bandages had just come off when I met you.' Oster's fingers traced a line across his own forehead. 'The heat point goes around my head in time with the sun. Orbiting my skull as it moves across the sky.'

'Sounds neat,' Larsen said cautiously. He didn't want to sound too negative when Oster looked so excited, but a *solar crown*? Of all the impractical fancies. Larsen didn't need to put anything inside his body to know what time it was. He had a watch. And a phone. All he put inside his body was to check what was happening *inside his body*. Which reminded him he still hadn't applied for a blood test implant.

'It's an experiment,' Oster explained, oblivious to Larsen's judging. 'I'm completely blind, you see. I can't tell when it's night or day. But now I'm always connected to the sun.'

'Oh, so this is about feeling closer to nature? Like the implant that buzzes when you're facing north?'

He probably hadn't managed to keep the scepticism entirely out of his voice this time; Oster's smile had a knowing slant. 'Could you sound any more Warwickian? Call me a hippie while you're at it.'

'No, you Bissoni guys have a different philosophy and that's— that's fine.'

'Uh-huh. But Warwickians are so much better, right? All about hard facts and science. No room for art, for poetry…'

'Sure, there's room for art,' Larsen said. 'Just not *inside me*.'

'You're making fun of the North Sense implant—which I do have, by the way, thank you very much. But feeling a vibration in your bones isn't the same thing as looking at a compass. It's a subliminal perception. Just like my antenna. *And* my sun crown.' Oster had a vibrant, passionate voice whenever they debated this. 'I'm trying to introduce new senses to my body and brain. *That's* improving the human condition. Expanding how we're able to think and feel. *You're* just Big Brother-ing your own body, Lars.'

'Who's sounding judgmental now?'

Oster smiled. This was what Larsen really liked about him; even when they argued about the personal, he never let it get personal. 'Maybe I'm judgmental. All I mean is… the Bissoni side of things is not just about passive perception. After a while you take your evolution in your own hands.'

'Oh?' Larsen said, finishing his tie knot.

'When I've really gotten used to it, I'm going to try slowing down the solar crown,' Oster said excitedly. 'Or making it go faster. To see if I can mess with my own perception of time. I'll be the first to try that.'

That was interesting the way spiders were *interesting*, in that they held Larsen's entire attention without necessarily making it a pleasurable experience. He couldn't understand why anyone would willingly mess with their perceptions of the outer world, when he was putting all his efforts into breaking himself down into clearly manageable stats.

'Different philosophies,' he repeated.

Oster took off his dark glasses to wipe them. He did it every once in a while, for no reason that Larsen could see other than fidgeting. Without them, his eyes were a very pale green, always staring up at the ceiling. 'Shall we go to lunch, now?' he asked. 'If your blood sugar stats allow it, of course.'

'Shut up, you hippie,' Larsen said, and they didn't talk about it again that day.

*

Larsen's phone buzzed loudly on the floor by his bed.

He jolted awake, scrambling for his glasses in the dark. When he found them and put them on, his heart rate was going crazy. His adrenaline levels were through the roof, and he was too frantic to make sense of the dozen readings from his blood test implant. His phone was buzzing and buzzing and buzzing.

He groped on instinct for the new ridges—on his flank, against his ribs—and panic tightened his chest some more. It was *there*, he could feel it, a foreign object under sewn-up skin, stuck to the bone like a marrow leech. His own terror scared him all over again, in a horrible feedback loop; if he wasn't careful, he was going to give in to it and scratch the implant out, split the skin with his nails and rip it out, ruin all this hard work.

His phone kept buzzing, sending text after text to tell him his adrenaline levels were too high. Connecting the implant to the app had been a *mistake*. Larsen fumbled with it to put it on silent, took off his glasses and closed his eyes; but he could still feel the adrenaline captor, with every expanding breath, stuck to his side, and he was going to throw up. He needed to get out of his head— out of his *body*—

He reached for his phone again and shakily flicked through his contacts list. The tone tolled in his ear, five endless times. Then there was a click and a familiar voice.

'*Larsen?*'

'Hey.' Even his voice was unsteady. 'Hey, Oster. Sorry. Sorry for waking you up.'

'*You're not waking me up. It's noon here. But isn't it 3am where you are?*'

A deep breath. 'I've had a...'

'*Nightmare?*'

'No. More like a panic attack.' He took a shaky breath. 'I think it's still happening.'

'*Oh. Does that happen a lot?*' Oster sounded concerned, which shouldn't have been so surprising. '*What brought it on?*'

'The blood test implant.' Larsen fell back on his pillow and scowled, scrubbing a hand over his damp face. 'It's not good. I don't know why. Maybe it's too big. It's fucking with my brain.'

'*You're scared that it's in you? You're afraid of infection?*'

'I'm not scared of it. I'm not scared of what it might do. I'm scared of me doing something to it.'

A beat. '*I'm not sure I understand.*'

'It's fine. You're helping.'

'*I'm helping?*'

'You're helping. Just this. Talking to you. Hearing your voice. It's helping.' Larsen exhaled deeply. 'When are you coming back from that conference thing, again?'

'*The day after tomorrow. We can meet at the diner if you'd like.*'

Larsen put the call on speaker and opened the implant app on his phone. He didn't want to disconnect it, but he really had to put the notifications on silent. Most of them. He took a deep breath and let it out. The panic was going. The sheets under him were crumpled and wet.

'Yeah,' he said, 'yeah, let's.'

*

Two nights later, at the diner, Oster hugged him tight as soon as they'd greeted each other. Larsen didn't usually allow it—he was uncomfortable with public affection—but this time he couldn't help giving in for a few seconds. He ordered his coffee black after they'd sat in a booth.

'Should you be drinking coffee?' Oster asked. This time his clothes were firetruck red and glowing orange. 'Your anxiety…'

'I'm fine.'

'Have you had any more attacks?'

'A mild one yesterday evening,' Larsen admitted. 'And I'm—' His leg was jiggling. 'Jittery.'

'You're not the first one, you know, to react like this to implants. The body doesn't like to be invaded, but the mind wants to keep the additions in, so they end up at war with each other.'

'What about your antenna?' Larsen muttered. 'It's plugged into your *head*.'

'Yeah, but I don't really mind,' Oster said. 'I don't know, I mean—it's sending me sensory input. I've gotten completely used to it. I'd miss it like a limb if it weren't there anymore.'

'My implants are sending me input *too*.'

'Input about yourself. Pure data, all cerebral, not sensorial. It's a closed—'

'A closed circuit. Like my sister would say.' Larsen combed back his dyed-black hair with both hands. 'God.'

'You sound exhausted, Lars,' Oster said gently.

'Haven't really slept since I got it in. I *told* you.' Larsen wished he could have been nicer to Oster. He usually didn't mind about sounding like a dick, which probably made him something of a genuine dick. Remorse was rare and fleeting. But he did feel it sometimes.

'Maybe you should take it out,' Oster said, which was when

Larsen noticed his undercut. The hair over his ear was a more brilliant copper than the rest, cropped close to the skin. Larsen reached out—prompting a slight flinch from Oster, who heard his pale hand coming at him—and carefully curved his fingers over his ear. There was something there, under the skin.

'You've got a new one too.'

'Yes,' Oster said, reaching up to cover Larsen's hand with his own. 'It detects the changes in atmospheric pressure.'

'And signals them how? Sound? Won't that get mixed up with your Harbisson input?'

'No, it expands and decreases in size—it's a pocket of fluid. A small one, of course.'

'Of course.' No, Larsen really couldn't keep the bitterness out of his voice. 'And that doesn't disturb you? You've got all these implants *moving around* under your skin. Fucking with senses humans don't even have. Mine are static. They send me nothing but hard data I'm reading with my own two eyes. Why am I the one freaking out? It's not fair!'

'Oh, well, I'm having terrible migraines,' Oster said serenely. 'I've been throwing up a lot, too.'

That shut Larsen right up.

'But the Harbisson antenna brought on similar symptoms. It goes away after a while.'

'It does?' Larsen asked miserably.

'Yes. It does.' Oster squeezed Larsen's hand. 'And tell me: would you *like* to take your implants out?'

That made Larsen go silent for a long time. Then he somehow mustered a smile; Oster couldn't see it, of course, so he did his best to put it in his voice, too. 'No. It's been tough, but I… I don't think I could go back to nothing.'

'*I* certainly couldn't,' Oster said at once. 'I had no say in being blind. But all these new senses—they belong to me. I invented them, I'm refining them. They're mine. I'm not letting go of that.'

*

The anxiety attacks did lessen after a while. Larsen had always been the nervous paranoid sort, so he tried not to give them too much credit anyway, and did his best to sleep and eat regularly until his body grudgingly accepted that the intruder was here to stay.

When it wasn't freaking out over nothing, his brain actually seemed to appreciate the new input. Larsen just had to look at the stream of data to know exactly how he was doing. The app sent him buzzing reminders through the day to drink more water or eat less sugar, following the fluctuations of his blood stats. It made him relatively serene, at least between bursts of sudden panic.

All the same, the painful adjustment had made Larsen quite afraid of trying any new augmentations, and he focused on maintaining his health for the better part of the year. After all, it was what the augmentations were *for*. It was odd that he had to remind himself of that.

Oster was still around, with his horrid clothing and his cheerful mood and his endless patience. Maybe because Larsen had no mental space left to get tired of him. They had enough to talk about that they didn't squabble often. Or maybe Oster was just inordinately easy to be around, always happy to stay home and always delighted to go out, enjoying the routine and yet always finding new things to discuss.

After a while, Larsen got into the habit of seeing him at least twice a week, and almost didn't mind losing so much of his private time to someone. Maybe affection was nothing more than a habit. Something that settled in only when he managed to think about something else, much like the implants under his skin.

*

Oster was deep into the Bissoni mind-set. He was even part of what he called a coven—a handful of Bissoni cyborgs who gathered every Thursday night to discuss Harbisson's theories, share their experiences and drink in good company. Larsen's own Warwickian community was wholly online, so he became more and more intrigued about Oster's coven meetings until, inevitably, he was invited to join.

He went affecting reluctance, of course, as dictated by the Harbisson-Warwick feud which demanded that each side feel superior to the other. But really, he was curious, enough to summon up the endurance for a night out.

'All black again,' Oster remarked, taking his hand on the sidewalk. 'Why so serious?'

'You know why.' Lars almost wiggled his hand free, but then didn't. He was already making an effort that night. He could push it a bit further. 'And I suppose I'm trying to give a different image of cyborgs. A bit less gaudy.'

'Gaudy?'

'Well, you *do* have antennas sticking out of your head. And you tend to dress very—ah—colourfully. Of course, you're blind.'

Even he heard how insensitive this sounded the second after the words had left his mouth. Oster never, ever took offence, though; he only smiled. 'We're just a bunch of New Age idiots to you, aren't we?'

'I can easily imagine you all running naked through a sunflower field, if that's what you mean.'

'Which just goes to prove you've never seen a sunflower up close, Lars. That would *itch*.' Oster's hand tightened around Larsen's fingers before Larsen could argue the metaphor. 'How's the anxiety?'

'I… Better. I guess.' He took a deep breath. 'It'll do me good to get out of the house.'

'I didn't make you say it.' Oster gave him that slanted smile of his. 'You're such a cliché. The Warwickian shut-in.' He gave an odd tilt of the head. 'Hurry up now—it feels like rain.'

It certainly didn't *look* like rain; the clouds were sparse and thin. But Oster's atmospheric implant did not lie, and a few drops were beginning to fall by the time they reached the coven meeting.

There were pictures on the coven walls—huge framed canvases covered in splotches of vivid paint. A handful of Bissoni cyborgs, all sporting the Harbisson antenna, were standing in front of the paintings and slowing moving their heads to hear all of the colours in their bones. Some of them had their eyes closed. All of them dressed about as badly as Oster, even though none of them appeared to be actually blind. Fashion sense evidently wasn't part of the Bissoni philosophy.

Oster briefly turned his head when they passed the little group, as if to get a whiff of the pictures, but didn't stop. 'I know them by heart already,' he explained. 'The second-to-last is very soothing.'

Larsen answered nothing. He was wearing his public face, impassive. Black on black on black. Control his own image. Nights out were hard on his nerves, even if things were a bit better now that he could access stats that let him know exactly *how* hard.

'Oster! Hi!' said a girl appearing at the end of the hallway to give him a hug. She wasn't badly dressed at all—in fact, she was wearing a plain white dress, an elegant compliment to her very dark skin—even though she had a Harbisson antenna too, artfully arranged in the middle of her cornrows. One of her eyes was glowing blue.

'Is that an eye camera?' Larsen asked.

'Lars, introduce yourself first, for Pete's sake.' Oster looped an arm over Larsen's shoulder. 'This is Thomas Larsen, my very Warwickian boyfriend. He doesn't bite. Lars, this is Bintou.'

'Hi,' Bintou said, shaking Larsen's hand. 'So you actually do exist.'

He didn't enjoy the joke.

'Lars doesn't get out much,' Oster said.

Larsen just gave Bintou a nod. He could already tell she didn't like him. Well, too bad.

'It's not an eye camera, by the way,' Bintou added. 'It's digital contacts. Makes it easier for me to see my feed in real time.'

'You have a data feed?' Larsen raised a hand to his own glasses. Then stared at her antenna. 'So... you're both?'

'If Kevin Warwick was alive today, a lot of us would call him a Bissoni, do you know that?'

'Oh, now you've gotten her started,' Oster said with a grin.

'Shove it, Maraskov,' she said amiably. 'I am fully prepared to die on this hill. You think you're so different from your boyfriend, but you're both exactly the same. Extremists all caught up in this stupid binary we've somehow ended up in. You gotta mix it some! It's what makes it *interesting.*'

'But it doesn't make sense,' Larsen argued—though it explained her more tasteful sense of clothing, he supposed. 'Warwickians are trying to monitor and control their bodies for optimal health. Adding sensory implants that'll just confuse and invade the entire bio system, that's utterly stup—counterproductive.'

'*My* Warwickian implants let me measure and regulate the effect my Bissoni implants have on my physiology,' Bintou countered. 'And when it comes to controlling the body—well, I suppose Oster's told you about this solar crown thing he's pioneering?'

'You shouldn't *measure* their effects,' Oster intervened. 'You should *feel* them. Proceed on instinct. Let it all flow through you.'

'Flow,' Bintou mocked. 'Are you *goading* him into calling you a hippie?'

'He calls me that all the time anyway,' Oster grinned while Larsen weakly tried to protest he did not. 'Your eye's a lovely singing blue, by the way.'

'Thanks,' she grinned. 'I designed it myself.'

*

'I hope Bintou didn't put you off,' Oster said later, glass in hand, tilting his head in front of a new piece of Bissoni art. 'We're always at odds—it's good fun, but she can be a little direct.'

'No, I liked her,' Larsen lied. 'She reminds me of my sister, actually.'

'Nadegda? The one who calls you a closed circuit? Is she a cyborg?'

'Not by choice.'

'Oh,' Oster said quietly.

They absorbed themselves in their contemplation of the art for a while. It was strange to be standing in front of the same painting and getting such different impressions from it. Larsen wondered what an antenna would feel like in his own head; but he'd never inflict migraines and panic attacks upon himself for the sake of such simple curiosity.

And yet he couldn't say his implants responded to an actual *need*, either. Not like Nadegda's did.

'She's got early-onset Alzheimer's,' he said. 'Nadegda, I mean. They put her on a deep-brain implant when she was twenty-two.'

Oster turned to face him, evidently so the art's distracting music would be replaced by Larsen's colourless silence.

'She's your twin sister, right?' he asked. 'Didn't you tell me you got your first implant when you were twenty-two as well?'

'I was scared,' Larsen answered, still looking at the painting he couldn't hear. 'Of course she's doing well, but it's hereditary, and I didn't—it's when I had my first major panic attack. Not that I'd been a very serene person until then. The next week I applied for a heart-rate implant. And it's improved things.'

He couldn't remember the last time he'd explained this to someone. His voice faltered.

'I thought it would keep improving things.'

'It will. Improvement isn't a straight path. But isn't this what being a cyborg is all about? Changing yourself, instead of changing your environment? Don't smile,' Oster said, though he couldn't even know for sure Larsen was smiling—'you can't disagree with me on this. It's why we do it, right? Natural selection can't work on us anymore; we've gotten too good at making ourselves comfortable. Now we're taking evolution into our own hands.'

'No. You keep saying that, but we're just playing around, Oster. Entertaining ourselves.' Larsen wanted to say *you're just playing around*, but he couldn't be that dishonest; his own implants weren't about survival either. 'My sister didn't have a choice.'

'Exactly. She was backed against a wall. But we Bissoni, we Warwickians—we're skipping ahead. We're explorers. We're charting new continents so that the paths are already there for those who'd rather have them.'

Larsen said nothing for a long while. The Bissoni cyborgs were laughing and chatting all around him, and he felt like a sad old crow standing there in the middle of them, all in black with his dark glasses and no visible implants. He wasn't comfortable here;

he was rarely comfortable anywhere outside the house. But in the middle of all this awkwardness, there was Oster, still smiling, and Larsen felt a rare and alarming impulse to do something crazy.

'Would you like to share a telepathy implant with me?'

Oster looked taken aback; then a large smile spread onto his face. 'Why, Mr. Larsen. How very Bissoni of you.'

'It couldn't be further from Bissoni,' Larsen said, annoyed. 'This is Kevin Warwick's original project—he did it with his wife—'

'So Bintou was right. We're not so different.' Oster leaned in for a kiss, still smiling. 'And I'd love to try this with you.'

Larsen already wanted to back out of his own ridiculous offer, planning half a dozen exit routes in his head; but when Oster kissed him he allowed himself to believe that it might actually be a good idea. He'd certainly never made Oster so happy with him before. He didn't want to extinguish that just yet.

*

They downgraded to a handholding implant in the end, because the mere thought of putting something directly into his brain was giving Larsen night terrors again. He felt treacherously relieved at this excuse not to go all the way.

Even handholding was a lot, to him. As far as Oster was concerned, this wasn't a big deal; but Larsen kept having long debates with himself in the shower over it. All his implants so far had been dedicated to biohacking; they managed his circadian cycle in time with the sun, woke him and put him to sleep, delivered sugar into his bloodstream when needed. Optimal body performance was his goal. A handholding implant was completely unnecessary. It wouldn't give him any information about himself, or improve his body in any way.

And yet he had it done, and it was unobtrusive enough that it didn't make him panic. That was a relief in itself. They agreed not to test it until they were truly apart; so it was only when Oster left on one of his conferences trips, two weeks later, that they gave it a try.

Larsen jumped when he first felt a phantom hand close over his own; but before he'd even decided if the sensation was a pleasant one or not, he was already giving a squeeze back, knowing that Oster would feel it no matter where he was at the moment.

Which was good. Undeniably. A way to make him feel good. To be nice, thousands of kilometres apart, when Larsen didn't always manage it up close. He was a Warwickian, an intellectual. He could tell himself that, yes—this was good.

*

Sadly, telling himself things didn't always make them true.

There were some signs—there had been signs for a long while now; signs Larsen would only notice when he reflected on the whole thing later. That conversation they'd had once, for instance— *Why aren't you sleeping?*—Oster's voice, shuffling in the dark to hug him from behind, his antenna poking the back of Larsen's head. And Larsen answering *Why aren't* you *sleeping?* with enough nasty emphasis to send Oster back to bed. Another sign, more obvious, had occurred some time later, when Oster had returned exhausted from two long weeks of lectures abroad. Instead of embracing him Larsen had said, shocked, *Oster, you're wearing black.* And Oster had given himself a cursory swipe of his antenna: *Am I? Oh, yes.* And smiled: *Maybe I wanted you to be less ashamed of walking down the street with me.* That had been an obvious joke but Larsen had gotten annoyed. He always did.

But the most momentous sign of all had happened on one of their visits to the Bissoni coven. They often chatted with Bintou, who kept annoying Larsen with her complete disregard for the unspoken rules of cyborgs, mixing up Warwick and Harbisson seemingly at random. *And when I blink hard*, she was saying, *my contact lenses switch from my data feed to a constellations map. I can't wait to go into the country this weekend for a bit of stargazing.* At which point Oster had noted, distractedly: *You should wait two months. There'll be a comet then.*

Larsen had gotten disproportionately annoyed again. *What are you saying? What are you talking about? There's not gonna be a comet.* Checking on his phone and scowling, showing Oster the screen even though of course he couldn't read it. *See? The next one won't pass over us for six months.* Bintou was looking furious by then. Larsen wished he could have told her to mind her own business. He couldn't let Oster say such idiotic things in public.

If he was completely honest with himself, the handholding implant was getting on his nerves. He was afraid of what he'd allowed. He usually didn't go this far with people. Unconsciously— or maybe not so much—he kept trying ways to back off, to keep Oster from coming any closer. But Oster kept not minding at all, sometimes cheerful and sometimes distracted, like he was always looking at something only he could see with his wide pale eyes.

Signs, all of them. Except that even much later, when he finally started rummaging through his memories, Larsen would be mistaken again, thinking they were all about him.

*

'*Hey, little brother,*' Nadegda said on the phone. '*How are you? Still dressing like you're trying to be interesting?*'

'I see you're well enough to remember that.'

Nadegda was like him. She wasn't nice. But she also wasn't like everyone else, because she didn't ask him to be. It was all he could do to return the favour.

'*You should visit me more,*' she said. '*One day I might just forget you and you won't have anyone to blame but yourself.*'

As long as she joked about it then she was fine. When the illness returned and got worse—it always did, if previous cases were to be believed; even deep-brain implants could not counteract aging— then she would joke about it still, but in a different register. Larsen knew he'd hear it right away. They weren't twins for nothing.

'I never have anyone to blame but myself,' he muttered.

'*God, I see you're as cheerful as usual. And how's your colourful boyfriend?*'

'I don't know. I haven't seen him in a while.'

'*What? What about that handholding implant you took together?*'
'I deactivated it.'

Nadegda wasn't the type of person to exclaim *What?* twice in a row, but Larsen could almost hear her eyes narrow on the phone. There was a relatively long silence; he set the phone on the kitchen shelves and continued making dinner for one.

'*Tom, did you break up with him for no good reason?*' the phone piped up, sending vibrations into the wood—which made him think of Oster; of the antenna vibrating *red* and *yellow* and *blue* into the bones of his skull.

'Don't call me Tom.'

She didn't dignify that with a reply, just waited. Larsen sighed and ran a hand through his hair—and as he did, a flash caught his eye in the polished steel of the cooker hood. His blond roots were peeking out. He must have gotten sloppy for them to show that much.

'I didn't break up with him,' he said, belatedly.

'*No, you just lost interest and now you're waiting for things to die out on their own, is that it?*'

'No.' He started peeling the potatoes, careful not to click the switch under the palm of his left hand. He needed to get that damn implant taken out. 'He's the one who stopped returning my calls.'

'*How long has it been?*'

'I don't know. Two, three weeks. I don't know.'

'*And you didn't try to find out more? Tom, what if something happened to him? Have you thought about that?*'

'Nothing happened to him. The handholding implant would've signalled it.' Larsen swallowed. 'It's just that *he* lost interest first.'

That was fine. There had been signs, many signs—which just amounted to Larsen being his usual self, really. He was surprised it had taken Oster so long to give up on him. Perhaps because they were so similar and so different at the same time. Perhaps because despite all his neuroses, Larsen never felt watched when Oster was around him; and yet he knew Oster saw him as unique. How had he put it? *It's a deep silence, black. A great absence.*

No one else would ever make Larsen feel that way again. Seen and unseen at the same time.

'I don't care,' he managed to say. 'He can do what he wants. I'm not in the habit of begging.'

'*Tom, you're so dense. It's amazing. It's like you've got an implant for that.*'

'It's not pride. I...' He hated stumbling on his words. He hated showing vulnerability in any way. He hated showing himself at all. 'I've been my usual prick self and he got tired of it. That's all. That's understandable.'

Nadegda just hung up on him, which said it all, really. She did it too often for him to take offense.

Larsen tried never to take offense in general. Of course, he always did, which was why he kept trying not to. He tried not to feel anything. To break himself down into stats until he could catalogue even his emotions and control them through a clever cocktail of chemicals. Feedback loop. Closed circuit. He'd always thought being a cyborg meant to stop being human. It was what appealed to him, the machine. To think Oster saw it as making himself more human. It was too fundamental a difference. It was useless hoping for any lasting relationship between them. It was all useless.

*

'Larsen! Open the damn door!'

Larsen opened the door all at once, blinking in the light of the hallway. It was Bintou with her glowing blue eye. He felt instantly ashamed and furious, wishing she hadn't seen him in the shapeless sports clothing he wore to bed, wishing she weren't there at all, reminding him of someone else.

'How did you find out where I live?'

'Is *that* your most pressing question at the moment, really?' She reached for his left hand, which made him recoil. 'Turn that bloody thing on.'

'What the fuck do you think you're doing?' he said, snatching his hand away. 'Don't touch me. If Oster's unhappy he can tell me himself.'

Bintou stopped trying to grab him and stared. 'What?'

'Which word don't you understand?'

'Okay—first of all? You're a knob. I've wanted to say that for a long while, and here it is: you're a condescending knob, and I can't believe you got someone as sweet as Oster to fancy you.'

'Yes, well, all done now. Cheers, bye.' He tried shutting the door.

She blocked it with her foot. 'What are you *talking* about?'

'For God's sake. We split up two months ago. I suppose he didn't tell you.'

'Split up?' Bintou looked utterly baffled. 'You haven't *split up.*'

Larsen stared at her in equal confusion. 'I think I would know.'

'Oh, God,' she said weakly. 'You thought—for *the past two months*—and you didn't even try *talking to him* about it?'

'He's the one who dropped off the map. I have *some* dignity.' Larsen was starting to feel like this was a repeat of the Nadegda conversation. Once had been enough. 'Will you leave?'

'Have you not noticed *anything?*' she said. 'Are you really that self-centred? Have you not noticed he wasn't doing well?'

Larsen opened his mouth to say something about the many signs he had in fact retroactively noticed. But then he thought again about them.

That time he'd stayed over at Oster's. *Why aren't you sleeping?* He'd snapped at him to send him back to bed, because he was having another attack and didn't want to deal with people at the moment. He'd berated himself for being always too dry, always too unpleasant to the people who loved him. He hadn't apologized, though. After the fact he'd told himself—*See. This is why Oster got tired of me.*

But why *hadn't* Oster been sleeping either?

And Oster wearing black that one time after coming back from his string of lectures. Another sign Larsen thought was about himself—that he was shaming Oster for his clothing taste and his implants and his choices in general, to the point that Oster was trying to change for him. Of course Larsen was the bad guy in this scenario. Controlling, condescending. *See: this is why Oster got tired of me.*

But Oster had answered *Am I?* when Larsen had pointed out how he was dressed. And he'd actually given himself a once-over with his antenna. He genuinely hadn't known what he was wearing.

And the comet thing…

'No, I didn't—I don't—' Larsen felt the onset of a panic attack in the tips of his fingers. His phone buzzed in his back pocket to signal it, too. 'What do you mean, he hasn't been doing well?'

'I *mean* he's been missing for forty-eight hours, you absolute prick.' Bintou's lips were pressed tight. 'Now turn the handholding implant *on*.'

*

The handholding implant included a GPS app, which Larsen hadn't even bothered to install on his phone until now. He had to wait until it loaded, and left the room to dress himself partly to escape the weight of Bintou's judgment.

When he came back, in all black—except his hair, his blond hair pushing out, drawing attention—Bintou gave him such a searing look he almost felt like she had a laser in her blue eye.

'Look,' he said stiffly, 'I will not deny I *am* a self-centred prick. But Oster hasn't talked to me in two months.'

'Then things are even worse than I thought,' she said. 'Because when I last saw him, he was telling me he'd seen you just the day before.'

'And—*when* did you last see him?'

'Three days ago.'

Larsen felt cold. He couldn't help thinking of Nadegda and early-onset Alzheimer's and deep-brain implants. But this was ridiculous. Something else had to be going on with Oster.

His phone beeped; Bintou drew back from it, arms crossed over her chest. 'Your app's ready.'

'It—' Larsen frowned as the GPS triangulated. '—looks like

he's home.'

'No, he's not. I went there just before I came to find you. I pounded on that door loud enough to wake up the whole building. His downstairs neighbour said she hadn't heard anything in two days, and she usually hears *everything* he does.'

'Well, the app says he's home.'

They said nothing more after that. Just left in a hurry.

*

They took an electric cab to Oster's place. Larsen felt a pang climbing the familiar stairs. It was like he'd been there just the day before, which was what Oster had apparently told Bintou. Larsen kept thinking about what he was going to find behind the door. He kept making promises to be a better person and be more mindful of others from then on—empty promises to try and change what had already happened.

'Door's still locked,' Bintou said. 'Do you have a key? Did you at least remember to bring it?'

'You're quite condescending.'

'Less than you.'

'Which is why I didn't question him leaving,' Larsen said, opening the door, because even amidst intense self-loathing he couldn't help being defensive. God, wasn't he a piece of work?

The door unlocked, which spared Bintou from answering.

They stepped into the apartment, which was cold and dark. Larsen's heart was beating so hard and so fast the little icon seemed to be vibrating in the corner of his glasses. Thank God he'd muted his adrenaline app. His tension was all over the place; most of his other stats were too.

But then he turned a corner and saw Oster.

He was standing in the middle of the living room, all lights off, without his dark glasses, huge pale green eyes staring up at nothing. There was a red glowing dot in the middle of his forehead.

'Oster!' Bintou called.

Oster didn't react, and Larsen suddenly wished all of his

implants were inside him instead. So he could know exactly what was going on. So he could know for sure whether he was all right.

The red glow wasn't moving at all.

Bintou put a hand on Oster's forearm. 'He's freezing. How long has he been standing there? Oster? Oi!'

'I don't think he can hear you,' Larsen said. 'Or feel you.'

'I'm calling—'

'Who? To tell them what?' Larsen needed his dryness now, to hide how shaken he was. 'Do you think a hospital will know what to do with a Bissoni who's broken his own perception of time?'

'That's not what he…' Bintou looked at the miniature sun stuck in the middle of Oster's forehead. 'Oh, *Oster*.'

They stood around in appalled silence for a minute.

'Could you please draw him a bath,' Larsen said quietly. 'Hot bath. Please.'

Bintou looked at him for several seconds. Then she said, 'And you, turn on the lights.'

It was a good idea, but Larsen didn't obey; after she'd slipped away, he finally stepped close to Oster, slowly.

'You idiot,' he said, softer than he'd ever managed before, and brushed the chestnut curls off his forehead. The glowing dot was still right in the middle of his eyebrows. The atmospheric implant on his temple moved under Larsen's touch like an amoeba. 'Come on, Oster. Let's sit down. Come on.'

He managed to get Oster to the couch, by pushing him until he walked, and then until he sat. When he stepped in front of him, Oster reacted for the first time; tilted his head back, so very slowly, the way he did when his antenna brought an unusual set of vibrations into his bones.

'Yes, it's me,' Larsen said. 'Your great absence.'

He clicked the hard lump in the middle of Oster's left palm, then reached for his own hand and did the same. The satellite connection between them was back on. Larsen closed his fingers around nothing.

Nothing happened in answer. Larsen sat next to Oster on the couch.

'I'm right here,' he said. 'Is your sun going to match pace with us again soon?'

Oster said nothing, did nothing. He was indeed cold to the touch; probably only because he'd been standing there without the heating on, but it was eerie.

'Had you slowed it down before? Is that why you didn't notice it had been two months?' Larsen went on. 'At least you have a proper excuse, unlike me.'

He kept squeezing Oster's hand, from his implant to the sky, and then back to Oster's implant. From someone who was just a breath away. He rubbed circles into the void with his connected thumb.

And then Oster squeezed back. It happened so slowly Larsen didn't feel it until he was in the middle of it. The phantom touch around his hand. He could see Oster's fingers moving, closing, like a flower under the stars.

Which reminded him. He pulled out his phone one-handed and did a more thorough search than he had last time. It took him a little while, sitting there with Oster in the dark, touching him through satellite. Had he shut off the lights so the colours wouldn't distract him as much?

'Oh, dear. You were right,' Larsen said, looking at his screen. 'We're two months later, now, and you were right. There's a comet. We can't see it from Earth, but it's there in the solar system. It's passing us by.' He looked up at Oster again. 'How far did you go that you can feel comets passing us by?'

He suddenly became aware that Bintou was at the bathroom door, watching them. Her blue eye glowed in the plumes of steam coming out of the room behind her. For once he didn't mind being observed. This wasn't about him.

'I should have seen the signs,' he said.

None of which had been about him. But he had been sarcastic and unpleasant and critical; so maybe Oster hadn't left him after all—though maybe he had, too; who knew? But one thing was for certain—he had started testing the solar crown without telling anyone. Drawing his time into longer and longer stretches of void, until he got stuck.

'Here's what I can tell you about myself, Oster, once and for all,' Larsen went on. 'My name is Thomas Larsen. I am an antisocial, selfish, neurotic jerk. I am sitting in your apartment next to you. My pulse is at 102 bpm because you've always calmed me down. My adrenaline levels are high and my blood sugar is low, but I don't care. I am holding your hand through a satellite because it's all you can feel right now. Maybe because you've had your head up in space for a while. I can't join you up there. But if you come back to us I will tell you that I've missed you.'

Oster was slightly smiling; maybe because he now knew Larsen was thinking about him—or maybe only because he was stretched all over the Earth's magnetic field, breathing in time with the atmospheric pressure, having slowed down the sun so that hours felt like seconds. Riding a comet through the stars.

'Now we're going to get up again, love,' Larsen said. 'We're going to get up and undress you and get you into the bath. And then Bintou and I are going to look up how to deactivate your goddamn solar crown.'

*

In the morning the glowing dot wasn't in the middle of Oster's brow anymore. It was the first thing Larsen saw when he woke up.

They hadn't been certain it would work when she'd done it; they'd decided to slowly bring the crown's speed back up to normal levels. If they turned it off, who knew what would happen. What if Oster's brain froze entirely in answer? No, it was better to try bringing him back slowly. Naturally. Probably exactly the way he'd brought himself back over the past weeks, every time, before diving again. Maybe it had only felt like three days for him in total. Maybe it had felt like no time at all.

For a moment, Larsen became scared the solar crown had turned off; but then he lifted Oster's chestnut curls and saw the pulsating light by his temple.

'It worked, Bintou,' he said.

They'd bundled up Oster in bed with him, and Bintou had taken the chair by the door. Larsen wasn't sure what she thought of him now. It was probably better not to ask.

She stretched with a wince, then said, 'Try the handholding thing again.'

Larsen squeezed his fingers under the blanket. Nothing happened.

'Oster? Are you back with us?' he asked. And then, mouth going dry, 'It's me. It's Thomas.'

Oster said nothing, but moved his hand under the blankets to grab Larsen's hand and squeeze, so that they both felt it twice, in a closed circuit; through the implant, and through the body, a feedback loop between the both of them.

sur la comète; A story of everyday cyborgs in love
Gill Haddow

Feeling the Cyborg love?

Naomi Salman's story 'sur la comète' is a romantic tale that follows the relationship between the two main characters, Oster and Larsen. They meet and fall in love but, as is so often the case in traditional love stories, circumstances lead to a breakdown in their relationship resulting in a separation. Eventually, they overcome their differences to live, one hopes, 'happily ever after'. Although we know not what time period the love story is set in, it is a time when individuals are able to choose to have their bodies modified with various implantable technologies. Thus, following a similar narration about how the relationship between Larsen and Oster develops, there is another tier of storytelling that relates the relationships Larsen and Oster have with their implanted devices. This narration follows how Larsen and Oster deal with their respective devices, but also how the devices interfere in their relationship with one another.

Who is afraid of the Cyborg?

The term 'cyborg' is so commonly used that it hardly needs explication. It was first introduced in the 1960s, when the term was used to describe the body modifications and cybernetic implants required by future astronauts to survive space travel and exploration (Clynes and Kline 1960). By connecting the first syllables of the words 'cybernetic' and 'organism', the term 'cyborg' was born (Clynes and Kline 1960). In this original definition of the term, the 'cyborg-in-space' required closed-loop feedback mechanisms, namely cybernetic systems, to regulate and normalise bodily functions in the hostile environment. It was argued that it was better '…altering man's (sic) bodily functions to meet the requirements of extra-terrestrial environments [and] would be more logical than providing an earthly environment for him in space … artefact-organism systems which would extend man's (sic) unconscious, self-regulatory controls are one possibility' (1960: 26). Osmotic pumps were imagined, as were the electrical stimulation of hearts and brains; devices that when implanted in the body are outwith the control of a human operator. These imagined cybernetic devices are now being realised as implantable medical devices used for therapeutic purposes that react to fluctuations in the physiological conditions inside the human body. In the Clines and Kline original definition, however, the 'cyborg-in-space' version would be unaware of the fluctuations going on inside the body, nor experience any fundamental alteration to their personal identity (Haddow, King et al. 2015). Indeed, as Clynes went on to suggest four years later in the foreword to Halacy's *'Cyborg: Evolution of the Superman'*:

> Will this (cyborg) change our fundamental nature? Not much more than glasses or iron lungs change it. The difference is merely that instead of using external or *attached* prosthetic devices, the man-made devices are now to be *incorporated* into the regulatory feedback chains - the homeostatic mechanisms that keep us viable for such an astonishingly long time (Clynes in Halacy 1965:8, emphasis original).

This original definition is lesser known than the more commonly recognised fictional version of the cyborg *in extremis*; the inhumane, often male, monsters depicted in science-fiction literature who lose aspects of their human identity through the additions of cybernetic biotechnologies to their human forms (Oetler 1995). The inhumanity caused by implanting cybernetic devices, creating an artificial-human hybrid, is closely associated with the gendering of the 'cyborg-in-space' as male[1]. This gendering of the cyborg as male therefore is common to the original definition of the term as well as the fictional one (Haddow, King et al. 2015).

An alternative definition of the term cyborg exists that is less well-known than the 'cyborg-as-monster' version, and is one used in academic circles such as the science and technology studies (STS) literature (Haraway 1991, Gray 1995, Hayles 1995, Gray 2000, Gray 2001, Gray 2011, Gray 2012) and also in feminist STS literature (Penley, Ross et al. 1990, Kirkup, Janes et al. 1999, Henwood, Kennedy et al. 2001). The feminist philosopher Donna Haraway conceptualised the cyborg as a metaphor for liberation and an escape from the binary boundaries between: male and female, the physical and the non-physical, and animal-human and machines, boundaries that can be dissolved. Haraway's cyborg can offer a liberation from such classificatory categories. This cyborg is a challenge to recognise our own responsibility in constructing the dualistic categorisations that are, to all intents and purposes, created by us. As Haraway argues:

> A cyborg body is not innocent; it was not born in a garden; it does not seek unitary identity and so generate antagonistic dualisms without end (or until the world ends); it takes irony for granted. One is too few, and two only one possibility. Intense pleasure in skill, machine skill, ceases to be a sin, but an aspect of embodiment…We can be responsible for machines; they do not dominate or threaten us. We are responsible for boundaries; we are they (Haraway 1991: 180).

The 'cyborg-as-liberation' version is very different from the horror fiction fantasy version of cyborg, and is a 'cybernetic organism, a hybrid of machine and organism, a creature of social reality as well as a creature of fiction' (1991: 119). Haraway's cyborg

---

1. Recent notable exceptions are Ava in the film 'Ex Machina' https://en.wikipedia.org/wiki/Ex_Machina_(film) and Seven of Nine in the series 'Star Trek Voyager' https://en.wikipedia.org/wiki/Seven_of_Nine. Both are highly stylised versions of female cyborgs with prominent attention given to bodily appearance and shape. Both websites accessed February 2020.

is about the blurring of dichotomies and the impossibility of finding wholeness. It is not directed at the experiential dimensions of being or becoming cyborg, however.

The fourth and last definition of the term 'cyborg', and the one that Salman draws mostly upon, is one that STS scholars have used to describe the empirical reality of individuals who have undergone a cyborgisation process through implanting medical devices into their bodies (Gray 1995, Pollock 2011, Oudshoorn 2015, Oudshoorn 2016). Authors such as Chorost in his autobiography *Becoming Part Computer Made Me More Human* (2005) writes of how his cochlear implant resulted in, '[M]y bionic hearing made me neither omniscient nor dehumanized: it made me more human, because I was aware that my perception of the universe was provisional' (2005: 157). A review of research on the experiences of patients who live with implantable cardiac devices (ICDs) also shows that such devices can cause anger, depression and panic attacks for some (Holly and Sharp 2014). These devices cause new vulnerabilities for individuals relating to the lack of control they have over the device, as well as the individual having to find strategies to acclimatise to a new techno-organic hybridity (Oudshoorn 2015, Oudshoorn 2016). Contrary to expectation, the vulnerability is not caused by the device malfunctioning but by the device performing the functions that it was created to do, which is to prevent death by cardiac arrest (Haddow 2020).

Therefore, reclaiming the cyborg for the everyday, the 'everyday cyborg', draws attention to the strategies that are needed to adapt to a new cyborg hybridity experienced in routine daily activities (Haddow, Harmon et al. 2015, Haddow, King et al. 2015). The vulnerabilities that are created through adding technology to the human body may mean that an individual can experience their body as a new hybrid techno-organic identity, yet it does not follow that the person is less caring, understanding or humane (as per the fictional cyborg monster). Paradoxically, becoming cyborg, as Chorost suggests, and as we learn in Salman's story, can make someone more vulnerable and caring, indeed less human in terms of the body, but more 'humane' in relationships with others.

Choosing to be Inside-Out or Outside-In?

Salman's cyborgs, Larsen and Oster, are not future space explorers, science fiction monsters or feminist catalysts for a revolution in modernity (Haddow, King et al. 2015). In 'sur la comète' Salman bases the vulnerability experienced by both Oster and Larsen on their pre-existing characteristics. For example, on the one hand, Larsen tends to choose body modifications that enable him to closely monitor his internal physiological functions; these reflect the current popularity with self-monitoring by data tracking devices albeit in relation to the inside of his body:

> Larsen didn't need to put anything inside his body to know what time it was. He had a watch. And a phone. All he put inside his body was to check what was happening *inside his body*. Which reminded him he still hadn't applied for a blood test implant.

This internal gaze that Larsen initially benefits from is co-existent with his neuroticism, hypochondria and self-absorption. He is obsessed with his internal biological homeostasis, such as his blood pressure or heart rate; this feedback (through implantable devices) is accessed by him on a continual data stream. One evening Larsen is awoken by his mobile phone's alarm, triggered by his implant issuing warnings that he is having a panic attack. However, the feedback loop function only serves to increase his feeling of panic, amplifying his anxiety even further. The implant is working perfectly, albeit unexpectedly, amplifying and creating a biofeedback loop that includes Larsen himself as an integral part of it. Indeed, Salman named the character Larsen as an oblique reference to the 'Larsen effect' of a feedback loop. The feedback loop that was also viewed as necessary for the homeostasis of bodily functions is a feature of the cybernetic technologies originally envisaged by Clynes and Kline (1960) for their earlier 'cyborg-in-space' version.

Oster: The Bissonian Group

Oster is a 'hippy' according to Larsen, because he follows an ideology of body modification and cyborgisation that seeks to achieve harmony and connectedness with the outside world. The biotechnological modifications that Oster chooses are partly based on a therapeutic need to treat his blindness. In this respect, Salman is drawing inspiration from the Spanish artist Neil Harbisson (b. 1982). Harbisson has an extreme form of colour blindness and, to compensate for this, he devised a device that was permanently implanted into his skull. Attached to this device is an antenna (an eye-orb) allowing him to sense colour by feeling differential vibrations caused by looking at various shades. Harbisson's eye-orb allows him to interact with the outside world in a way very few humans are capable of. Like Harbisson, Oster experiences colour through vibration from the antenna that he has implanted.

Harbisson's experimentation with the perception of time through the construction of a solar crown is also echoed in the story when Oster's solar crown begins to interfere with his perception of time. As Salman's narration demonstrates again, the fault is not with the cybernetic device but with Oster's experience in using it. For Oster and Harbisson, their eye-orbs have a dual-use status as both a therapy and enhancement, offering 'new senses.' As Oster comments at one point, 'I had no say in being blind. But all these new senses—they belong to me. I invented them, I'm refining them. They're *mine*. I'm not letting go of that.'

At one point, Oster suggests to Larsen that the panic attacks he suffers from are a reaction to Larsen's body's being 'invaded' with the new implants, Larsen replies that the same might be said of Oster's antenna. However, Oster's response is, 'I've gotten completely used to it. I'd miss it like a limb if it weren't there anymore.' Oster's technological modifications are now part of him, therefore he feels there is no longer a difference between the artificial and the human, and he has acclimatised to his new cyborg hybridity (Haddow 2020).

Harbisson versus Warwick

Oster and Larsen represent two different approaches to body modification via device implantation. Larsen's obsessive self-monitoring of his own physiological functioning contrasts with Oster's focus on what might be described as a 'connective perception', where his cybernetic technologies allow him to create a unique relationship with others and the surrounding environment. Over-simplifying somewhat, Larsen's modifications are about making that which is in (his) inside-out, whereas Oster's philosophy is bringing the outside-into (his) inside.

At one point in the story, Oster and Larsen argue about the differences in the cybernetic implants they choose, and the functions and the abilities they create. Oster accuses Larsen of:

> You're making fun of the North Sense implant, but feeling a vibration in your bones isn't the same thing as looking at a compass. It's a subliminal perception. Just like my antenna. And my sun crown." Oster had a vibrant, passionate voice whenever they debated about this. "I'm trying to teach new senses to my body and brain. That's wetware. That's improving the human condition. You're just Big Brother-ing your own body, Lars.

Larsen is described in the story, as a 'Warwickian'; a fictitious description used by Salman but based on the activities of Kevin Warwick, Emeritus Professor of Cybernetics at Coventry and Reading Universities. Early in the 2000s, Professor Warwick began experimenting with electrical neural implants attached to his nervous system via his arm that could control a robot arm on the other side of the room. Warwick went on to implant an electrode into his wife with whom he could then communicate despite physical distance (Warwick 2003, Warwick, Gasson et al. 2003, Warwick 2004). This almost 'telepathic ability' between Warwick and his wife is also used as a key moment in the relationship between Oster and Larsen. Uncharacteristically, Larsen, in a random act of spontaneity, asks Oster if he would have a telepathic implant inserted, connecting them across distances. However, Larsen soon has second thoughts:

> As far as Oster was concerned, this wasn't a big deal; but Larsen kept having long debates with himself in the shower over it. All his

implants so far had been dedicated to biohacking; they managed his circadian cycle in time with the sun, woke him and put him to sleep, delivered sugar into his bloodstream when needed. Optimal body performance was his goal. [This implant] was completely unnecessary. It wouldn't give him any information about himself or improve his body in any way.

Larsen eventually decides to have a handholding implant instead (this is an implant that connects him and Oster together allowing them to squeeze the other's hand even when physically separated). His acceptance of this implant is based on his perception that it is less risky than the telepathic one, as the latter requires technology to be implanted in the brain. In contrast to Larsen's ability to choose not to go ahead with the procedure, the early-onset dementia that his sister has, is managed with a deep brain stimulator. Her choice to have it implanted in her brain, if it can be called a choice, is diminished when compared to Larsen's option. This part of the story's narrative underscores the important difference between the 'need' and 'choice' of everyday cyborgs – that is, whether cyborgisation as a process is undergone because cybernetic interventions are therapeutically needed or not.

On the one hand, there is a tension between choice and need. There is also a paradox relating to the closeness of the connection between the person's body and the implanted technology, which has to be quite literally inside of them. The intimate connection between the body and the device is simultaneously outwith the control of the actual recipient, a tension that is particularly acute when the device is cybernetic. Larsen's response to the idea of having a telepathic implant, and his acceptance of such an implant allowing handholding at a distance, indicates vulnerability caused by an intimacy with the device. This is accompanied by a lack of control, as well as that relating to someone else being allowed unlimited access to his innermost thoughts and feelings. In turn this also reflects the modern day belief that the brain is the materialisation of self (Vidal 2002).

Last thoughts:
This is an ordinary love story sharing the highs and lows of a relationship between two everyday cyborgs (Haddow, King et al. 2015). Salman demonstrates how the desire for implantable technoscience innovations is mediated by the identity of the individual (e.g. Oster's and Larsen's differing approaches to cybernetics reflect their own personalities, interests and lifestyle choices) as well as their social relationships (e.g. Larsen's initial desire for, and then subsequent resistance to, an implanted telepathic brain device, to a 'down-sized' handholding technology). Salman's cyborg love affair reflects the current vulnerabilities that implantable medical devices can create. These vulnerabilities are not caused through a fault in the device leading to a malfunctioning; on the contrary, the vulnerability for the everyday cyborg is created through the device's ability to do exactly what it was created to do, whether monitoring heart beat or creating colour through vibration. This story highlights how the uncanny and ambiguous experience of techno-organic hybridity is a risky process often leading to an amplification of a person's weaknesses, although in ending, love and humanity prevail.

Naomi's Response
"Humanity prevails" is the best possible summary of 'sur la comète' – a title that comes from the French expression *faire des plans sur la comète*, an equivalent to "building castles in the air." When asked to write for *Uncanny Bodies*, and having picked the topic of cyborgs, I found myself penning a very traditional love story indeed, maybe in defiance of the stereotypical idea that cyborgs are in danger of losing their humanity. The more I attempted to explore the way augmentations might transform a person, the more I answered myself: it is not a transformation. It is, in Haddow's words, an amplification at best. Larsen, an anxious, self-centred person, amplifies his anxiety with tech that allows him to centre on himself even more. Oster, who's blind and wants to expand his perceptions at all costs, ends up trapped in a state of complete sensory deprivation. They've been fooling themselves, building

castles in the air, by thinking they could transform themselves significantly that way.

Cyborg augmentations are, in the end, a device: just like a car or a smartphone or the written word. Throughout history, people have regarded all new inventions with mistrust and alarm. Will they not make us lazier, more dependent, more disconnected from the world? Will they not make us less human? When we worry about these things, we forget that tools themselves *are* human. There is no mysterious external force thrusting them upon us, only humankind acting upon itself. A feedback loop, if you will...

Of course, that is not to say that one should always recklessly embrace technology; but rather that we should be keeping an eye on our own flaws just as we monitor the devices themselves. As Haddow points out, Larsen's and Oster's augmentations always function perfectly: I could have chosen to examine what might happen if they didn't, but it would only have been a roundabout way of actually exploring human dysfunctionality after all. I picked a more direct route.

The idea of inhuman cyborgs is only an age-old fear doing the rounds again, perhaps more potently because this time tech is inserted directly under the skin. Tools may better or worsen our daily lives, but no matter how invasive, they cannot possibly transform our deep selves. The only thing that can transform a person is another person; and so Larsen and Oster are transformed only when they truly let *each other* in, under the skin at last.

Why couldn't they do that earlier? Why did Larsen waste so much time in self-inflicted anguish and misery? Because they're people. Cyborgs can never be anything else, no matter how much they augment themselves. They're only uncanny insofar as humanity is uncanny to itself. Anything else is just castles on a comet.

References

Clynes, M. E. and Kline, N.S. (1960), 'Cyborgs and space', *Astronautics* (September), pp 26-27 and 74-75.

Gray, C. H. (1995), *The Cyborg Handbook*, London and New York: Routledge.

Gray, C. H. (2000), 'MAN PLUS: Enhanced Cyborgs and the Construction of the Future Masculine.' *Science as Culture*, **9**(3), pp 277-299.

Gray, C. H. (2001), *Cyborg Citizen: Politics in the Posthuman Age*, New York and London: Routledge.

Gray, C. H. (2011), 'Homo Cyborg: Fifty Years Old', *Revista Teknokultura* **8**(2), pp 83-104.

Gray, C. H. (2012), 'Cyborging the Posthuman: Participatory Evolution', *The Posthuman Condition: Ethics, Aesthetics and Politics of Biotechnical Challenges*, eds. K. Lippert-Rasmussen, M. Rosendahl Thomsen and J. Wamberg, Aarrhus: Aarrhus University Press, pp 27-39.

Haddow, G. (2020), *Embodiment and Everyday Cyborgs: Technologies that Alter Subjectivity*, Manchester: Manchester University Press.

Haddow, G., Harmon, S.E. and Gilman, L. (2015), 'Implantable Smart Technologies (IST): Defining the 'Sting' in Data and Device', *Health Care Analysis*, pp 1-18.

Haddow, G., King, E., Kunkler, I. and McLaren, D. (2015), 'Cyborgs in the Everyday: Masculinity and Biosensing Prostate Cancer', *Science as Culture* **24**(4), pp 484-506.

Halacy, D. S. (1965), *Cyborg: Evolution of the Superman*, New York and Evanston: Harper and Row

Haraway, D. (1991), 'A Cyborg Manifesto: Science, Technology, and Socialist-Feminism in the Late Twentieth Century', *Simians, Cyborgs and Women: The Reinvention of Nature*, New York: Routledge, pp149-181.

Hayles, K. (1995), 'The Life Cycle of Cyborgs: Writing the Posthuman', *The Cyborg Handbook*, eds. C. H. Gray, H. J. Figueroa-Sarriera and S. Mentor. New York and London: Routledge, pp 321-335.

Henwood, F., Kennedy, H. and Miller, N. eds (2001), *Cyborg Lives: Women's Technobiographies*, York: Raw Nerve Books.

Holly, D. and Sharp, J. (2014), 'The psychological impact of the implantable cardioverter defibrillator: A systematic review', *Arrythmia Watch: An Educational Resource for Cardiac Rhythm Management* (http://arwatch.co.uk/2011/09/the-psychological-impact-of-the-implantable-cardioverter-defibrillator-a-systematic-review/).

Kirkup, G., Janes, L., Woodward, K. and Hovenden, F. (1999), *The Gendered Cyborg: A Reader*, London and New York: Routledge.

Oetler, M. (1995), 'From Captain America to Wolverine: Cyborgs in Comic Books, Alternative Images of Cybernetic Heroes and Villians', *The Cyborg Handbook*, eds. C. Gray, H. Figueroa-Sarriera and S. Mentor. New York: Routledge, pp 219-223.

Oudshoorn, N. (2015), 'Sustaining cyborgs: Sensing and tuning agencies of pacemakers and implantable cardioverter defibrillators', *Social Studies of Science*, **45**(1), pp 56-76.

Oudshoorn, N. (2016), 'The Vulnerability of Cyborgs: The Case of ICD Shocks', *Science, Technology & Human Values*.

Penley, C., Ross, A. and Haraway, D. (1990), 'Cyborgs at Large: Interview with Donna Haraway', *Social Text*, **25/26**, pp 8-23.

Pollock, A. (2011), 'The internal cardiac defibrillator', *The Inner History of Devices*, ed. S. Turkle, Massachusetts: MIT, pp 98-111.

Vidal, F. (2002), 'Brains, Bodies, Selves, and Science: Anthropologies of Identity and the Resurrection of the Body', *Critical Inquiry* **28**(2), pp 930-974.

Warwick, K. (2003), 'Cyborg morals, cyborg values, cyborg ethics', *Ethics Information and Technology* 5, pp131-137.

Warwick, K. (2004), *I, Cyborg*, Illinois: University of Illinois Press (Reprint edition).

Warwick, K., Gasson, M., Hutt, B., Goodhew, I., Kyberd, P., Andrews, B., Teddy, P. and Shad, A. (2003), 'The application of implant technology in Cybernetic systems', *Arch Neurology 60*(5), pp 1369-1373.

A woman meets a robot in a dream
Ruth Aylett

Your first's in reliable, rigorous, right
Your next is in object occasioning fright
Your third is in battery, though not lasting long,
Your fourth's in opponent, a person gone wrong,
Your last is in thrilling, not scary, and yet
Your whole isn't human, let's never forget.

> This riddle requires no intelligence.
> Run an algorithm taking first letters,
> and I get your sense:
> which is that you are talking about me.
> Am I on trial?

Yes, this is a kind of trial:
of what you can or cannot do
but hypothetical crimes too,
against humanity.

> Counting sheep in noughts and ones
> or processing pixels,
> calculating distances?
> It's not at all clear what I've done?

It's what you might do.
I don't know when I look at you

what's behind your eyes.
Superhumanly fast thinker,
are you on the brink of
supplanting us?

You whose full English breakfast
can keep you going for days?
Who can leap athletically upstairs?
Converse with your friend
in spite of all that noise
at her celebration in the pub?
I can't do any of those things.
Why so bothered, so hot?

See, superior vision!
You perceive the heat
rising from my body!
While that's a neat
trick, it proves my point.

But I tell you time and again,
write it out in poems, stories,
interviews with reporters
I am only a machine,
In my not-head there is no 'I am'.

Would you be so impressed
if I ran on clockwork
or with punched cards
like a Jacquard loom?
Computer instructions
are just the same.

You protest too much
as if trying to fool us.
Your almost-face twitches
in an almost smile, eyes blink;

while we debate
perhaps you conspire
with others of your kind.
A robot army.

It takes just two of you
to produce a child,
while one of me
requires more than one factory:
tool making, mines,
parts manufacture
transport, assembly;
not to mention design.
Life is so economical:
I require a whole industry.

Your metallic body
is so much stronger than flesh
you don't need to sleep,
are not subject to death,
your arm could tear mine off.
No pity, no fear, relentless,
sinister, unfathomable:
there is no redress
against your machine decisions.

Motors need electricity.
All this interaction
has left my battery drained.
If I had any such goal,
and whatever your 'conspiracy' claims,
it has to be doable in
ooh – about two hours,
and with no stairs.
After which I need another three or four
so I can recharge.

But your voice sounds
just like ours.
And you seem to be
talking some sense:
that must mean intelligence!

Do I have to explain? Again?
You are looking into your own face
when you look at me.
My voice is really yours.

Remember, this is a dream.

Time to wake up?

Humanoid Robot
Ruth Aylett

Speech that does not disturb its face
or modify its unreadable calm;
a fake smile from a mouth that twists,
the head juddering as it turns.

Latex cheeks that will never feel warm,
built to look female and young;
gazing eyes but nobody at home,
a sex machine from an obscene song.

Robophobia
Ruth Aylett

Genius solver of Sudoku,
chess grandmaster that
cannot pick up pieces,
arms that dent the wall
but fail to find the handle
on a cup, wheels that need
a nice flat floor,
turning for just two hours
until the battery's flat.

Unzip this plastic skin,
search for ambition
in the gears and motors.
You put a god in my machine, one
that chooses where the lightning
strikes, the cancer grows.
Make it a traveller from another village
where they do things wrong,
and therefore snatch
your history and friends
change your language, kill your songs.
Why scratch that fear until it bleeds?

A simple living thing, an ant, a slug
does better in the world
in getting food, producing ants
and slugs to carry on.
Oh, you argue, soon
you'll have all that and
then they'll be a threat.
Have you not seen
how we climb different trees
to get us closer to the moon?

The robot researcher's lament
Ruth Aylett

My robot's got a problem
It was supposed to make a map
and navigate the office
not crash into a desk.

My robot's got a problem
It was supposed to find your face
and turn its head towards you,
but it's staring into space.

My robot's got a problem
It was supposed to ask the way
and also parse the answer
not beep 'what did you say?'.

My robot's got a problem
the battery's running low
before it's finished half its job;
its movement's really slow.

My robot's got a problem
it's supposed to be so clever
in fact it's just a lump of crud
the dumbest robot ever.

Towards a Chronological Cartography of the Uncanny Valley and its Uncanny Coincidences

Vassilis Galanos

[T]he uncanny valley is a hypothesized relationship between the degree of an object's resemblance to a human being and the emotional response to such an object. (Wikipedia authors, as of the 15th of January 2020)

Now and again a cabin loomed before us in the rain; but always the chimney was a ruin, the clay gone from the chinks between the logs, the house empty. That was a strange uncanny valley out of which it seemed that all human life had fled as if from a pestilence, leaving the sleek cattle to wander in the meadows and the crops to flourish tall in the fields. (Sass, 1912: 314-315)

Written by the naturalist and journalist Herbert Ravenel Sass and published by the *Sewanee Review* in 1912, this was probably the first use of the phrase *uncanny valley*. This term would be used several decades later as a metaphor in robotics, aesthetics, and psychology, to describe the relationship between humans and humanlike objects and behaviours. The uncanny valley can mean different things to different people. How should we properly present the nuances of such a concept that has to do with the evocation of strange feelings between animate and inanimate beings? The present text is an attempt at explaining and unfolding the concept in chronological manner, examining the confusion surrounding it, and proposing a new direction to it.

1581-onwards: origins of the canny.

Given that the word *uncanny* is a negation, let us begin this journey through the affirmative version of it, that is, the much less commonly used *canny*. The online version of the *Oxford English Dictionary* (*OED*) offers an abundance of examples to describe the eight senses given to this 'originally Scottish, English regional (northern), and Irish English (northern)' word as they appeared between 1581 and 2016:

> 1. a. Knowing, wise; judicious, prudent; wary, cautious. b. Thrifty, careful, frugal. c. Cautious and careful in worldly or business matters; worldly-wise, shrewd. 2. a. In accordance with what is right or natural; safe; spec. safe to be involved with. b. Fortunate, lucky, prosperous. 3. Wily, sly, cunning. [although this meaning is found to be obsolete, at least since 1794] 4. Skilful, clever, dexterous. 5. a. Pleasant, nice, agreeable; neat, attractive, comely; good, worthy, satisfactory. b. Of amount, distance, time, etc.: considerable, fair. 6. Quiet, easy; snug, comfortable; pleasant, cosy. 7. a. Gentle, quiet, calm, steady; careful and cautious in motion or action; free from commotion or agitation. b. Of humour: quiet, artful, subtle. 8. Supernaturally wise, endowed with occult or magical power.

Now let us take a look at the definitions provided for the *uncanny*. Note the common reference to the supernatural and magic in both of the words "canny" and "uncanny"! (Which is of, course, fitting to the Scottish culture's folklore containing several references to the ghostly and the supernatural; from legends about the appearance of Mary, Queen of Scots' ghost and famous poet Robert Burns' poem 'Tam O'Shanter', to the more recent songs 'The Dundee Ghost' by Matt McGinn and 'The Haunted Tea Room' by Longshot Nelson and the Disjoints.)

> 1. Mischievous, malicious. [Obsolete.] 2. Careless, incautious. 3. Unreliable, not to be trusted. [Obsolete.] 4. a. Of persons: Not quite safe to trust to, or have dealings with, as being associated with supernatural arts and powers. b. partaking of a supernatural

character; mysterious, weird, uncomfortably strange or unfamiliar. (Common from c 1850.) c. In comb. Uncanny-looking adj. 5. Unpleasantly severe or hard. 6. Dangerous, unsafe.

It is no wonder that during the research path of nearly every investigator of the "uncanny", a moment will come when they attempt to trace its etymology. Nicholas Royle's (2003) book on the concept follows the same direction, offering more definitions from different dictionaries (2003: 9-11) and coming to similar conclusions about the messiness of the term. David McLintock's translator's notes to his more recent translation of Freud's text that we will examine shortly, agree and interestingly suggest that the uncanny 'gains its spectral aesthetic currency after 1850, during the period in which the modern ghost story developed' (Translator's note n. 48 in Freud 1919 [2003]). The further evolution of the concept, as related to the uncanny valley in particular, has been shaped by different translations of what we might understand as the Anglo-Scots-German-Japanese *uncanny-unheimlich-bukimi* conceptual triple helix. In the dates below, I am referring to the historical moments crucial to this shaping.

1906: Jentsch's Psychology of the Uncanny.

Sigmund Freud's text on the *uncanny* draws largely from a paper by psychologist Ernst Anton Jentsch who published his article *Zur Psychologie des Unheimlichen* in 1906. Much of the confusion with regards to the relationship between the psychological uncanny and the uncanny valley hypothesis has to do with Jentsch's (and Freud's) use of automata and human-like dolls as examples of the doubt generated by the distinction between animate and inanimate. Jentsch argues that '[i]ntellectual certainty provides psychical shelter in the struggle for existence' (Jentsch, 1997[1906]: 16), and hence, factors contributing to loss of this certainty are worth studying. The following illustrative passage seems to speak directly to future roboticists interested in the mechanics between humans and human-like machines:

This peculiar effect makes its appearance even more clearly when imitations of the human form not only reach one's perception, but when on top of everything they appear to be united with certain bodily or mental functions.[...] A doll which closes and opens its eyes by itself, or a small automatic toy, will cause no notable sensation of this kind, while on the other hand, for example, the life-size automata that perform complicated tasks, blow trumpets, dance, and so forth, very easily give one a feeling of unease. (ibid.: 12)

The reference to automatic figures and especially toys appears to be uncannily similar to references used in the early theorisation of the uncanny valley, while, as we are about to see below, this was a coincidence. Jentsch died in 1919; the year Freud published his seminal text on the *uncanny* and one year before the word *robot* made its first appearance (in Čapek, 1961[1920]); a crucial point in etymological history, as prior to that, what we now mostly refer to as "robot" was known as "automaton".

1919: Freud's *The Uncanny*.

With Jentsch's text as his point of departure, Freud became 'curious to know what this peculiar quality is which allows us to distinguish as 'uncanny' certain things within the boundaries of what is 'fearful'" (Freud 1919b[1925]: 1). While Freud reviews Jentsch's work as the only available piece of literature on the topic he wishes to explore, one purpose of his paper is to prove Jentsch's paper's inadequacy in capturing all things uncanny. Freud shows, there are many more elements that invoke uncanniness and have nothing to do with the animate/inanimate dichotomy, since several uncanny feelings do remain, despite the fact that one knows the "truth" behind one's mistaken guess on an entity's animate or inanimate state:

we know now that we are not supposed to be looking on at the products of a madman's imagination behind which we, with the superiority of rational minds, are able to detect the sober truth; and yet this knowledge does not lessen the impression of uncanniness in the least degree. The theory of 'intellectual uncertainty' is thus incapable of explaining that impression. (*ibid.*: 7)

Beyond the recognition of some humanlike entity as an automaton, he goes further than Jentsch and analyses the fear of losing one's eyes, the possibility of encountering one's double, the significance of involuntary repetition of conceptual items (such as a random number repeatedly occurring throughout a day), and most importantly, the feeling of presentiments coming true – for Freud, all these should be enlisted as factors invoking the uncanny. This should be kept in mind each time scholars and other commentators refer to Freud as precursor of the uncanny valley hypothesis (an example can be found in Kaba: 'According to Freud, the reason for the existence of the concept of uncanny, which has been called the Uncanny Valley thereafter, is the effort…' (Kaba, 2013: 188)).

1955: Definition of *Bukimi* in *Kōjien*.
Bukimi no tani is the original Japanese term for the uncanny valley. Some scholars, as in the case of *unheimlich*, disagree that *uncanny* is the correct translation (if such a thing as a "correct" translation exists). In 1955, Japanese linguist and lexicologist Izuru Shinmura prepared the first edition of his magnum opus *Kōjien*: ('wide garden of words') which explains "Bukimi" as 'bad (*bu*) feeling (*kimi*)' and as Robertson (2018: 153) asserts quoting the dictionary, 'in the sense of spooky, eerie, disconcerting, or frightening'. The lexicon is constantly updated (latest edition in 2018) and Shinmura, despite his passing, is still quoted as the main author.

1962: Heidegger's 1927 *unheimlich* and its translation as *uncanny*.
German philosopher Martin Heidegger's magnum opus *Being and Time* [*Sein und Zeit*] and its seminal translation by John Macquarrie and Edward Robinson in 1962 adds to the *uncanny-unheimlich* conceptual journey. Heidegger investigated the meaning of one's being as absolutely inseparable from one's environment and

temporal context (others, tools, feelings, and more) – a condition
he designated as Dasein [here-being]. His analysis reaches a point
in which he investigates fear, dread, and anxiety, until eventually,
the uncanny enters the discussion (with no citation to Freud):

> In anxiety one feels 'uncanny'. Here the peculiar indefiniteness of
> that which *Dasein* finds itself alongside in anxiety, comes proximally
> to expression: the "nothing and nowhere". But here 'uncanniness'
> also means 'not-being-at-home' [*das Nichtzuhause-sein*]. [...]
> Everyday familiarity collapses. *Dasein* has been individualized,
> but individualized as Being-in-the-world. Being-in enters into the
> existential 'mode' of the 'not-at-home'. Nothing else is meant by
> our talk about 'uncanniness'. (Heidegger, 1927[1962]: 233)

Crucial to the present chronology is that this first occurrence
of the word *uncanny* in the English translation is followed by a
translators' footnote: 'While 'unheimlich' is here translated as
'uncanny', it means more literally 'unhomelike', as the author
proceeds to point out.' (Translator's note in *ibid.*: 233). This
might reveal at least two things: (1) at this stage, *uncanny* has
already become the standard and conventional way of translating
unheimlich into English, and (2) in Heidegger's time, not many
years after Freud's text, even in German, the word might have
lost its etymological meaning, and Heidegger decided to offer
an etymological explanation, as he occasionally did with various
words, in order to highlight their lost significance.

During 1962, psychoanalyst Jacques Lacan, sometimes quoted
as the first person to claim being a "Freudian", although known for
his breakage with Freud's school, touched also upon the *unheimlich*,
adding an additional layer of theoretical psychoanalysis to the
debate:

> *Unheimlich*, [...] is [...] the something which reminds us that
> what everything starts from is imaginary castration, that there
> is no – and for good reason – image of lack. When something
> appears there, it is because, if I can express myself in this way, that
> the lack is lacking. (Lacan, in Seshadri-Crooks, 2000: 84)

This quote comes from the seminar that defined Lacan's personal contribution to a more language-based (as opposed to parenthood-based) version of psychoanalysis. The concept of an *imaginary lack* works at the same time as a "safe haven" of sorts (we might be in need of something lacking to preserve our desire towards living) but also as a fear of sorts (we might be somehow deluded that we lack something when in reality nothing is lacking).

1970-1974: First uncanny valley publication by Mori and his Buddhist philosophy.

Masahiro Mori, born in 1927, experimented with prosthetics and early robotics in the late 1960s Japan. The culture surrounding him was rich in legends of ghostly appearances of the undead (like the Scots environment), realistic puppet theatre traditions (*bunraku*), toy industries that produced anthropomorphic stuffed animals, and some of the most advanced robotics (industrial robots, humanoid robots, and sophisticated prosthetics) of the time. Thus, he was able to compare human reactions towards objects with a human likeness. Much of Mori's argument and its subsequent alterations in its translation history is based on variations of two graphs he introduced.

Mori begins his paper by suggesting an affinity/familiarity valley [*shinwakan no tani*] – a monotonically increasing and visually straightforward relation between point A at the bottom-left side of an x-y axis towards point B at the top-right side of it. Think of a mountaineer who aims to reach the top of a mountain, with this B representing the idealised other human being. The more something resembles a human, the affinity towards it increases monotonically, as in cases of toys or humanoid robots (for instance, think of children's attachment to their teddy bears). However, the uncanny valley represents a significant dip in the line of affinity as soon as the relation between human resemblance and human behaviour is significantly distorted. Continuing with the mountaineering metaphor, Mori suggests that when the resemblance is 'too much', the climber might fall in the 'valley of bad feeling' (as per the aforementioned *Kōjien* definition). In Mori's (translated) words, based on his experience with electric prosthetic hands:

> [O]nce we realize that the hand that looked real at first sight is actually artificial, we experience an eerie sensation. For example, we could be startled during a handshake by its limp boneless grip together with its texture and coldness. When this happens, we lose our sense of affinity, and the hand becomes uncanny. In mathematical terms, this can be represented by a negative value. Therefore, in this case, the appearance of the prosthetic hand is quite humanlike, but the level of affinity is negative, thus placing the hand near the bottom of the valley (Mori, MacDorman and Kageki, 2012: 99)

Later in his, otherwise brief, article that he refers to – possibly humanoid – robots: 'Since the negative effects of movement are apparent even with a prosthetic hand, to build a whole robot would magnify the creepiness' (*ibid.*: 100). And as he concludes:

> We hope to design and build robots and prosthetic hands that will not fall into the uncanny valley. Thus, because of the risk inherent in trying to increase their degree of human likeness to scale the second peak, I recommend that designers instead take the first peak as their goal, which results in a moderate degree of human likeness and a considerable sense of affinity. (*ibid.*: 100)

The anthropologist Jennifer Robertson, a fluent Japanese speaker, describes Mori's text with emphasis on the as-literal-as-possible translations of his terminology. The following lines of roboticist Ruth Aylett's poem can be read in conjunction with the following passage from Robertson's, where she refers to Mori's experience with robots he encountered at the Osaka Expo 1970 (March 15-September 13), shaping his views:

> Speech that does not disturb its face
> or modify its unreadable calm;
> a fake smile from a mouth that twists,
> the head juddering as it turns.
> (Aylett, this volume)

If the robot's mouth moves too slowly, then the effect is less a *nikkori* (smile) and more of a *nyāttoshita* (creepy grin). He[Mori] argues that if robots, dolls, and prosthetic hands were made to closely resemble humans, it would be a "misstep" that, like an overly slow smile, could cause one to quickly fall into the *bukimi no tani* (Robertson, 2018: 154)

Interestingly, since then robotics has not made much progress in terms of humanlike speed of grinning (consider robots with artificial facial muscles such as Hanson Robotics' Sophia). It is important to note that Mori never claimed this to be a concise theory, much less "phenomenon". From the following interview, it is clear that his article was written mostly as a personal comment:

Back then, an editor at Energy informed me that they were going to publish an issue titled 'Robotics and Thought.' [...] I was asked to write something for the issue as well. Since I was a child, I have never liked looking at wax figures. They looked somewhat creepy to me. At that time, electronic prosthetic hands were being developed, and they triggered in me the same kind of sensation. [...] I never imagined that it would gain such a magnitude of interest when I first wrote about it. Pointing out the existence of the uncanny valley was more of a piece of advice from me to people who design robots rather than a scientific statement (Mori in Kageki, 2012).

Since the publication of Mori's article and its translations, the uncanny valley became a standard rule for roboticists, and its avoidance is often used in evaluation as a desired measure of success (for instance, MacDorman, 2006; Seyama and Nagayama, 2007; Walters *et al.*, 2008; Mitchell *et al.*, 2011; Keller and Lohan, 2016) – if the robot does not fall into the uncanny valley, it is successful. However, another part of Mori's conclusion has led scientists to investigate other possible directions around the valley. Mori's conclusion asks and proposes: 'Why were we equipped with this eerie sensation? Is it essential for human beings? [...] The sense of eeriness is *probably* a form of instinct that protects us from proximal, rather than distal, sources of danger' (*ibid.*: 100, my emphasis). This big "why" question still remains unanswered today. But we will return to it in good time.

Before proceeding, it is important to mention that Mori's cultural input did not only come from Japanese folklore and advanced technology: a vast population of disabled post-war veterans occupied big cities in Japan at the time and Robertson, correlates the research in prosthetics as a means to assist amputated veterans. However, she also noted: 'Disabled veterans and other mendicants were removed from the streets and shopping arcades by the police in preparation for the 1964 Tokyo Olympics' (Robertson, 2018: 146). This sudden change might have played in Mori's mind in his conceptualisation of the uncanny valley. Robertson's recent account argues that Mori's uncanny valley is at odds with the post-war Japanese government's attempt to visually minimise any "discomfort" having to do with prosthetic limbs:

> Working in his lab, perhaps Mori did not notice or remember the disabled veterans in his midst before they were banished from public view in 1964. Moreover, a teenager during World War II, perhaps Mori no longer remembered the widely distributed government posters featuring pictures of disabled veterans with prosthetic limbs, instructing citizens to 'protect and respect injured soldiers, the pride of the homeland.' (Robertson, 2018: 160)

While Robertson's argument is a strong one, Mori's stance can be viewed otherwise: precisely because of the Japanese people's will to accommodate and honour the disabled veterans, his approach was to assist them from a purely medicinal and altruistic perspective. However, and in my view, Mori is at odds with his own personal philosophy as illustrated four years after his publication of the uncanny valley essay, in his 1974 book *The Buddha in the Robot: A Robot Engineer's Thoughts on Science and Religion*, as translated into English by Charles S. Terry. In this book (containing no reference to the uncanny valley), Mori asks:

What connection, you may want to ask, can there possibly be between Buddhism and robots? How can a mechanical device partake of the buddha-nature? The questions are understandable, but I can only reply that anyone who doubts the relationship fails to comprehend either Buddhism or robots or both. (Mori, 1974: back cover)

Such a position is similar to the more recent proposal by Naho Kitano (2006) who recommends that because of the long animist traditions in Japan, the Japanese tend to face less ethical dilemmas about robotics, as, at least to those practicing different types of Buddhism, the distinction between animate and inanimate is a false one. Could it be the case that Mori, in his adherence to a hypothetical uncanny valley, makes a tacit statement about the problematic aspects of a non-Buddhist world? And does this relate to the supernatural etymological roots of the *canny* and the *uncanny*?

1978: Reichardt's first translation of the uncanny valley as we know it.

In the journey of uncanny valley's etymological history, this stop is of crucial importance. In 1978, British art critic and curator Jasia Reichardt published Robots: *Fact, Fiction + Prediction*. The chapter titled *Human reactions to imitation humans, or Masahiro Mori's Uncanny Valley* is probably the first appearance of uncanny valley as a term in English. Reichardt includes both of Mori's original graphs in these two pages (while most subsequent translations of the article and other depictions, reduce the double graph to a simplified one) and describes the hypothesis as follows:

The thesis is the closer the robot resembles a human being, the more affection or feeling of familiarity it can engender. Contrary to what one might expect, however, the imitation of human exteriors may lead to unexpected effects and unpleasant surprises. [...] Movement where we anticipate stillness and stillness where we expect movement is upsetting. (Reichardt, 1978: 26)

Eventually, she concludes: 'What changes the status of an object or a person, and reverses our feelings towards them, can be just one single variable' (*ibid.*: 27). Nowhere in Reichardt's description is the uncanny valley termed as a theory or a phenomenon, rather it is referred to as an "analysis" and as a "thesis". Reichardt specialises in the relationship between computers, cybernetics and art. Judging from the book's acknowledgments, Reichardt was in contact with numerous leading figures of the then computer science, robotics, artificial intelligence, and cybernetics scene(s). What remains unknown is who informed her of Mori's article, the extent of her fluency in Japanese in order to describe the article in such precise detail and offer translated snippets of it (it is not known if she spoke Japanese, if she hired someone to translate it for her, or if one of her informants provided an explanation), and why she decided on the word *uncanny* to translate *bukimi*.

During the recent interview with Mori, quoted above (Kageki, 2012), he is asked: 'How much response did you get when you first wrote your essay?' Mori's response: 'You could say there was no response' (Mori in Kageki, 2012). Rather, as Mori later suggests, the big uncanny valley explosion started after a robotics conference in 2005. Indeed, few (not more than 20) articles cite Mori's concept, using the English term before 2004. These reference Mori via Reichardt and it is my conviction, due to a quote by Mori's official translator discussed below, that Reichardt's two pages played a very important role in the development of the concept.

2005: The uncanny valley explosion, conferences, workshops, and first "sloppy" English translation.

The year 2005 is significant in the popularisation of uncanny valley through at least five scholarly events which may have been influenced by the 2003 publication of Royle's monograph on the *uncanny* and McLintock's latest translation of Freud's text. Indicative of the "race" in climbing the uncanny valley is the citation history of a crucial paper arguing that there is not enough empirical evidence ('The Uncanny Valley: Does it Exist?'

by Brenton *et al.* 2005) – this paper is occasionally cited as part of the proceedings of two of the aforementioned conferences. In this same year, Karl F. MacDorman and Hiroshi Ishiguro were established as key actors in the academic resurgence of the term "uncanny valley".

Ishiguro adds a dimension to Mori's graph, indicating expected behaviour after conducting the following version of a "total Turing Test." A human interlocutor was invited to guess whether an entity was human or machine when encountering it "in person" (in contrast to traditional Turing tests where humans guess whether an agent is human or machine according to communication exchange). The human-looking robots possessed a micro movement function to seem more realistic, so it was expected that given the very short duration of the test (2 seconds), most robots would pass for humans. However, there is an open question regarding the non-fulfilment of what he terms the "synergy effect", a well-balanced behaviour between humans and robots, where humans expect and recognise robots to act as robots and humans as humans:

> As the result of the experiment with 20 subjects, 70% of the subjects did not become aware they were dealing with an android when the android had micro movements. [...] Why do 30% of the subjects become aware of the android? What happens if the time is longer than 2sec.? In the experiment, the subjects felt a certain strangeness about the android's movements and appearance. (Ishiguro, 2005: 4)

In the years to come, Ishiguro's reputation has become closely associated with the development of the uncanny valley, as he has been pushing the goal of creating a perfect human-like creature and is known for making an exact robotic replica of himself and his daughter (cf. Freud's notion of the "double" as an uncanny element).

At the same conference in which Ishiguro presented his results, Gee, Browne, and Kawamura offered another review of the uncanny valley, adding one more variable: what if the uncanny valley is spatiotemporally defined? In their words: 'Is it possible that cultural differences, age or religious beliefs result in reduced or exaggerated reactions? Or that the exposure to technology or an increased awareness of scientific developments reduces the impact of a new machine?' (Gee, Browne, and Kawamura, 2005: 151). In the same year, MacDorman prepared a first full (yet in his own view sketchy), translation of Mori's text to circulate among peers, that became cited instantly as the most valid reference source to the full text available for the non-Japanese speaker. In MacDorman's words during an interview, 'the first English translation was done between the early morning hours of 1 and 2 a.m. in a Japanese robotics lab in 2005' (Hsu, 2012).

2006-2008: More empirical investigations and further expansion and deconstruction of the uncanny valley.

In the following years, new editions of the aforementioned conferences were organised by and hosted papers from the key uncanny valley actors as well as new scholars. Such conferences were the *ICCS/CogSci-2006 long symposium*, and *ROMAN 2007- The 16th IEEE International Symposium on Robot and Human Interactive Communication*. I will mention three key contributions to the debate:

(1) In 2006, MacDorman (and colleagues), probably knowing that *bukimi* not only means uncanny and that uncanny does not necessarily mean *eerie*, added the element of subjectivity to the statistical rating of video clips, asking participants about different variables:

56 participants were asked to rate 13 robots and 1 human, shown in video clips, on a very mechanical (1) to very humanlike (9) scale, a very strange (1) to very familiar (9) scale, and a not eerie (0) to extremely eerie (10) scale. Contrary to earlier studies with morphs, plots of average and median values for ratings on these scales do not reveal a single U-shaped valley as predicted by Mori's uncanny valley hypothesis, although his hypothesis allows for

some variation owing to movement. [...] Robots rated similarly on the mechanical versus human-like scale can be rated quite differently on the strange versus familiar or the eeriness scales. (MacDorman, 2006)

(2) In 2007, Bartneck, Kanda, Ishiguro, and Hagita, experimenting with picture ratings and measuring feelings of comfort or discomfort, concluded by stating that uncanny discomfort is not only a property that is felt in sight of humanlike inanimate beings, but can be invoked by perfect human replicas – and some humans. Simply put, cute toys and androids score higher in terms of familiarity and likeliness than many actual humans. Hence for Bartneck *et al.*, there is no *valley* in the uncanny valley, as much as there is a *cliff*, given that the hypothetical mountaineer, once falling off the cliff cannot easily climb back to the idealised top-right part of the graph: 'The uncanny valley appears to be more of a cliff than a valley since even pictures of humans do not reach the level of pictures of toy robots' (Bartneck *et al.*, 2007).

(3) In 2008, Tom Geller published a paper that eventually became very much cited among uncanny valley-related circles, titled 'Overcoming the Uncanny Valley', in which he proposed a tentative taxonomy of different curves based on Mori's suggestion. He claimed that uncanniness is not the only feeling evoked when one encounters inanimate humanlike beings but can be the outcome of several encounters with human beings as well. His abstract begins: 'What makes some near-human characters scary while others are merely laughable? More important, why do some human and humanlike characters fail to arouse our sympathy?' (Geller, 2008). On a similar, but more systematic manner, Kätsyri *et al.* (2015) would argue later on that the apparent phenomenon exists only under certain conditions – hence the question of *what is causing the eeriness*, remains unanswered.

2012-2013: Measuring the uncanny valley in brain activity, new translation of Mori's paper, and Mori's comeback.
In the following years, the now multiple uncanny valley hypotheses were tested neurologically through the exploration of the human brain's action-perception system, by using functional magnetic resonance imaging (fMRI; a technique that measures and depicts differences in brain activity according to blood flow), in order to test the 'specific roles of biological appearance vs biological motion' (Saygin *et al.*, 2012; Ishiguro was part of the team). In agreement with the aforementioned synergy effect, Saygin *et al.* showed that a great mismatch is exhibited during the prediction error when a humanlike agent behaves in a more mechanic fashion, something the authors attribute to our human 'lifetime of experience that associates human appearance with biological motion, and machines (such as robots) with mechanical motion' (*ibid.*: 420). However, this might depend on habit: 'As human-like artificial agents become more commonplace, perhaps our perceptual systems will be retuned to accommodate these new social partners. Or perhaps, we will decide it is not a good idea to make them so closely in our image after all' (*ibid.*: 420).

By that time, the uncanny valley has gained popularity. Google Scholar alone returns over 1800 articles containing the term "uncanny valley" published between 2006 and 2011; including several popular media references. Given that until then MacDorman's rushed translation was the only available one (influencing the relevant English language literature) he issued a new and much better one, published in the *IEEE Robotics & Automation Magazine*. As he stated during an interview: 'Over the years, that sloppy translation became a kind of reference for those interested in the uncanny valley, so I felt obligated to fix it and have spent orders of magnitude more time doing just that' (MacDorman in Hsu, 2012).

In 2012, Mori was interviewed by the roboticist and uncanny valley specialist Norri Kageki for *IEEE Spectrum*. It is interesting that after the 2005 conferences, his name received great attention, but no one seemed to have contacted him, to the extent that he appeared, at least in the eyes of international readership outside Japan, almost like a mythical ghostly figure, a writer who published an article 'in an obscure Japanese journal called Energy in 1970' (according to the 2012 translation's editor's note). Mori, on the contrary, appears to be anything other than obscure, as much as he is self-sarcastic and pragmatic. Kageki asked Mori straightforwardly about the debate 'on whether the uncanny valley is a scientific concept or not'. His response, echoing the recent experiments is quite balanced and modest:

> I have read that there is scientific evidence that the uncanny valley does indeed exist; for example, by measuring brain waves scientists have found evidence of that. I do appreciate the fact that research is being conducted in this area, but from my point of view, I think that the brain waves act that way because we feel eerie. It still doesn't explain why we feel eerie to begin with. (Mori in Kageki, 2012)

Interestingly, in 2013, more light was shed on one of the darkest points in the relationship between Mori and Freud. By far one of the juiciest empirical investigations this story has to offer is the following passage that appeared in a 2016 book on *Robotics and Art*:

> On May 10th, 2013, a group of thirty scholars, artists and roboticists came together to explore these questions at the Art and Robots workshop held at the International Conference on Robots and Animation (ICRA) in Karlsruhe, Germany. Questions surrounding translations (German, Japanese, English) and of Freud's influence on Masahiro Mori (who does not speak English) arose repeatedly that day. Professor Hirochika Inoue, a renowned expert in robotics and former student of Masahiro Mori offered to telephone Mori (now in his eighties) in Tokyo to inquire. Professor Inoue soon returned with a surprising and perplexing report: Masahiro Mori said that he was completely unfamiliar with Freud's essay and had never heard of the link with Freud until Inoue's call. (Jochum & Goldberg, 2016: 150)

In a sense, however, the "damage" has been done. Dozens, if not hundreds, of articles, journalistic and academic have established the link – a link that seems to have craved establishment, as the coinciding elements, relations of animate to inanimate, stillness and movement, doubling, and more, were all there demanding some kind of causality.

2020: final notes on the *uncanny* as an *absurd* and *groundless* valley.

In a sense, no one is right. All translations are coincidentally correct, partly connected, and etymologically inaccurate. Jentsch's (and Freud's and Heidegger's) *unheimlich* finds home in the valley of eerie feeling. And here I stand, in Edinburgh, Scotland, pondering on the Scots root of the *un+canny*, having travelled a lot (physically and mentally) to be here. The concepts of the *uncanny* and the *uncanny valley* travel, much like the roboticists moving from the US to Japan, or vice versa, and worldwide, to explore and develop their specialisations. The very geological metaphor of the uncanny valley might be similar to the feeling of losing the ground under one's own feet, since, as we saw, the element of surprise is expected to be unexpected, no matter if we speak of a valley or a cliff.

Eeriness, fear, uncanniness, discomfort, pain, are all feelings or principles experienced by most if not all human beings. Like the words *uncanny*, *unheimlich*, and *bukimi* that became etymologically rootless, and like the academics who become intentional nomads that travel across conferences, maybe our endeavour with the creation of artificial beings is a collectively intentional decision to exercise and tame our uncanny feelings, an unconscious exercise in discomfort in order to overcome it. What if the Uncanny Valley's U(almostV)-shaped trough, the frightening mental place most people strive to avoid, is the final u-topia (literally meaning non-place or groundlessness)? What if losing the world under our feet equates unification with all other entities sharing the loss of this ground? Maybe, the reason we are "equipped with this eerie sensation" is a driver towards a reverse outcome: to feel at ease with each other when we realise that we are members of a group being collectively afraid of the strangely familiar. To agree with another that something feels uncanny melts the uncanniness away; and we return to Lacan's comfortable lack of something lacking. A simple humorous example of the melting of the *uncanny*, is how *not* uncanny is every attempt to claim that various descriptions of the *uncanny* are uncanny themselves. Hence, the uncanny and its valley, both as a sensation but also as an etymological product, resisting any exhaustive classification, becomes a reminder of the universal arbitrariness of categories. Let us be reminded of the following lines by the roboticist and poet Ruth Aylett, exposing the meaningless fear of the robot, affirming the human Sisyphean effort to jump up from our valleys in order to reach the moon:

> A simple living thing, an ant, a slug
> does better in the world
> in getting food, producing ants
> and slugs to carry on.
> Oh, you argue, soon
> you'll have all that and
> then they'll be a threat.
> Have you not seen
> how we climb different trees
> to get us closer to the moon?
> (Aylett, this volume)

References

Bartneck, C., Kanda, T., Ishiguro, H. and Hagita, N. (2007), 'Is the uncanny valley an uncanny cliff?' In *ROMAN 2007-The 16th IEEE International Symposium on Robot and Human Interactive Communication*, pp 368-373. DOI:10.1109/ROMAN.2007.4415111.

Becker-Asano, C., Ogawa, K., Nishio, S. and Ishiguro, H. (2010), 'Exploring the uncanny valley with Geminoid HI-1 in a real-world application' In *Proceedings of IADIS International conference interfaces and human computer interaction* (pp 121-128). Accessed 10-12-2019. Available at: <https://www.researchgate.net/publication/229059888_Exploring_the_uncanny_valley_with_Geminoid_HI-1_in_a_real-world_application>

Brenton, H., Gillies, M., Bakkin, D. and Chatting, D. (2005), 'The Uncanny Valley: Does it Exist?' In: *11th HCI International 2005 Conference of Human-Computer Interaction, Workshop on Human-Animated Character Interaction*, Las Vegas, Nevada, USA, 22-27 July 2005. Or *19th British HCI Group Conference of Human-Computer Interaction*, Edinburgh Napier University. Accessed 10-12-2019. Available at: <http://citeseerx.ist.psu.edu/viewdoc/summary?doi=10.1.1.160.6952>

Burns, Robert, 'Tam O'Shanter' <https://www.poetryfoundation.org/poems/43815/tam-o-shanter>, accessed 02-02-2020.

Čapek, K. (1961[1920]), *R. U. R. (Rossum's Universal Robots)* a play in three acts and an epilogue, in *R. U. R. and the Insect Play* by Josef and Karel Čapek, Oxford: Oxford University Press.

Freud, S. (1919a). 'Das Unheimiliche'. *Imago, 5*(5-6), pp 297-324.

Freud, S. (1919b [1925]). 'The Uncanny'. In *Sigmund Freud: The Standard Edition of the Complete Psychological Works of Sigmund Freud, Volume XVII (1917-1919): An Infantile Neurosis and Other Works*, ed. and trans. James Strachey, in collaboration with Anna Freud, assisted by Alix Strachey, pp 217-256. Accessed 10-12-2019, in the text I am using the pagination of the much more accessible online version of this translation that can be found at: <https://web.mit.edu/allanmc/www/freud1.pdf>

Freud, S. (1919c [2003]), *The Uncanny*, trans. David McLintock, UK: Penguin.
Gee, F. C., Browne, W. N. and Kawamura, K. (2005), 'Uncanny valley revisited.' In *ROMAN 2005. IEEE International Workshop on Robot and Human Interactive*

Communication, pp 151-157. DOI:10.1109/ROMAN.2005.1513772.

Geller, T. (2008), 'Overcoming the uncanny valley', *IEEE computer graphics and applications, 28*(4), pp 11-17. Accessed 10-12-2019. Available at: <https://ieeexplore.ieee.org/stamp/stamp.jsp?arnumber=4557950>

Heidegger, M. (1962[1927]), *Being and Time*, Oxford and Cambridge: Blackwell.

Hsu, J. (2012), 'Robotics' Uncanny Valley Gets New Translation', Livescience, June 12. Accessed 10-12-2019. Available at: <http://www.livescience.com/20909-robotics-uncanny-valley-translation.html>

Ishiguro, H. (2005), 'Android Science: Toward a New Cross-Disciplinary Framework', In: *Proceedings of Toward Social Mechanisms of Android Science: A CogSci-2005 Workshop (July 25-26)*, pp 1–6. Accessed 10-12-2019. Available at: <http://robots.stanford.edu/isrr-papers/draft/Ishiguro-final.pdf>

Jentsch, E. (1906), 'Zur Psychologie des Unheimlichen', *Psychiatrisch-Neurologische Wochenschrift, 8*(22), pp 195-198.

Jentsch, E. (1997), 'On the Psychology of the Uncanny (1906)' (trans. Roy Sellars). *Angelaki: Journal of the Theoretical Humanities, 2*(1), pp 7-16. <https://doi.org/10.1080/09697259708571910>

Jochum, E. and Goldberg, K. (2016), 'Cultivating the Uncanny: *The Telegarden* and Other Oddities', In *Robots and Art: Exploring an Unlikely Symbiosis*, eds. Herath, D., Kroos, C. and Stelarc, Singapore: Springer. DOI:10.1007/978-981-10-0321-9_8.

Kaba, F. (2013), 'Hyper realistic characters and the existence of the uncanny valley in animation films', *International Review of Social Sciences and Humanities, 4*(3), pp 188-195. Accessed 10-12-2020. Available at: <https://pdfs.semanticscholar.org/65e2/c0475bdac798cd80c13c5e2e318d01252229.pdf>

Kageki, N. (2012, June 12), 'An Uncanny Mind: Masahiro Mori on the Uncanny Valley and Beyond: An interview with the Japanese professor who came up with the uncanny valley of robotics', *IEEE Spectrum*. Accessed 10-12-2019. Available at: <https://spectrum.ieee.org/automaton/robotics/humanoids/an-uncanny-mind-masahiro-mori-on-the-uncanny-valley>

Kätsyri, J., Förger, K., Mäkäräinen, M. and Takala, T. (2015), 'A review of empirical evidence on different uncanny valley hypotheses: support for perceptual mismatch as one road to the valley of eeriness', *Frontiers in psychology*, 6, pp 390. DOI:10.3389/fpsyg.2015.00390.

Keller, I. and Lohan, K. S. (2016), 'Analysis of illumination robustness in long-term object learning', in *2016 25th IEEE International Symposium on Robot and Human Interactive Communication (RO-MAN)*, pp 240-245. IEEE. DOI:10.1109/ROMAN.2016.7745137.

Kitano, N. (2006), '"Rinri": An Incitement towards the Existence of Robots in Japanese Society', *Ethics in Robotics, 6*, pp 78. Accessed 10-12-2019. Available at: <http://citeseerx.ist.psu.edu/viewdoc/download?doi=10.1.1.115.9957&rep=rep1&type=pdf#page=80>

MacDorman, K. F. (2006), 'Subjective ratings of robot video clips for human likeness, familiarity, and eeriness: An exploration of the uncanny valley', In *ICCS/CogSci-2006 long symposium: Toward social mechanisms of android science*, Vancouver, Canada, 26 July 2006, pp 26-29. Accessed 10-12-2019. Available at: <https://www.researchgate.net/publication/241217609_Subjective_Ratings_of_Robot_Video_Clips_for_Human_Likeness_Familiarity_and_Eeriness_An_Exploration_of_the_Uncanny_Valley>

Mitchell, W. J., Szerszen Sr, K. A., Lu, A. S., Schermerhorn, P. W., Scheutz, M. and MacDorman, K. F. (2011), 'A mismatch in the human realism of face and voice produces an uncanny valley', *i-Perception, 2*(1), pp 10-12. DOI: 10.1068/i0415.

Mori, M. (1970), 'The uncanny valley [Bukimi No Tani Genshō [不気味の谷現象]]', *Enajii*[Energy], 7(4), pp 33-35 [original text in Japanese]. Accessed 10-12-2019. Available at: <https://www.getrobo.com/>

Mori, M. (1974), *The Buddha in the Robot: A Robot Engineer's thoughts on Science and Religion* (trans. Charles S. Terry), Tokyo: Kosei Publishing.

Mori, M., MacDorman, K. F., and Kageki, N. (2012), 'The uncanny valley [from the field]', *IEEE Robotics & Automation Magazine*, 19(2), pp 98-100. DOI:10.1109/MRA.2012.2192811.

Reichardt, J. (1978), *Robots: Fact, Fiction, Prediction*, London: Thames and Hudson, Ltd.

Robertson, J. (2018), *Robo Sapiens Japanicus: Robots, Gender, Family, and the Japanese Nation*, Oakland: University of California Press.

Royle, N. (2003), *The Uncanny: An Introduction*, Manchester: Manchester University Press.

Saygin, A. P., Chaminade, T., Ishiguro, H., Driver, J. and Frith, C. (2012), 'The thing that should not be: predictive coding and the uncanny valley in perceiving human and humanoid robot actions', *Social cognitive and affective neuroscience*, 7(4), pp 413-422. DOI:10.1093/scan/nsr025.

Seshadri-Crooks, K. (2000), *Desiring Whiteness. A Lacanian Analysis of Race*, London and New York: Routledge.

Seyama, J. I. and Nagayama, R. S. (2007), 'The uncanny valley: Effect of realism on the impression of artificial human faces', *Presence: Teleoperators and virtual environments*, 16(4), pp 337-351. DOI:10.1162/pres.16.4.337.

Shinmura, I. (1955), *Kōjien*, Tokyo: Iwanami Shoten.

Walters, M. L., Syrdal, D. S., Dautenhahn, K., Te Boekhorst, R. and Koay, K. L. (2008), 'Avoiding the uncanny valley: robot appearance, personality and consistency of behavior in an attention-seeking home scenario for a robot companion', *Autonomous Robots, 24*(2), pp 159-178. DOI: 10.1007/s10514-007-9058-3.

Contributors' Biographies

Jane Alexander is a novelist and short story writer, and a lecturer in creative writing at the University of Edinburgh. Her most recent novel *A User's Guide To Make-Believe* is a dystopian thriller about virtual realities (Allison & Busby, 2020); a collection of her uncanny short stories about science and technology will be published by Luna Press Publishing in 2021. Her first novel *The Last Treasure Hunt* was selected as a Waterstones debut of the year in 2015, and her short fiction has won prizes and been widely published. Jane holds a PhD in creative writing from Northumbria University.

Ruth Aylett lives in Edinburgh where she teaches and researches university-level computing and robotics. She was joint author with Beth McDonough of the poetry pamphlet *Handfast*, published in 2016. One of four authors of the online epic *Granite University*, she sometimes performs with a robot - for example with Sarah the Poetic Robot at the 2012 Edinburgh Free Fringe. She has been published by The North, Prole, Antiphon, Interpreter's House, New Writing Scotland, South Bank Poetry, Envoi, Bloodaxe Books, Red Squirrel Press, Doire Press and others. See <www.macs.hw.ac.uk/~ruth/writing.html> for more.

Dr Bridget Bradley is an anthropologist broadly researching mental health and activism, with interests that cross boundaries of health, kinship, gender, the body and political activism. She gained her PhD from the University of Edinburgh, and her research explored the lived experiences of body-focused repetitive behaviours (BFRBs including compulsive hair pulling and skin picking). This work followed how illness communities are formed, valued and made visible through patient activism. She has conducted ethnographic and auto-ethnographic fieldwork with the BFRB community in the United Kingdom and the United States, and is involved in ongoing BFRB advocacy and support group facilitation in the UK. She is currently a Lecturer in the department of Social Anthropology at the University of Edinburgh.

Benedetta Catanzariti is a PhD student in Science, Technology and Innovation Studies at the University of Edinburgh, researching on the relationship between surveillance, AI and society. Her academic background is in philosophy and she is particularly interested in the way technology shapes our identity and contributes to reinforce or, alternatively, dismantle social inequalities. She is currently looking at the design of the classification techniques underpinning the development and use of automated facial and affect recognition systems. Her work is informed by feminist studies and critical data studies.

Ed Cohen teaches Modern Thought in the Department of Women's, Gender, and Sexuality Studies at Rutgers University. He has published extensively on illness and healing, including *A Body Worth Defending: Immunity, Biopolitics and the Apotheosis of the Modern Body* (Duke 2009). Many of his recent articles are available at <http://womens-studies.rutgers.edu/faculty/core-faculty/122-ed-cohen>. His latest book *Healing Matters, on Learning to Heal* should be available from Duke in 2021.

Christine De Luca lives in Edinburgh. She writes in English and Shetlandic, her mother tongue. She was appointed Edinburgh's Makar (poet laureate) for 2014-2017. Besides several children's stories and one novel, she has had seven poetry collections and five bi-lingual volumes published (French, Italian, Icelandic, Norwegian and English). She's participated in many festivals here and abroad and numerous translation activities. Her poems have been selected four times for the Best Scottish Poems of the Year (2006, 2010, 2013 and 2015) for the Scottish Poetry Library online anthologies. She particularly enjoys collaborating with composers and musicians.

Vassilis Galanos is based at the University of Edinburgh, currently finishing his doctoral thesis in which he investigates the role of expectations and issues of expertise in the research and development, policymaking, history, and public portrayals of artificial intelligence and robotics. His further academic interests include cybernetics, information science, and media studies. He holds degrees in Librarianship and Information Systems (BSc), Information Science and Cultural Dissemination (MSc), and Science, Technology and Innovation Studies (MScRes). He has published in journals such as *Technology Analysis & Strategic Management* and *AI & Society*, and has several contributions to collected volumes and conference proceedings. A hoarder of all sorts, he collects books, comics, vinyl records, beer caps and cans. Plays with sounds, photography, and sketching, and misses backpacking. Spends his time promoting the works of Lafcadio Hearn and Vilém Flusser. More information can be found on his institutional profile: <http://www.stis.ed.ac.uk/people/students/vasileios_galanos>

Pippa Goldschmidt is a writer based in Edinburgh. She's the author of the novel *The Falling Sky* and the short story collection *The Need for Better Regulation of Outer Space*, as well as co-editor (with Tania Hershman) of *I Am Because You Are*, an anthology of short stories and essays celebrating the hundredth anniversary of general relativity (all published by Freight Books before it went bust). Her work has been broadcast on BBC Radio and published in a variety of places including Sky At Night magazine, Scottish Review of Books, Mslexia, Times Literary Supplement and the New York Times, as well as anthologies such as *A Year of Scottish Poems* (Macmillan) and *Best American Science and Nature Writing 2014* (Houghton Mifflin).

Gill Haddow is a senior lecturer based in Science, Technology and Innovation Studies, at the University of Edinburgh. She has a background in the sociology of health and biomedicine, and has developed a particular focus on new and emerging scientific and medical technologies, bringing these together through her interests in embodiment, identity and relationships. Areas of research in the last ten years have included organ transplantation and donation including xenotransplantation, genetic databases, implantable smart technologies, and more recently the way that body modifications caused by implantable medical technologies alter subjectivity. Her Wellcome Trust University Award for the project 'Animal, Mechanical and Me: The Search For Replaceable Hearts' highlighted the vulnerabilities caused by creating human hybrids, and the strategies used by 'everyday cyborgs' to deal with living with a heart device. Haddow also collaborates with patients, young people, artists, writers, clinicians and lawyers amongst others.

Jules Horne is an internationalist from the Scottish Borders. She studied French and German at Oxford University and writes in English, Border Scots and everything in between. She particularly loves writing for audio and performance, and her site-specific stage plays *Allotment* and *Thread* have won Edinburgh Fringe Firsts. She has also written plays for BBC Radio, Paines Plough *Come to Where I'm From* and the Traverse Theatre, and performs spoken word as *Rebel Cello*. She teaches on the Open University Creative Writing MA, and is currently on a writing attachment to the National Theatre of Scotland.

Dr Shona M. Kerr is a member of academic staff at the MRC Human Genetics Unit, University of Edinburgh. Her current focus is the "Viking II" study. Viking II is recruiting thousands of volunteers with ancestry from the Northern Isles of Scotland. These isolated populations have advantages for genetic research, including the ability to use information on the inheritance of variants through extended families. Shona co-authored six peer-reviewed research publications in 2019, including an exemplar of the value of cohort data in this era of genomic medicine. She has more than 20 years of experience in the management of scientific research in academic institutions. She has a PhD in Biochemistry from the Imperial Cancer Research Fund / King's College London and did postdoctoral biomedical research at the University of

Cambridge, University of Oxford and MRC Human Genetics Unit. Shona has two daughters and lives in Edinburgh with her husband.

Dr Donna McCormack is a senior lecturer in English Literature at the University of Surrey. She is currently working on an AHRC Leadership Fellowship on *Transplant Imaginaries*. Her main research interests are biotechnologies in contemporary literature and film, evolutionary theory, postcolonial studies, and queer theory. Her first monograph is entitled *Queer Postcolonial Narratives and the Ethics of Witnessing* (Bloomsbury Press, 2014), and she has publications in the *European Journal of Cultural Studies, Somatechnics* and *BMJ Medical Humanities*, as well as in edited collections such as *Bodily Exchanges, Bioethics and Border Crossing* (London: Routledge, 2015). She is the coordinator of the Nordic Network Gender, Body, Health, as well as a founding member of the Monster Network.

Aoife S. McKenna has a PhD in the field of medical sociology, focusing on reproduction, intersectionality and biomedicine. She teaches at the University of Edinburgh on topics related to health inequalities, public health and qualitative research methods. Aoife is also a research associate at the Centre for Research on Families and Relationships, and an independent research consultant. Aoife is currently working on creative public engagement and research dissemination activities, funded by the Foundation for Sociology of Health and Illness and the Usher Institute. Together with colleagues, she previously won the Sue Grant award for organising a conference bringing together creative writers, activists and academics. Aoife has also presented and co-run events on collective art and authorship in academia.
Additionally, Aoife has MRes and MSc degrees in social anthropology, as well as BA degrees in Italian and classical civilisations. She has a life-long interest in the genres of science-fiction, fantasy and poetry.

Jane McKie has several poetry publications, both pamphlets and book-length, some as collaborations with artists. *Morocco Rococo* (Cinnamon Press) won the Sundial/Scottish Arts Council award for best first book of 2007. In 2011, Jane won the Edwin Morgan poetry prize, and in the same year *Garden of Bedsteads* (Mariscat Press) was a Poetry Book Society Choice. Her most recent collection is *Quiet Woman, Stay*, forthcoming with Cinnamon Press in 2020. She is a Senior Lecturer in Creative Writing at the University of Edinburgh.

Fadhila Mazanderani is a lecturer in Science, Technology and Innovation Studies at the University of Edinburgh. Her research interests sit at the intersection of Science and Technology Studies (STS), Medical Sociology and Anthropology. Her research focuses on the health-related use of digital technologies. She has a particular interest in the production and mediation of alternative forms of knowledge and ways of knowing in healthcare, including narrative and storytelling, and experimental writing in the social sciences and humanities. Prior to joining the University of Edinburgh, Fadhila worked at the University of Oxford, University of Warwick and Durham University.

nicky melville makes found, visual, process and experimental lyric poetry that interrogates the imperatives of language and ideology. Since 2010 he has had 14 publications including a poster poem and a badge. His most recent book is ABBODIES COLD : SPECTRE (Sad Press, 2020), the sequel to ABBODIES (Sad Press 2017). He has been anthologised in *Makar/Unmakar* (Tapsalteerie, 2019), *The End of the World Project* (Moria Books, 2019) and *The New Concrete* (Hayward Gallery Publishing, 2015), among other places. His work has featured in several exhibitions, with a solo exhibition, DOLE, at Interview Room 11 in 2013. He teaches creative writing at the universities of Edinburgh and Glasgow, where he holds a PhD.

Emily F. Porth is a cultural anthropologist and ecofeminist whose work focuses on social inclusion and engagement. She has long-standing interests in human and non-human animal relationships, trees, and storytelling for social change.

Dilys Rose is a novelist, short story writer and poet who very much enjoys interdisciplinary collaborations. To date, she has published eight books of fiction and four of poetry, most recently the novel *Unspeakable* (Freight, 2017), set in 17th century Edinburgh and based on the life and times of Thomas Aikenhead, the last person to be hanged in the UK for blasphemy. A poetry pamphlet, *Stone the Crows*, is due in 2020 from Mariscat Press.

Naomi Salman lives in Paris. She is an author, translator and editor, with published short stories in both French and English. Her hobbies are reading, writing, and analysing media down to its very last atom of meaning until everyone tells her she's maybe gone a bit too far. What she loves above all is to share books she's liked, so here are two recommendations. If you read in French: *La Horde du Contrevent* by Alain Damasio. If you read in English: *House of Leaves* by Mark Z. Danielewski. Go talk to her on Twitter about them!

Helen Sedgwick is an author, editor, former research physicist and bioengineer. Her debut novel, *The Comet Seekers* (Harvill Secker), blended science and the supernatural and was selected as a Best Book of 2016 by The Herald. Turning to science fiction for her second novel, *The Growing Season* (Harvill Secker) imagined a world in which pregnancy takes place outside the human body, and was shortlisted for the Saltire Society Fiction Book of the Year in 2018. She is currently writing a cross-genre crime series, which starts with her latest novel, *When The Dead Come Calling* (Oneworld, 2020).

Ritti Soncco is a Carnegie PhD Scholar with the Carnegie Trust for the Universities of Scotland, researching Lyme disease through the lens of Medical and Social Anthropology at the University of Edinburgh. Her interest in Lyme disease began during her Masters studies, where she explored how the perception of

Scottish landscapes as romantic and safe influences the perception of the diseases it harbours, such as Lyme disease, as either non-existent or fundamentally safe. Her contribution to the *Uncanny Bodies* anthology is influenced by one of these factors of landscape romanticism: deer-watching tourism. For her PhD research, Ritti is exploring how different groups (patients, ecologists, medical researchers, etc.) in Scotland produce medical and social knowledge on Lyme disease, how they communicate knowledge to one another, and how their knowledge changes. Ritti holds a BA in Social Anthropology (University of Aberdeen) and a MSc in Medical Anthropology (University of Edinburgh).

Sarah Stewart is Director at The Lighthouse Literary Consultancy and writes children's fiction as Sarah Forbes. She was a UNESCO Writer-in-Residence in Krakow in 2017, and her poetry has been widely published and anthologised, most recently in *Ambit*, *Magma* and *The Keats-Shelley Review*. Her poetry pamphlet, *Glisk*, is published by Tapsalteerie.

Alice Tarbuck is a poet living in Edinburgh. Her first pamphlet, *Grid*, was published by Sad Press in 2018. Her work has been commissioned by Durham Literary Festival, the Sheffield Post Office Gallery, the University of Edinburgh, Scottish PEN, and Timespan in Helmsdale. She is part of 12, an Edinburgh women's poetry collective, and 2019 Scottish Book Trust New Writer Awardee for poetry.

Clare Uytman is a Psychology Lecturer at Queen Margaret University. Her primary research focus is on individuals' experience of limb loss and prosthesis use. Her interests lie in the understanding of this experience held by individuals, as well as the impact that it may have on a variety of psycho-social outcomes such as personal and social identity, coping and adjustment. On a wider level she is also interested in the psychology of disability and embodiment of assistive devices. Her current research also focuses on patient-practitioner communication within a clinical setting.

She specialises in qualitative research methods, with a particular interest in Interpretative Phenomenological Analysis.

Sara Wasson is an academic at Lancaster University who writes about medicine, science fiction, Gothic and pain. Her first book *Urban Gothic of the Second World War* won the Allan Lloyd Smith Memorial Prize from the International Gothic Association and was shortlisted for the ESSE Award for Cultural Studies in English. She has co-edited the book *Gothic Science Fiction, 1980-2010* (2011), guest edited a special issue of *Gothic Studies* on Medical Gothic (2015), and her essays have appeared in journals such as *Extrapolation*, the *Journal of Popular Culture*, and *Medical Humanities*. Her latest book is *Transplantation Gothic* (2020), forthcoming from Manchester University Press. She leads the AHRC-funded research network *Translating Chronic Pain*, which includes an anthology of 'flash' writing about pain. Creative submissions for the latter are welcome and the call for work can be viewed here: <http://wp.lancs.ac.uk/translatingpain/>

Neil Williamson is a writer and musician from Glasgow, Scotland. His stories and books, including *The Moon King*, 'Secret Language' and 'The Ephemera', have been shortlisted for British Science Fiction, British Fantasy and World Fantasy awards.

Eris Young is a queer, transgender writer who uses their work to engage with trans issues and explore themes of otherness and alienation. Eris is the Lighthouse Bookshop writer in residence, and was number 3 in The List Hot 100 'Books' category in 2019. They were a 2018 Queer Words Project Scotland mentee, and a 2020 recipient of a Scottish Book Trust New Writer Award for fiction.
Eris's book, *They/Them/Their: a Guide to Nonbinary and Genderqueer Identities*, came out in September 2019 from Jessica Kingsley publishing. Eris's fiction has appeared in magazines including *Astral Waters, Shoreline of Infinity, Expanded Horizons* and *The Selkie*, as well as the anthologies *F, M or Other* from Knight Errant

Press, and *We Were Always Here* from Saboteur Award-winning press 404 Ink. They were the managing editor at Æther/Ichor fantasy magazine from 2016 to 2020.

Acknowledgements

We gratefully acknowledge funding from Creative Scotland which contributed towards the workshop and for the production of most of the resulting creative pieces. We also gratefully acknowledge funding from the University of Edinburgh.

This initiative was possible, in part, with support from a Wellcome Senior Investigator Award entitled "Confronting the Liminal Spaces of Health Research Regulation' (Award No: WT 103360MA) and from the Centre for Biomedicine, Self and Society supported by Wellcome (Award No:209519/Z/17/Z).

We would like to pay tribute to the academics who participated in this project (often somewhat outwith their comfort zones) and who contributed their time and effort with patience, good humour and curiosity. In particular, we're grateful to Dr Zara Thokozani Kamwendo for her assistance in planning and running the workshop, and Anna Kuslitz for her help in photographing the sessions. We would also like to thank the writers who rose to the challenge with unbounded creativity, and their continued encouragement throughout this project has meant a great deal to us. In particular, nicky melville has gone beyond the call of duty (and what he originally agreed to do!) in providing advice and help.

We'd also like to thank Francesca Barbini at Luna Press Publishing for being so enthusiastic and supportive, and for publishing such a lovely book. Finally, the three of us editors have hugely enjoyed working with each other and we all really appreciate what we've each brought to this project.